Accession
36188197

KU-743-277

DISTANT READING

DISTANT READING

FRANCO MORETTI

LIS - LIBRARY

Date	Fund
14/12/15	Shr - xl

Order No.
2671311

University of Chester

VERSO

London • New York

First published by Verso 2013
© Franco Moretti 2013

Most of the chapters in this book first appeared in the pages of *New Left Review*: 'Modern
European Literature: A Geographical Sketch', July–August 1994; 'Conjectures on World
Literature', January–February 2000; 'Planet Hollywood', May–June 2001; 'More
Conjectures', March–April 2003; 'The End of the Beginning: A Reply to Christopher
Prendergast', September–October 2006; 'The Novel: History and Theory', July–August
2008; 'Network Theory, Plot Analysis', March–April 2011
'The Slaughterhouse of Literature' appeared in *Modern Language Quarterly*, 61: 1, March 2000.
'Evolution, World-Systems, *Weltliteratur*' appeared in *Review*, 3, 2005
'Style, Inc.: Reflections on 7,000 Titles (British Novels, 1740–1850)' appeared in *Critical
Inquiry*, Autumn 2009

All rights reserved

The moral rights of the author have been asserted

5 7 9 10 8 6 4

Verso

UK: 6 Meard Street, London W1F 0EG
US: 20 Jay Street, Suite 1010, Brooklyn, NY 11201
www.versobooks.com

Verso is the imprint of New Left Books

ISBN-13: 978-1-78168-084-1 (PBK)
ISBN-13: 978-1-78168-112-1 (HBK)

British Library Cataloguing in Publication Data
A catalogue record for this book is available from the British Library

Library of Congress Cataloging-in-Publication Data
Moretti, Franco, 1950-
[Essays. Selections]
Distant reading / Franco Moretti.
pages cm
Includes bibliographical references and index.
ISBN 978-1-78168-084-1 (pbk. : alk. paper) — ISBN 978-1-78168-112-1 (hardback : alk. paper)
1. Criticism. 2. Literature—History and criticism—Theory, etc. I. Title.
PN81.M666 2013
801'.95—dc23
2012047274

Typeset in Fournier by Hewer Text UK Ltd, Edinburgh
Printed in the US by Maple Vail

To D.A. Miller
l'amico americano

Contents

Modern European Literature:
A Geographical Sketch

In the spring of 1991, Carlo Ginzburg asked me to write an essay on European literature for the first volume of Einaudi's Storia d'Europa. *I had been thinking for some time about European literature—in particular, about its capacity to generate new forms, which seemed so historically unique—and in a book I had just finished reading I found the theoretical framework for the essay: it was Ernst Mayr's* Systematics and the Origin of Species, *where the concept of 'allopatric speciation' (allopatry = a homeland elsewhere) explained the genesis of new species by their movement into new spaces. I took forms as the literary analogue of species, and charted the morphological transformations triggered by European geography: the differentiation of tragedy in the seventeenth century, the novel's take-off in the eighteenth, the centralization and then fragmentation of the literary field in the nineteenth and twentieth. The notion of 'European literature', singular, was replaced by that of an archipelago of distinct yet close national cultures, where styles and stories moved quickly and frequently, undergoing all sorts of metamorphoses. Creativity had found an explanation that made it seem easy, and almost inevitable.*

This was a happy essay. Aimed at a non-academic audience, and on such a large topic, it asked for a balance between the abstraction of model-building and the vividness of individual examples—a scene, a character, a line of verse—that would make it worth reading in the first place. Somehow, I found the right tone; possibly, because of my total reliance on the canon of European masterpieces (as a colleague pointed out, the word 'great' seemed ubiquitous in the essay; and it was, I used it fifty-one times!). The canon allowed for comparative analysis to take place: Shakespeare and Racine, the conte philosophique *and the* Bildungsroman, *the Austrians and the avant-gardes . . . As the years went by, I would move increasingly away from this idea of literature as a collection of masterpieces; and in truth, I feel no nostalgia for what it meant. But the conceptual cogency that a small set of texts allows for—that, I do miss.*

This was a happy essay. Evolution, geography, and formalism—the three approaches that would define my work for over a decade—first came into systematic contact while writing these pages. I felt curious, full of energy; I kept studying, adding, correcting. I learned a lot, and one day I even had the first, confused idea of an Atlas of literature. And then, I was writing in Italian; for the last time, as it turned out— though, at the time, I didn't know it. In Italian, sentences run easier; details, and even nuances, seem to emerge all by themselves. In English, it would all be different.

Years ago, Denis de Rougement published a study entitled *Twenty-eight Centuries of Europe*; here, readers will only find five of them, the most recent. The idea is that the sixteenth century acts as a double watershed—against the past, and against other continents— after which European literature develops that formal inventiveness that makes it truly unique. (Not everybody agrees on this point, however, and so we will begin by comparing opposite explanatory models.) As for examples, the limited space at my disposal has been a great help; I have felt free to focus on a few forms, and make definite choices. If the description will not be complete (but is that ever the case?), at least it will not lack clarity.

I. A MODEL: UNIFIED EUROPE

> Those were beautiful times, those were splendid times, the times of Christian Europe, when one Christianity inhabited this continent shaped in human form, and one vast, shared design united the farthest provinces of this spiritual kingdom. Free from extended worldly possessions, one supreme ruler held together the great political forces . . .

What you have just read are the first sentences of *Christianity, or Europe*, the celebrated essay written by Novalis in the very last months of the eighteenth century. As its underlying structure, a very simple, very effective equation: Europe is Christianity, and Christianity is unity. All threats to such unity—the Reformation, of course; but also the modern nation states, economic competition, or 'untimely, hazardous discoveries in the realm of knowledge'— threaten Europe as well, and induce Novalis, who is all but a moderate thinker, to approve of Galilei's humiliation, or to sing a hymn in praise of the Jesuits—'with an admirable foresight and constance, with a wisdom such as the world had never seen before . . . a Society appeared, the equal of which had never been in universal history . . .' Here, let me just point out how this intransigent conception of European unity—one Christianity, one design, one ruler—is also the backbone of the only scholarly masterpiece devoted to our subject: Ernst Robert Curtius's *European Literature and the Latin Middle Ages*, published in 1948. 'This work aims at grasping European literature as a unified whole, and to found such unity on the Latin tradition,' reads Auerbach's review.[1] And thus

---

1   Erich Auerbach's review article was published in *Romanische Forschungen*,

Curtius himself: 'We must conceive of the Middle Ages in their continuity both with Antiquity and with the modern world. This is the only way to construct what Toynbee would call 'an intelligible field of study'—the field being precisely European literature.[2]

Onto Novalis's spatial order (Rome as the centre of Europe), Curtius superimposes the temporal sequence of Latin *topoi*, with its fulcrum in the Middle Ages, which again leads to Rome. Europe is unique because it is one, and it is one because it has a centre: 'Being European means having become *cives romani*, Roman citizens.'[3] And here's the rub, of course: because Curtius's Europe is not really Europe, but rather—to use the term so dear to him—'Romania'. It is a single space, unified by the Latin–Christian spirit that still pervades those universalistic works (*The Divine Comedy*, *Faust*) which seem to establish separate 'national' literatures, but in fact pre-empt them. In Europe, for Curtius, there is room for one literature only, and that is European literature.

If circumscribed to the Middle Ages—where most of the evidence comes from—this model may well be invulnerable. But Curtius has something else in mind: not the delimitation of the Middle Ages, but their permanence well into modernity. The line about European literature being 'intelligible' only because of medieval continuity leaves no doubts about it. And yet, 'in today's spiritual situation', that very unity which has survived for twenty centuries is threatened as never before:

> This book is not the result of purely scientific concerns; it arises out of a preoccupation for the safeguard of Western civilization. It is an attempt at clarifying . . . the unity of this tradition across time and

---

1950, pp. 237–45.
2   Ernest Robert Curtius, *Europäische Literatur und Lateinische Mittelalter*, 1948, 2nd edn, Bern 1953, p. 387.
3   Ibid., p. 22.

space. In the spiritual chaos of our age, proving the existence of such unity has become necessary . . . [4]

Chaos. Reviewing *Ulysses* in 1923, Eliot had evoked 'the immense panorama of futility and anarchy which is contemporary history';[5] while for Novalis, chaos was at work already in the sixteenth and seventeenth centuries. And the reason for the crisis is at bottom always the same: the modern nation state, which from its very inception—'irreligiously', as Novalis puts it—has rejected a supernational spiritual centre.

Historical conjunctures have certainly contributed to this hostility: Novalis is writing during the Napoleonic wars, Eliot and Curtius immediately after the First and Second World Wars. But above and beyond specific events, the distrust of the nation state is probably the logical outcome of their overall model: to the extent that European culture can exist *only as unity* (Latin, or Christian, or both), then the nation state is the veritable *negation of Europe*. No compromise is possible, in this pre-modern, or rather *anti*-modern model; either Europe is an organic whole, or else nothing at all. It exists if states do not, and vice versa: when the latter arise, Europe as such vanishes, and can only be visualized in the elegiac mode. Novalis's essay, in fact, is already a dirge for a world that has lost its soul; no longer 'inhabited' by the great Christian design, his Europe has been damned to be mere matter: space devoid of sense. The 'continent shaped in human form' turns into the world of 'total sinfulness' described by the *Theory of the Novel* (which opens with an unmistakable allusion to the first lines of *Christianity*). And even though Lukács never explicitly says so, his novelistic universe, which is no longer 'a home' for the hero, is precisely modern Europe:

---

4   Ibid., p. 9 (the passage belongs to the preface to the second edition).
5   '*Ulysses*, Order and Myth', *The Dial*, November 1923, p. 201.

Our world has become infinitely large, and each of its corners is richer in gifts and dangers than the world of the Greeks, but such wealth cancels out the positive meaning—the totality—upon which their life was based.[6]

The withering away of a unified totality as a loss of meaning . . . But is this inevitably the case?

2. ANOTHER MODEL: DIVIDED EUROPE

1828. A generation has gone by, and the German catholic Novalis is countered by the French protestant Guizot:

> In the history of non-European peoples, the simultaneous presence of conflicting principles has been a sort of accident, limited to episodic crises . . . The opposite is true for the civilization of modern Europe . . . varied, confused, stormy from its very inception; all forms, all principles of social organization coexist here: spiritual and temporal rule, the theocratic, monarchic, aristocratic, democratic element; all classes, all social positions crowd and overlap; there are countless gradations of freedom and wealth and power. Among these forces, a permanent struggle: none of them manages to stifle the others, and to seize the monopoly of social power . . . In the ideas and feelings of Europe, the same difference, the same struggle. Theocratic, monarchic, aristocratic, popular convictions confront each other and clash . . . [7]

For Novalis, disparity and conflict poisoned Europe; for Guizot, they constitute it. Far from lamenting a lost unity, his Europe owes its success precisely to the *collapse* of Roman–Christian universal-

---

6   Gyorgy Lukács, *Theory of the Novel*, Cambridge, MA 1968 (1916), p. 34.
7   François Guizot, *Histoire de la Civilisation en Europe*, 6th edn, Paris 1855 (1828), pp. 35, 37–8.

ism, which has made it polycentric and flexible.[8] No point in looking for its secret in *one* place, or value, or institution; indeed, it's best to forget the idea of a European 'essence' altogether and perceive it as a polytheistic field of forces. Edgar Morin, *Penser l'Europe*:

> 'All simplifications of Europe—idealization, abstraction, reduction—mutilate it. Europe is a *Complex* (complexus: what is woven together) whose peculiarity consists in combining the sharpest differences without confusing them, and in uniting opposites so that they will not be separated.'[9]

Like all complex systems, Europe changes over time (especially from the sixteenth century on), and therefore, Morin again, 'its identity is defined not *despite* its metamorphoses, but *through* them'. This polycentric Europe, decidedly accident prone, no longer shuns disorder, but seizes upon it as an occasion for more daring and complex patterns. In the field of literature, this implies a farewell to Curtius's 'Romania', with its fixed geographical centre, and the

---

8   Thus also Geoffrey Barraclough (*European Unity in Thought and Action*, Oxford 1963, pp. 7, 12–13): 'The idea of Europe as a distinct unity is post-classical. It was created in the Middle Ages. In the most general terms, it may be described as a result of the collapse of the universalism of the Roman Empire. [The Carolingian Empire] was not a "starting point," but a conclusion . . . it was necessary for the Carolingian Empire to collapse for Europe to come into being . . . European unity could henceforward only mean the articulation—not the suppression—of ingrained regional diversity.' Similar considerations inform another work largely influenced by Guizot, Federico Chabod's *Storia dell'idea di Europa*, Bari 1961. Immanuel Wallerstein has developed this insight in terms of economic history, defining modern capitalism as that social formation which 'operates within an arena larger than that which any political entity can totally control': the *divided* states of seventeenth-century Europe were therefore capable of that take-off which proved impossible for the politically united Asiatic empires (Immanuel Wallerstein, *The Modern World-System*, New York 1974, pp. 348, 61–3). In the same direction, see also Eric Jones, *The European Miracle*, Cambridge 1981.

9   Paris 1987.

diachronic chain of *topoi* linking it to classical antiquity. His 'European literature' is replaced by a 'system of European literatures': national (and regional) entities, clearly different, and often hostile to each other. It is a *productive* enmity, without which they would all be more insipid. But it never turns into self-sufficiency, or mutual ignorance: no deserts, here, no oceans, no unbridgeable distances to harden for centuries the features of a civilization. Europe's narrow space forces each culture to interact with all others, imposing a common destiny, with its hierarchies and power relations. There are resistances to the establishment of this system, as with Russian literature, which splits between westernizers and slavophiles, in a beautiful instance of the geographical reality of Europe: of its being not really a continent, but a large Asian peninsula, with the area of conjunction—Russia—understandably doubtful about its own identity. But Europe's attraction is too strong, and from *Fathers and Sons* to *The Brothers Karamazov*, from *War and Peace* to *Petersburg*, the dramatization of the uncertainty becomes in its turn a great theme not only of Russian, but also (as in Thomas Mann) of European culture.

National literatures, then, in a European system: and among them, what relationship? According to many, the rule lies in a sort of duplication, with national cultures acting as microcosms of Europe; thus England for Eliot, France for Guizot, Italy for Dionisotti, Austria for Werfel . . . There is some truth, of course, in this discovery of common European features in all great continental cultures. But when a hypothesis is always on target, it stops being interesting, and here I will propose a different model. Literary Europe will be in the following pages a kind of ecosystem that defines different possibilities of growth for each national literature. At times its horizon will act as a brake, pre-empting or slowing down intellectual development; at other times, it will offer unexpected chances, which will crystallize in inventions as precious as they are unlikely. Let us see a first instance.

3. BAROQUE TRAGEDY, EUROPE OPENS UP

Nothing conveys the idea of a polycentric Europe as sharply as the genesis of the great baroque tragedy. In the mid sixteenth century, one still encounters figures such as George Buchanan: a Scot, who works in London and Paris, and writes his tragedies, in Latin, on well-known biblical subjects: an excellent instance of the lasting unity—across time and across space—of European drama. For cultivated tragedy the model is almost always Seneca, while medieval traditions, rooted in popular religion, tend to be very similar everywhere. Shared by all of western Europe is also the figure of the tragic hero (the absolute sovereign), and the 'memorable scene' (the court), where his downfall shall take place.

From this space and hero arises however the first discontinuity with the classical heritage. The new sovereign—*ab-solutus*, untied, freed from the ethico-political bonds of the feudal tradition—has achieved what Hegel will call 'self-determination': he can decide freely, and thus posit himself as the new source of historical movement: as in the *Trauerspiel*, and *Gorboduc*, and *Lear*, where everything indeed begins with his decisions; as in Racine, or *La Vida es Sueno*. The new prince has unburdened himself—writes Kierkegaard— 'of substantial determinations, like family, stage, or bloodline [which constitute] the veritable Fate of Greek tragedy'.[10] And yet, this king that has freed himself from Fate has become himself his own Fate: the more absolute he is, the more energetic and self-determined, the more he will resemble a tyrant, and draw the entire kingdom to its ruin. The sovereign act which breaks with the past is a jump in the dark: Hamlet striking behind the arras, Sigismundo ruling in his 'dream'. It is modern literature's first look at the future: an accursed horizon, and an inevitable one. Phèdre's first sentence— 'N'allons point plus avant'—is a useless wish, for tragedy has set

---

10   Søren Kierkegaard, *Either/Or*, Princeton 1971, vol. I, p. 141.

history on a sliding plane—'tomorrow, and tomorrow, and tomorrow'—which offers no turning back.

If the tragic hero cannot hold himself back, the space he inhabits is endowed for its part with an extraordinary force of gravity. 'My decision is taken: I am leaving, dear Théramène', reads the opening line of *Phèdre*; but of course no one is allowed to leave Trezene. 'In *Iphigenie*'—writes Barthes in *Sur Racine*—'a whole people is held captive by tragedy because the wind does not rise.' In *Hamlet*, characters scatter between Wittenberg and Paris, Norway and Poland (and the other world); Hamlet himself wants to leave Norway, is sent to England, and kidnapped by pirates. But it is all in vain; Fortinbras and Horatio, Hamlet and Laertes (and the Ghost) all keep their appointment in Elsinore to celebrate the great hecatomb. Rosaura's horse gets out of control, and 'therefore' leads her straight to Sigismundo's tower; in *La Vida es Sueno*, after all, jail and court are the only real spaces, and in a sense—as for the 'prison Denmark', or the serail in *Bajazet*—they are the *same* space. 'In the last analysis'—Barthes again—'it is tragic space that generates tragedy . . . every tragedy seems to consist in a trivial *there's no room for two*. Tragic conflict is a crisis of space.' Perhaps, a crisis of space produced by a reorganization of space that has been *too successful*: that has taken the claims of absolutism too seriously. 'The theory of sovereignty', writes Benjamin, 'positively demands the completion of the image of the sovereign, as tyrant.'[11] True, and the same applies to the court; the strengthening of the nation state (with its uncertain boundaries, and lack of internal homogeneity) required first of all an indisputable centre of gravity: small, powerful, undivided, where indeed there should be 'no room for two'. The space of the court: but, for the same reasons, of tragedy too.

Although many other elements contribute to the formation of

---

11   Walter Benjamin, *The Origins of the German Baroque Drama*, London 1977 (1928), p. 69.

baroque tragedy, the two I have discussed are probably the most important ones, and they both convey the same historical message: tragic form is the paradoxical outcome of the violence required by the formation of the nation state. It is the form through which European literature is first touched by Modernity, and in fact *torn apart* by it: for within a couple of generations, the stable, common features of European drama are replaced by a rapid succession of major formal mutations. By the mid seventeenth century, the tragedy of western Europe has branched out in three or four separate versions, where everything has changed: the relationship between word and action, the number of characters, stylistic register, temporal span, plot conventions, spatial movements, verse forms. In fact, not even the name of 'tragedy' is shared any longer.

It's the 'speciation' of evolutionary theory: the genesis of distinct forms where there used to be only one. But what made it possible? The separate national cultures? Yes, and no. Yes, in the obvious sense that each version of baroque tragedy is rooted in a specific national context—one of the three great western nation states, or the German and Italian territories. But if this space is ideal for the existence of *one* form, it is already too centred and homogeneous, too *narrow* to allow for the branching out of mutations we have to explain. In the Spain of the *siglo de oro* there is no room for German *Trauerspiel*, just as, in the eyes of the *tragédie classique*, Shakespeare is an absurdity to be avoided (let alone the Jacobeans). Morphological variety needs a broader space than the nation; with more cultural 'niches' for mutations to take root, and later contribute to literary evolution.[12] 'It's a well-known fact'—writes Jacques Monod—'that

---

12 'Later' means here: even centuries later. Of three tragic variations which arose almost simultaneously, the Spanish one achieved its European hegemony between the sixteenth and seventeenth centuries; the French one, during the *âge classique*; the English one, from the *Sturm und Drang* to the end of the nineteenth century. And had Benjamin been a little more lucky, the twentieth century might well have been the century of the *Trauerspiel*.

the important turning points in evolution have coincided with the invasion of new ecological spaces.'[13] And Stephen Jay Gould: 'Diversity—the number of different species present in a given area—is strongly influenced, if not controlled, by the amount of the habitable area itself.'[14]

A larger habitat, then: Europe. But which Europe? In an interesting analytical page (to which I shall return), Curtius delineates a sort of literary relay, a secular rotation of the literature that dominates the rest of Europe; in our period, for him, Spanish literature. Yet had Europe been really as united as Curtius would have it—had it been a sort of Spain writ large—then it would present the same limitations of the Spanish nation state: and there would be no room for the French or the English version of tragic form. Once more, the Europe we need is Guizot's, with the constitutive dis-union of its cultural scene.[15] And this means that Europe doesn't simply offer 'more' space than any nation state, but especially a *different* space: discontinuous, fractured, the European space functions as a sort of archipelago of (national) sub-spaces, each of them specializing in one formal variation.[16] If seen 'from within', and in isolation, these national spaces may well appear hostile to variations; they 'fix' on one form, and don't tolerate alternatives. But if seen 'from the outside', and as parts of a continental system, the same nation states act as the *carriers* of variations; they allow for the formal galaxy of

---

13   Jacques Monod, *Chance and Necessity*, London 1972, p. 121.

14   Stephen Jay Gould, *Ever Since Darwin*, New York 1977, p. 136.

15   'It is evident that this civilization cannot be found, nor its history fully appreciated, within the boundaries of a single state. If European civilization has its own unity, its variety is not less prodigious, and has never fully manifested itself in a single country. Its several features are disseminated here and there; one must look for the elements which constitute European history in France just as in England, in Germany just as in Italy or Spain.' Guizot, *Histoire*, pp. 5–6.

16   Archipelagos are posited as models of geographic speciation in Ernst Mayr's classic *Systematics and the Origin of Species*, New York 1942.

baroque tragedy which would have been unthinkable in a (still) unified Europe.

Would there be Shakespeare, had England not been an island? Who knows? But that the greatest novelties of tragic form should arise away from the mainland, and from someone with 'small Latin and less Greek', is quite a sign of what European literature had to gain from losing its unity, and forgetting its past.

In the spatial model I have begun to outline, geography is no longer the speechless onlooker of the—historical—deeds of the 'European spirit'. The European space is not a landscape, not a backdrop of history, but a *component* of it; always important, often decisive, it suggests that literary forms change 'in' time, no doubt, but not really 'because' of time. The most significant transformations do not occur because a form has a lot of time at its disposal: but because at the right moment—which is as a rule very short—it has *a lot of space*. Just think again of baroque tragedy; is its formal variety the result of passing time—of history? Little or nothing: English tragedy and *Trauerspiel*, Spanish drama and *tragédie classique* all achieve rather quickly a stable structure, which remains unchanged for decades, until it becomes sterile and disappears. A form needs time in order to reproduce itself; but in order to arise it is space that it needs most. Space, spaces, plural, of neighbouring, rival cultures; where the exploration of formal possibilities may be allowed, and in fact encouraged as a sort of patriotic duty. Once more: the space of a divided Europe.[17]

---

17   The principle of spatial dispersion applies to literary styles and movements as well as genres. Thus Van Tieghem on Romanticism: 'to consider these three literatures [German, English, and French] a sufficient manifestation of European Romanticism would underestimate its rich variety; actually, several of its most characteristic features are better represented in other literatures, less well known than the major ones'. Paul Van Tieghem, *Le Romantisme dans la littérature européene*, Paris 1948, p. 115.

4. The Republic of Letters

Baroque tragedy is among the first expressions of European poly-centrism. For several generations, however, isolation and mutual ignorance are still very strong: the case of Shakespeare—whose influence on the continent must wait till the end of the eighteenth century—is a clear sign of this state of affairs. The continental system is still at a potential stage; the elements are all there, but there's no switch to connect them yet. And that literary Europe is the sum of its parts, but not much more, is after all the picture offered by its first historian, Henry Hallam, in the four long volumes of his *Introduction to the Literature of Europe in the Fifteenth, Sixteenth, and Seventeenth Centuries*.[18] With implacable punctuality, Hallam slices the historical continuum every ten (or thirty, or fifty) years, and subjects each of the five great areas of western Europe to a meticulous investigation. But spatial proximity never turns into functional interaction: Hallam's Europe is a mechanical sum of its separate parts, and nothing more.[19] Bereft of internal links, it is a

---

18   London 1837–39, New York 1970.

19   Just one instance, drawn from the section entitled 'History of the Literature of Taste in Europe from 1520 to 1550', second part, 'State of Dramatic Representation in Italy—Spain and Portugal—France—Germany—England'. This is how the various national chapters begin: 'We have already seen the beginnings of the Italian comedy, founded in its style, and frequently in its subjects, upon Plautus . . .'; 'Meantime, a people very celebrated in dramatic literature was forming its national theatre. A few attempts were made in Spain . . .'; 'The Portuguese Gil Vicente may perhaps compete with Torres Naharro for the honour of leading the dramatists of the peninsula . . .'; 'We have no record of any original dramatic composition belonging to this age in France, with the exception of mysteries and moralities . . .'; 'In Germany, meantime, the pride of the meister-singers, Hans Sachs, was alone sufficient to pour forth a plenteous stream for the stage . . .'; 'The mysteries founded upon scriptural or legendary histories . . . continued to amuse the English public . . .' (*Introduction*, pp. 601–8). The connection between national spaces is established through the annalistic convention of the 'meantime'; temporal simultaneity, here, implies no structural interaction.

large, yet structurally fragile construction; an easy prey to the great classicist counter-attack, as a consequence of which the development of the European system comes to a halt for over a century.

To be sure—as suggested by the metaphor of the Republic of Letters, coined precisely in this age—cultivated Europe has never been so united as in the *âge classique*. But it's a unity gained at the price of diversity. Think of the semantic destiny of the epoch's keyword: cosmopolitan. 'Citizen of the world' is the definition of Johnson's *Dictionary* in 1755. It's not easy, however, to give a concrete, positive meaning to such citizenship, and a few years later, in 1762, the Académie Française follows the opposite strategy; a negative definition: cosmopolitan is he '*qui n'adopte point de patrie*', who adopts no country at all. Instead of belonging everywhere, he belongs nowhere; and if Johnson aimed at including the entire planet, the Académie proceeds by contrast to erase all national states. 'To aim at the good of mankind', writes Leibniz, 'the cosmopolitan will have to be indifferent to what characterizes a Frenchman, or a German.'[20]

But what may 'mankind' mean, in the concrete context of eighteenth-century Europe? Fatally, it will be the idealized version—abstract and normative at once—of a national literature of unique power and ambition. Isn't the *République des Lettres* after all the legitimate heir of the *Res publica Christiana*, just as French is replacing Latin as the sacred language of the spirit? 'The classical age', writes Paul Van Tieghem, 'coincides with the literary hegemony of France: it begins with it, it ends with it . . . The French spirit embodies to such an extent the classical ideal that, in several

---

20   Leibniz's passage is drawn from a 1697 letter, reported by Thomas J. Schlereth, *The Cosmopolitan Ideal in Enlightenment Thought*, Notre Dame 1977, pp. xxiv–xxv.

European countries, classical and French will become synonyms.'[21] French literary hegemony, then; nor literary only, as the Napoleonic wars will point out. It's the last attempt to make Europe one, imposing upon it the same uniformity of national cultures which Benjamin Constant denounces in his tract on the spirit of conquest. The attempt does not succeed, obviously; but it is nonetheless interesting that it was still possible to conceive it, or more precisely: that it was possible *for France* to conceive it. Because France plays indeed a unique role in the cultural history of Europe. Erich Auerbach:

> The preponderance of Romance materials in *Mimesis* is due to the fact that—on a European scale—Romance literatures are in the great majority of cases more representative than Germanic ones. In the twelfth and thirteenth centuries the lead is undoubtedly France's, and Italy's for the two following ones; during the seventeenth century it returns to France, and it stays there for the following century and for the nineteenth century as well, at least for what concerns the genesis and development of modern realism.[22]

One may disagree on details here, but hardly on the general picture. A great *national* mechanism, engaged in 'civilizing' its interior, and brilliant *cosmopolitan* enterprise, read and imitated everywhere, French literature has indeed played a unique role in European history—because it has played with unique brilliance (and luck) on the continental chequerboard. The reason for its success, in other words, lies less in what France 'is', than in what it is *in respect to others*. Because France is a great nation state, first of all, and this gives it an edge over Italy—its closest rival during the Middle Ages—and over the German territories. As for Spain and England,

---

21   Paul Van Tieghem, *Histoire littéraire de l'Europe et de l'Amérique*, Paris 1946, p. 67.

22   Erich Auerbach, 'Epilegomena zu *Mimesis*', *Romanische Forschungen*, 1954, pp. 13–14.

it is more populated than they are, and its language has a wider currency: it has a wider audience—and a wider audience means more space, more life, more inventiveness, more forms. And then position, decisive when books and ideas move still very slowly: France is right there, at the centre of the great western 'X'. To go from Spain to Holland and Germany, or from England to Italy, one must cross it, let it know of all new ideas, and spread its influence in the opposite direction. Then again, a literary tradition unencumbered by a Dante or a Shakespeare, a Goethe or a *siglo de oro*: free from the weight of unrepeatable models, French literature is more agile than others, it plays on more tables, always ready to place its bet on the novelties that crop up in the European space. And finally, a great nation state, yes, but never hegemonic in the political or economic arena; this eternal second best, always under pressure, may well have overinvested in the realm of culture, in the hope of finding there the extra stimuli necessary to succeed in the European rivalry. There is then still another reason, and I shall return to it soon.

5. THE NOVELISTIC REVOLUTION

Where does the European novel begin? In Spain, with the explorations of the *picaros* and the irony of *Don Quixote* . . . In France, with its brilliant anatomy of passions . . . In England (and Germany), with the sober simplicity of spiritual autobiography . . . In baroque adventures, which abound in Italy and elsewhere . . . Or maybe in Holland, in the luminous, lively everydayness of Vermeer, or the serious, withdrawn visages of Rembrandt . . . [23]

---

23 The latter hypothesis, quite dear to the writer of these pages, will have to wait for another occasion. In a discussion of the origins of the novel, however, the presence of two Dutchmen is far from casual. The novel's main topic—the bourgeois private sphere—takes its definitive form in seventeenth-century Holland, which is also, for over a century, the economic centre of the world. It would be perfectly logical, then, if the novel were to originate in Holland—except that, as we know, this was not in the least case. And why not? Perhaps, precisely

Where does the European novel begin? Behind this question lies a view of literary history as a sort of 'ladder', with steps that follow each other at a regular distance. But we should borrow a different metaphor from evolutionary theory, and think of literary development as a large bush: branches that coexist and bifurcate, that overlap and at times obstruct each other—but that, whenever one of them withers away, are ready to replace it with an ever thicker and stronger organism.

Where does the European novel begin? Who knows, who cares? But where it managed to survive and to grow, this is relevant, and this we do know: in Europe. In the European archipelago: a space discontinuous enough to allow the simultaneous exploration of widely different paths. And in the European bush, with the thickly woven network of its national literatures: where each new attempt immediately circulates, no longer running the risk of being forgotten for centuries. At this point, diversity joins forces with interaction, and after Hallam's paratactic Europe, and the French Republic of Letters, it is the turn of the European literary *system* in the proper sense. Neither European literature, nor merely national ones, but rather, so to say, national literatures of Europe.

The development of the European novel as an evolutionary bush, then. Fernand Braudel:

> All sectors are interconnected here, and they are all so developed that there is no danger of jams or obstructions. Whatever the chosen direction may be, or the concrete opportunity, the European novel

---

because the visual representation of the everyday had been so successful. Among similar symbolic forms (just as among similar animal species) there is an inevitable rivalry, and if one of them 'captures' a new historical experience, the life of rival forms becomes very difficult. On the other hand, what language would a 'Dutch' novel have used? Flemish? Frisian? A German dialect? French perhaps? Or Latin, even? (On the linguistic heterogeneity of seventeenth-century Holland, see Simon Schama, *The Embarrassment of Riches*, Berkeley 1988, p. 57.)

is ready to take off . . . and its growth will take the form of slower runners catching up with the leader of the race.[24]

The European novel? Not exactly, there's a little trick here; Braudel is describing the mechanics of the Industrial Revolution, and the subject of his sentences is, of course, 'the English economy'. But the overall pattern holds true for the sudden surge of the novel in the late eighteenth century. In twenty years, with a striking rapidity, all the forms that will dominate Western narrative for over a century find their masterpiece. *The Mysteries of Udolpho*, 1794, for the Gothic; *Wilhelm Meister's Apprenticeship*, 1796, for the *Bildungsroman*; *Elective Affinities*, 1809, for the novel of adultery; *Waverley*, 1814, for the historical novel. In another fifteen years, with Austen and Stendhal, Mary Shelley and Pushkin, Balzac and Manzoni, almost all the main variations on the basic forms are also in place.

It's a spiral of novelties—but of lasting novelties, with long-term consequences: hardly an exaggeration, in fact, to speak here of a veritable 'novelistic revolution'.[25] Like the economy, literature has indeed developed, by the end of the eighteenth century, the necessary precondition for its take-off: a (largely) new writer, the woman-novelist, and a quickly growing audience; a complex of national variations, well known to each other, and an Anglo-French core of great morphological flexibility; a new system of distribution

---

24   Fernand Braudel, *Civilisation materielle, économie et capitalisme*, vol. III, *Le Temps du monde*, Paris 1986, part 6.

25   As in the case of industry, it is only at some point in the course of the nineteenth century that people realize that the novel is destined to stay; and that it embodies, for better or worse, the essence of a new civilization. From this point onwards, a talented young man will no longer dream of writing a great tragedy, but a great novel; and as for old men, Goethe will rewrite his *Wilhelm Meister* three times over forty years, to make sure that it turns out as a modern novel ought to.

(the circulating library), and a precocious, recognizable early canon. And then, chance enters the historical scene, offering the novel the right opportunity at the right moment: the French Revolution. But don't think of a mechanical universe, where the ball of politics hits the ball of literature and passes its own spin over to it. This is rather a living system, of stimuli and responses, where the political sphere creates symbolic problems for the entire continent, and the literary sphere tries to address and to solve them. In the traumatic, fast-moving years between 1789 and 1815, human actions seem to have become indecipherable and threatening; to have—quite literally—lost their meaning. Restoring a 'sense of history' becomes one of the great symbolic tasks of the age: and a task uniquely suited for novelists, because it asks for enthralling stories (they must capture the explosive new rhythm of Modernity), but also well-organized ones (that rhythm must have a direction, and a shape).

The very difficulty of the historical scenario acts thus as a great chance for formal renewal, at all levels. The enigmatic quality of the new times, for instance, is channelled within the techniques of suspense, and reduced by the retrospective meaningfulness established by the narrative closure. The political and social struggle, transformed into an emotional conflict among concrete characters, loses its dangerously abstract nature (and it doesn't rule out a happy ending). The multiplication of languages and ideologies, finally, is curbed by the middle style of educated conversation (the most typical of novelistic episodes), and by the all-encompassing voice of the omniscient narrator.

Each problem stimulates a technical device, which retroacts upon it in an attempt to solve, or at least contain it. It is an effort to bridge a many-sided symbolic rupture, and to restore—through the narrative convention of individual biography—the *anthropomorphism* that modern history seems to have lost. And yet, in a beautiful instance of the heterogenesis of aims, in doing so the European novel invents an infinity of new stories that dismiss the narrative inheritance of antiquity, and project readers further and further into the future. A few generations later, the cost of the attempt will become clear, and we will return to it.

Uneven rhythm of literary evolution: it had taken two long centuries to collect the many ingredients of the new form; then, under the pressure of conjuncture, a generation or so is enough to create the continental unity of modern 'realism', where previously exceptional successes (such as *Clarissa*'s, or *Werther*'s) are replaced by a steady flow of communications. The unification that the *âge classique* had only accomplished for the thin layer of the very educated is thus achieved, in depth, and only a few decades later, by the novelistic revolution. And why so? Because of merely conjunctural reasons— because the *âge classique* had never had an opportunity such as the one offered to the novel by the French Revolution? Not really, conjuncture is a necessary ingredient of long-term change, but never a sufficient one, and the most typical narratives of the two epochs—*conte philosophique* and *Bildungsroman*—suggest structural reasons for the two different destinies. The *conte*'s sarcastic, nonchalant plot seems designed to frustrate narrative interest, which it thoroughly subordinates to philosophical abstraction; this is a novel by and for philosophers, almost at war with itself, where the sparkling language of criticism forces readers to endlessly question the meaning of the story. By contrast, the *Bildungsroman* draws from the uncertainties of youth an inexhaustible narrative potential, often in open defiance of all reflexive wisdom. Narration is here as relevant as comment, and a society overwhelmed by change wants precisely this: a worldview arising in and out of narrative structures, to be assimilated almost unconsciously, and possibly with the help of an unchallenged *doxa*. And then again, for the *conte*'s cosmopolitan nimbleness the national dimension is irrelevant, perhaps even contemptible; but Europe is inventing its nations and its nationalisms, and the socialization stories of the *Bildungsroman*, solidly rooted in the national community, are a much apter dispositive for the new situation.[26]

To sum it up in a formula, the *conte philosophique* had offered a (French) form for the whole of Europe; the *Bildungsroman* a (European) form pliant enough to adapt itself to each national space. And to represent this space, extending it well beyond the narrow centre of the court: launching a wide exploration, geographical and social—the many masters of the picaresque, the local lore of the historical novel, the phenomenology of emotions of the novel of adultery, the stages of social mobility of the *Bildungsroman* . . . If the novel still occasionally has a centre—Paris, 'the city of a hundred thousand novels', the world of extremes and melodrama—this is however no longer the rule. Apart from Dickens, English narrative draws its rhythms and its problems from the countryside, and its masterpiece—*Middlemarch*—bears the name of a mediocre provincial town. Germans and Italians tell of a world narrowed and impoverished by localism, while the Russian novel oscillates between Petersburg, the restless border with western Europe, and Moscow, capital of a boundless and almost timeless countryside.

Furthermore, even where the uniqueness of the capital is clearly emphasized—*The Red and the Black*, *Lost Illusions*, *A Sentimental Education*—its value is always of a relative kind, fixed through a wider equation; Paris acquires its meaning by its interaction with the provinces, where the young heroes have left mothers and sisters, friends and ideals—and where they will almost always return after their defeat. Paris is thus no longer an absolute space, as the court had

---

26   On the novel's contribution to the establishment of national cultures, there are some very convincing pages in Benedict Anderson, *Imagined Communities*, London 1983 (especially pp. 30–9).

been; it's only the capital of a nation, and the latter's existence can never be forgotten. Rather than working along the vertical axis, to erect the 'Tragick Scaffold' for the fall of princes, the novel proceeds horizontally, as a sort of literary railway, to weave the network capable of covering a country in all its extension. By the end of the nineteenth century, the task has been basically accomplished.

6. THE NORTH-WEST PASSAGE

I have spoken of a polycentric Europe, of evolutionary bushes and literary relays. In a page of his *European Literature*, Curtius seems to be heading in the same direction:

> From 1100 to 1275 (from *Chanson de Roland* to the *Roman de la Rose*), French literature and culture set the pace for all other nations . . . After 1300, however, the literary lead moves to Italy, with Dante, Petrarca, and Boccaccio . . . France, Spain, England are under its influence; it's the age of 'Italianism'. With the sixteenth century, the Spanish *siglo de oro* begins, which will dominate European literatures for over a hundred years . . . France liberates itself from Spanish and Italian influences only during the seventeenth century, when it again achieves a supremacy which will not be challenged until 1780. In England, in the meantime, a great poetical current had come into being as early as 1590; but it will arouse the interest of the rest of Europe only in the course of the eighteenth century. As for Germany, it was never a rival of the great Romance literatures. Its hour will come with the age of Goethe; before, German culture is often under external influence, but it never exerts its own.[27]

It is a very interesting passage: one of the very few where Curtius addresses the issue of the nation state. And yet—what states?

---

27 Curtius, *Europäische Literatur*, p. 44.

France, Italy, Spain, France again; 'Romania' (and within it, for four centuries out of seven, France). The opening up of the model is only an appearance; from 1100 to 1780, in fact, literary hegemony never leaves the Latin world. And after '1780'?

The Elizabethans are already quite a puzzle for Curtius; but if it cannot be solved, it is at least possible to postpone it by invoking England's isolation. Once it reaches the Age of Goethe, however, *European Literature* stops altogether, because its explanatory power has run its course. There's no way around it, Curtius's Europe really cannot accept the modern world, and even less the northern climate. Ours is exactly the opposite; it originates with the attack waged by absolutism against tradition; it rises to the challenge of 1789; it leaves the world of 'Romania' without ever turning back; it crosses the Channel, the Rhine, it spends its summers at Travemunde . . .

In this new old world, after the Thirty Years' War, two out of three of the great Romance literatures have forever lost their hegemonic chances. Italian literature, because Italy is less than a nation, and a provincial culture, however educated, is below the new European standards and needs. Spanish literature, for the opposite reason; because Spain is more than a nation, and the empire of the Americas tears it away from European issues. When European literature again achieves a unity, it is no longer in the name of the classical and Romance past, but of the bourgeois present; novels from the north, English, French, German; later, Russian.

This geographical drift is even more visible for post-Enlightenment tragedy, especially if one bears in mind the baroque moment. Then, the influence of the Reformation in England, and of Jansenism on Racine, was largely balanced by the Jesuitical element in Spain and France, Italy and Germany; but from the mid eighteenth century onwards, the Protestant component occupies virtually the entire stage. Romance tragedy disappears, and Germany holds for over a century—Lessing, Schiller, Hölderlin, Kleist, Büchner, Hebbel, Wagner, Hauptmann . . . —a veritable monopoly of tragic invention. At the end of the nineteenth century, the north-eastern trend is further accentuated; it's the moment of Ibsen, a Norwegian; of Strindberg, a Swede; of Chekhov, a Russian.[28] With expressionism, and then Brecht, we are back in the German area.[29]

Several processes are at work here, interwoven with each other. Following wealth, literature abandons the Mediterranean for the Channel, the North Sea, the Baltic. Novelistic 'realism' would be much more difficult without this movement, which distances the memories of the classical world, and enhances by comparison the prosaic (but not at all poor) bourgeois present. 'Serious imitation of the everyday', reads Auerbach's celebrated formula; and one thinks of the unadorned cheeses of Dutch still lifes, which resurface—appropriately saved from the shipwreck—on Robinson's island. It is Lotte's bread and butter in *Werther*, Hjalmar's bread and butter in *The Wild Duck*, Toni Buddenbrook's bread and

---

28   Even the main literary war of the nineteenth century—the conflict between tragic and novelistic conventions, culminating in the great Ibsen controversy—takes place almost entirely outside of the boundaries of 'Romania': France and England entrenched against tragedy, Germany and Scandinavia on the opposite side, and Russia somewhere in between.

29   From the eighteenth to the twentieth century, tragedy is thus the dominant form in the only northern culture which hasn't yet achieved its national unity. 'Germany', we read in *Reflections of an Unpolitical Man*, 'is the battleground of Europe': in a physical sense, from the Thirty Years' War to 1945, but even more so in a symbolic sense. In the absence of a stable political structure, and of the atmosphere of compromise which usually follows from it, all political values and anti-values of modern Europe achieve in Germany a metaphysical purity which makes their representation *sub specie tragica* almost ineluctable. The pitiless bourgeois honesty of *Emilia Galotti* and the abstract political idealism of *Don Carlos*; the Jacobin organicism of *Danton's Death* and the intractable heroism of *Herod and Mariane*; the dark mythical appeal of the *Ring* and the inflexible Stalinism of Brecht's *Lehrstücke*; one generation after another, the story of German drama is the extreme echo of the ideological history of Europe.

butter (and honey) on the morning of her engagement. It is the discoloured furniture of the Vauquer pension, the slightly super-fluous furniture of Flaubert's pages, the dark furniture of Ibsen's drawing rooms . . .

But this poetics of solidity (great keyword of the bourgeois ethos) has its price: losing the Mediterranean, European literature also loses adventure. Its security robs it of the unknown. In the Mediterranean 'civilizations had overlapped by way of their armies; myriad stories of adventures, and of remote worlds, had been circu-lated in this space . . .'[30] Very little of this up in the north, where wonders will have to wait for magic realism; works written in Spanish, in Portuguese, and often mediated by France. A new continent entering the literary scene, to be sure: but perhaps it is also the revenge of an imaginary still loyal to the internal sea.

A differently shaped, slightly wider Europe, where the silence of some Romance cultures—those most plagued by economic decline and religious reaction—is balanced by the productivity of the north. But there is one literature for which at bottom nothing changes, because it is at home in both worlds, and the great north-ward drift, which eliminates a couple of traditional rivals, does in fact even strengthen its position within the European system. This is French literature: the only survivor of 'Romania', because only in France has the Romance past—which, by itself, would have never been enough—joined forces with the logic of a great modern state (and the result is the *tragédie classique*), with a capitalist economy (and it is nineteenth-century realism), with a metropolis which is a true palimpsest of history: and it will be, with Baudelaire, modern poetry. Only in a Janus-faced city could this creature be born, itself a double, 'laughable and sublime', crudely contemporaneous and defiantly classical; where 'unhealthy demons / Heavily awake, like

---

30   Louis Gillet, *Dante*, Paris 1941, p. 80.

so many businessmen', and an old hunchback is also the phoenix, just like a barren stretch on the outskirts of town is the plain of Troy. 'New buildings, scaffolds, stones / Old suburbs, all for me turns into an allegory . . .'

Movement towards the bourgeois north. Permanence of France (and of Paris). Finally, the European system puts into words its lack of a centre. This is the great theme of Austrian literature, facing an imperial catastrophe which duplicates on a smaller scale, and several centuries later, the destiny of Europe as a whole.[31] Loss of the centre, in the Hapsburg Empire—where well into the nineteenth century Latin is still the official bureaucratic language, to be later replaced by a spectral German—loss of the centre means, first and foremost, a breaking apart of language. For Hofmannsthal's Chandos, it's the discovery of the gaps between signs and things; for Malte Laurids Brigge, the anxiety of a hidden meaning lying in ambush behind every word; for Schnitzler, the crazy discrepancy between aggressive drives and the impeccable style of good manners. In *The Radetzky March*, it's the incomprehensible insults in Hungarian which greet the news from Sarajevo; in *The Man Without Qualities*, the pompous nonsense of that 'collateral campaign' which longs to reunify the many languages of the empire; in Kafka, the desperate exhaustion produced by the too many, and too different, meanings of the Scripture.

What this literature is saying is in fact experienced throughout Europe. We should abandon the metaphor of the continental relay,

---

31 'We have received as our inheritance', writes the young Hugo von Hofmannsthal, 'an ancient European land; we are here the successors to two Roman empires, and must endure our destiny, whether we want it or not . . .' The passage is quoted by Curtius in his 1934 essay *Hugo von Hofmannsthal and Calderon*. Curtius is predictably in great syntony with this Roman–imperial image of Austria, and Hofmannsthal is indeed for him the most representative European author of the twentieth century.

where the torch of invention, although moving from hand to hand, is nevertheless always one. With the twentieth century, the time of *polarization* has come: simultaneous and conflicting attempts, which radicalize the technical potentialities of each form, and don't come to a halt—'consequentiality which spurns any compromise', in Adorno's phrase—until they have reached extreme results. One of the cornerstones of Guizot's Europe, its inclination to compromise, here comes to an end:

> Unable to exterminate each other, it was inevitable for conflicting principles to coexist, and to tacitly agree on some sort of mutual accommodation. Each of them implicitly accepted to develop only in part, and within well defined boundaries . . . No trace, here, of that imperturbable boldness, of that ruthless logic, which character- ize ancient civilizations.[32]

No trace of boldness? True, how true for realistic narrative. But for modernism?

7. New Spaces of an Old World

Polarization . . . James Joyce and Franz Kafka; the two greatest innovators of the twentieth-century novel. Does this mean—as in the decades of the novelistic revolution—that they are proceed- ing in the same general direction? Not in the least. Unknown to each other, they do indeed begin to write their masterpieces in the very same months; but *Ulysses* opts then for the noisy freedom of polyphony, while *The Trial* tells the story of a secret, monological Law. In the one, the omnivorous euphoria of the stream of consciousness; in the other, the wary subtlety of scriptural inter- pretation. The total irony of pluristilism—the terrible seriousness of allegory. The private space of a metropolitan psyche—the

---

32 Guizot, *Histoire*, pp. 40, 38.

public, hieratico-political space of the law court . . . And if we move from the novel to poetry, *The Waste Land* and the *Duino Elegies*, both published in 1922, repeat exactly the same configuration. Fragments from all ages piled up in a super-language endlessly meaningful, in Eliot; in Rilke, the renunciation of all evocative seduction, in the hope of finding the sober language of the present. There, a thousand words, and no voice to utter them; here, a voice very close by, looking in vain for the few right words.

The pattern of polarization may be followed within the visual arts (Picasso and Kandinsky; Chagall and Klee); the idea, after all, was first expressed in *The Philosophy of Modern Music*, organized around the opposition of Schoenberg and Stravinsky. But rather than multiplying examples, let us ask ourselves: why is all of this happening? What is the reason for this sudden, insistent repetition of the same technical configuration? Are there at work here—as Benjamin and Adorno suggest—the laws of historical dialectics?[33] But if that were the case, polarization ought to be the rule in literary history; whereas it's a very unusual exception, and clearly circumscribed in time. Should one then invoke the truly unique radicalism of the artistic world at the turn of the century? Fine; but what is the reason for that radicalism? Perhaps, the best thing is to turn once again to evolutionary theory, which, when it has to account for extreme forms, does not investigate 'the intrinsic character or meaning *of the*

---

33 'Philosophical history, the science of origin, is the form which, in the remotest extremes and the apparent excesses of the process of development, reveals the configuration of the idea—the sum total of all possible meaningful juxtapositions of such opposites. The representation of an idea can[not] be considered successful unless the whole range of possible extremes it contains has been virtually explored.' Walter Benjamin, *The Origin of German Baroque Drama*, p. 47. As Adorno wrote in *The Philosophy of Modern Music* (London 1973), 'only in such extremes can the essence of this music be defined; they alone permit the perception of its context of truth. "The middle road", according to Schoenberg . . . "is the only one which does not lead to Rome"' (p. 3).

extreme values themselves', but rather the conditions, and behaviour, of the system as a whole: 'When systems first arise they probe all the limits of possibility. Many variations don't work; the best solutions emerge, and variation diminishes.'[34]

When systems first arise; and this is fine, for we are discussing the beginnings of modernism. But then Gould adds that the 'early experimentation' is more varied and extreme the more 'empty' the given world is. And how can this specification apply to twentieth-century Europe, which has already been for centuries, in Braudel's formula, 'a world filled up'? Sure, we may say that not all of Europe is equally full, and that modernism sets in motion atypical and relatively empty areas, such as Joyce's Dublin, or Kafka's Prague; capitals of states that don't exist. But this novelty may be explained just as well (and probably better) with the general tendency towards a wider Europe—from 'Romania' to the first nation states, from the bourgeois north to the new nineteenth-century nations to the full incorporation of Russia. And so?

So, the reason for the modernist explosion shouldn't be sought in a new geographical space, but in new social spaces within the old geography. A space in terms of audience, first of all; as for baroque tragedy, and then for the novel, a new audience offers a freer, more

---

34   Stephen Jay Gould, *The Flamingo's Smile*, New York 1985, pp. 219–20. 'Many variations don't work'; today, we all know of Joyce's stream of consciousness; yet *Les lauriers sont coupées*, *The Making of the Americas*, *Berlin Alexanderplatz* are already novels for specialists; and some French texts of the 1920s, written under the spell of *Ulysses* (*Yeux de dix-huit ans*, *5,000*, *Amants, heureux amants*), are totally forgotten. If we are ever going to have a literary palaeontology, these library fossils will help us to understand why a certain technical solution was selected over others, and to have a better grasp of our cultural evolution. Like the history of life, the history of literature is a gigantic slaughterhouse of discarded possibilities; what it has excluded reveals its laws as clearly as what it has accepted.

hospitable ecosystem, with greater chances for formal experimentation. And especially *this* new audience, Pierre Bourdieu's 'intellectual field', which is a sort of anti-market, and flatly rejects the standardization of taste. It is following—whether it knows it or not—the slogan coined by Viktor Sklovski, the critical genius of the age: estrangement. Serious imitation of the everyday? Not in the least; defamiliarization, disfiguration, disautomatization . . . What has happened to European literature?

What has happened is that—let us open a short parenthesis—in the course of the nineteenth century, the urban audience has split. Poe, Balzac, Dickens are still appealing both to Baudelaire and to his philistine double. But the synthesis does not last, and in France and England (always there) a handful of new narrative forms—melodrama, *feuilleton*, detective fiction, science fiction—quickly capture millions of readers, preparing the way for the industry of sound and image. Is it a betrayal of literature, as cultivated critics have long maintained? Not at all; it is rather the coming to light of the limits of realism; at its ease in a solid, well-regulated world, which it makes even more so, the realistic temper doesn't know how to deal with those extreme situations, and terrible simplifications, that at times history forces one to face. Realism does not know how to represent the Other of Europe, nor yet—which is perhaps even worse—the Other *in* Europe: and so, mass literature takes over the task. Class struggle and the death of God, the ambiguities of language and the second industrial revolution; it is because it deals with all these phenomena that mass literature succeeds. And because it knows how to encrypt them, of course, in rhetorical tropes and plot devices that hide their deeper meanings, and foster a basic *unawareness* in readers. But literature always works like this, at least to a certain extent, and the excommunication of mass culture is truly a thing of the past.

But more: isn't there a sort of pact between mass literature and modernism—a sort of silent division of labour? Where the latter plunges into abstraction, decomposing the character to the point of making it vanish (Musil's 'qualities without the man'), the former strengthens anthropomorphic beliefs, filling the world with ghosts and Martians, vampires and great criminals. Modernism drops the 'linear plot' (Gide), and the 'story's thread' (Musil), to produce immense, immobile works; mass literature places plot in first place, gravitates towards the ending, has a tendency for short narratives (and thus prepares the conventions of film). Modernism, especially in poetry, exploits linguistic polysemy, stressing hermeneutic ambiguity and indecision; mass literature, especially detective fiction, is a dis-ambiguating machine, which aims at restoring the univocity of signs, to reimpose a rigid causality in all things human.[35]

Farewell, middle way of realism; farewell, educated nineteenth-century reader . . . Here one finds much less, or much more; formal automatisms for the majority, but all sorts of novelties for an over-educated aggressive minority. It's the first 'empty' space needed for the genesis of modernism, and it interacts with a political space, or more precisely, a space *liberated* from politics. Following Mannheim's hypothesis on the relationships between capitalism and culture, as the economic network of European societies becomes more diffuse and solid, a rigid symbolic orthodoxy is no longer needed to keep them together. Contrary to the great prophecy of the Dialectic, of Enlightenment, the 'unity of the Western system' does *not* 'grow increasingly stronger' as capitalism succeeds. Culture is freed from political obligations; surveillance decreases,

---

35   The metaphor used earlier—'division of labour'—is not completely satisfactory. In the 'epic' projects of the early twentieth century (Mahler, Joyce), where all sorts of 'low' conventions are conscripted for the edification of the aesthetic totality, mass culture and *avant-garde* techniques lie side by side—as Adorno put it—'like two halves that no longer form a whole'. The proximity multiplies dissonances and irony; it radicalizes the complexity of the formal system. Their blending at all costs—quite a triumph of entropy—will be the great achievement of postmodernism.

selective pressure grows weaker—and the strangest experiments are free to take place.[36]

It is not an uneventful process, of course: there are the book-burnings of degenerate art and the persecution of the Russian avant-garde; on a more bland note, the scuffle at the première of the *Sacre du Printemps*, the banning of *Ulysses*, fistfights and insults at each Dada event. But the trend is clear, and, within capitalist democracies, never really called into question. Art has become a protected, a neutralized space; as Edgar Wind observed, 'Art is so well received because it has lost its sting.'[37] In a sort of unspoken pact with the devil, nothing is forbidden any longer, because nothing is significant any longer. For the first generation, this is an exhilarating discovery: in the beginning was the scandal, as Mann's Mephisto will put it, and the scandal was made into a success. But in the perfect void one cannot breathe, and it won't take long for European literature to discover that it has nothing left to say.

8. Cité pleine de rêves . . .

An audience space. A politically neutralized space. And a geographical space: after the Europe of courts, the *République des Lettres*, the Lutheran world of eighteenth- and nineteenth-century tragedy, the nation states of the novel, it's time for the Europe of capitals.[38]

---

36   It goes without saying that the aesthetic sphere had begun to move towards autonomy three or four centuries earlier. A relative security against arbitrary acts of power has thus been almost a constant of modern European literature, and must have encouraged its formal inventiveness.

37   Edgar Wind, *Art and Anarchy*, London 1963, p. 9.

38   These many Europes arise successively, one after the other, but they later coexist for long stretches of time, and the cohabitation of diverse formal spaces within a fixed geography has induced a growing complexity in the European literary system. The form of the present essay—which does not begin with a fully given concept of European literature, but constructs it in the course of time, adding new determinations along the way—tries to reproduce the historical evolution of its object.

Better still, of metropolises: Milan more than Rome, Barcelona more than Madrid, Petersburg more than Moscow. Their true bond is no longer with the interior (towards the provinces, or the countryside), but with Europe: with the wealthy north-west, and even more so with other metropolises, at times quite far removed in physical space, but close and congenial in the space of culture. Under their sign, in fact, the very boundaries of Europe begin to lose their relevance; for the *avant-garde*, Paris is closer to Buenos Aires than to Lyon; Berlin more akin to Manhattan than to Lübeck.

This syntony between modernism and the metropolis arises first and foremost out of a common enthusiasm for the growing division of labour. In the theoretical field, it's the analytical breakthrough of the Formalist school; in the artistic field, techniques such as polyphony, rooted in the proliferation of professional jargons and sectorial codes. Specialism, for this happy generation, is freedom; freedom from the (narrow) measure of the (bad) taste of the (bourgeois) nineteenth century. Specialism emancipates sound, meaning, colour, line, time; whole worlds to be explored with no fear for the equilibrium of the whole. And specialism is radicalism; it plays with daring hypotheses, which would never pass the rigid controls of the provinces, but in the niches of the metropolis (in the garrets of the *bohème*) may survive and prosper. It is the big city that protects what is unusual, writes a sociologist at the turn of the century, and that makes it more unusual still:

> The city is the spectroscope of society; it analyses and sifts the population, separating and classifying the diverse elements. The entire progress of civilization is a process of differentiation, and the city is the greatest differentiator. The mediocrity of the country is transformed by the city into the highest talent or the lowest criminal. Genius is often born in the country, but it is brought to light and developed by the city [just as] the boy

thief of the village becomes the daring bank robber of the metropolis.[39]

Division of labour aside, the metropolis of the early twentieth century is also a great meeting-place, which multiplies the 'artists of world-literary formation' first perceived by Nietzsche, and spreads what Enzensberger has called 'the universal language of modern poetry':[40] this strange *lingua franca*, obscure but effective, and capable of travelling any distance; the Italian futurists, who write their manifestos in French, and are immediately read by their Russian contemporaries; the Rumanian Tristan Tzara, who invents in German-speaking Zürich the antilanguage of Dada; French surrealism, which will give its best on American soil, in narratives written in Spanish . . .

This is Raymond Williams's 'City of Strangers': where language has lost its naturalness and must in a sense be reinvented. It's the story of Joyce's English, 'familiar and foreign' as early as *Portrait*; and then, as years go by, less and less comparable to a national language. *Ulysses*, with its Latin title referring to a Greek hero, and

---

39   Adna F. Weber, *The Growth of Cities in the Nineteenth Century*, New York 1899, p. 442. The textual history of *Hamlet* offers a lovely instance of the role of the metropolis in literary invention. The first printed versions of *Hamlet* are, as is well known, three; the first in-quarto (Q1), of 1603; the second in-quarto (Q2), of 1604; and the in-folio (F) of 1623. The *Hamlet* we read is based on Q2 and F; it's from them that it draws its 'strangeness', its tragi-comic web, the enigmatic structure which has turned it into a key text of modernity. Q1, on the other hand (the bad Quarto, as philologists affectionately call it), apart from other major defects, ruthlessly simplifies everything; it gives us a one-dimensional tragedy, lacking in the heterogeneity and complexity of *Hamlet*. And where does Q1 come from? In all likelihood, from the sudden need to prepare a text for a tour in the provinces. Formal inventiveness, tolerated in London, and in fact rewarded with a great success, is deemed implausible as soon as the play has to leave the metropolis.

40   Nietzsche's phrase, on Wagner and French late Romanticism, is from *Beyond Good and Evil* (1886); Enzensberger's essay is collected in *Einzelheiten*.

written by an Irishman moving between 'Trieste-Zurich-Paris' (a
Trieste that was still the Italian port of the Austro-Hungarian
Empire . . .), is the clearest sign of a literature for which national
boundaries have lost all explanatory power.

Intrinsic to the City of Strangers, then, is a great literature of exiles:
the final chapter in a long-term tendency, a true constant, of
European history. Dante leaves Florence for Verona, and Galilei
(mistakenly, as Brecht would say) Padua for Florence; the great
philosophy of the seventeenth century finds a refuge in wealthy
Amsterdam ('That *Bank of Conscience*, where not one so strange /
Opinion but finds Credit, and Exchange': Andrew Marvell); the
Romantic movement swarms across the continent; there is Paris
capital of the nineteenth century, the central European migration to
England, Scandinavia and the United States, and the Jewish
diaspora, of course, a little everywhere.[41] See here how Europe is
more than the sum of its parts; it is only thanks to the diversified
system of its nation states that what each *individual* state would
gladly silence forever can survive and flourish. And as for national
literatures, this pattern suggests that their strength is directly
proportional to their *impurity*; hegemony does not belong to those
that produce exiles, but to those that welcome them. Some great
twentieth-century techniques, such as *collage*, or intertextuality,

---

41   According to a classic study by Carlo Dionisotti, the Italian literary
canon (the first to be established in Europe) was entirely the product of exile: 'the
work of an exile' Dante's *Comedy*, 'a voluntary exile' Petrarch at the time of the
Canzoniere, 'exile in the midst of his own fatherland' the situation out of which
arises the *Decameron*. See *Geografia e storia della letteratura italiana*, Turin 1967
(1951), p. 32. Dionisotti wrote the essay in London, after Fascism had forced him
too into exile. At the other end of the European development, Perry Anderson
has redefined the great 'English' culture of the twentieth century as almost
entirely the work of emigrés; see his 'Components of the National Culture', *New
Left Review* I: 50 (July–August 1968). The most ambitious overall description of
the European canon—*Mimesis*—was in its turn written by Auerbach during his
exile in Istanbul.

will even display a kind of foreignness as an essential ingredient of literary experiments—as will also, in a related field, the key Formalist concept of 'estrangement'.

Such is the lesson coming from the great English modernism—if English is the right word for a Pole who navigates around the world, an Irishman who wanders across half of Europe, but keeps away from London, and two Americans, one of them promptly ensconced in Fascist Italy. And if English is, again, the word for Conrad's style, unstable meeting-place of so many European languages, eroded and overdetermined by life in the colonies; for the opening of *Cantos*, translation into high English of a late Latin translation of an archaic Greek original; for *The Waste Land*, with four languages encased into each other already in its title-page; or finally, but it's too easy, for *Finnegan's Wake*. A Babel of places, languages, times; Europe is breaking out of Europe. Where to?

9. WELTLITERATUR

Against Curtius, I have explained the greatness of European literature by its relative distance from the classical inheritance. 'Relative' distance, as from the nineteenth century onwards a new geopolitical reality—Western, yet not European—emphasizes this new state of affairs. America, reads a lyric of the old Goethe:

> America, you have it better
> Than our continent, the old one;
> You have no fallen castles
> And no basalts.

> You in your inmost are not worried,
> When it is time to live,
> By useless memories
> And vain disputes.

Useless memories and vain disputes . . . 'I have more memories than if
I were a thousand years old', opens one stanza of Baudelaire's *Spleen*.
But European modernity cannot escape the fate described by Hans
Blumenberg in his great study on *The Legitimacy of the Modern Age*; it
cannot simply begin anew, ignoring previous history. Even though the
past no longer dominates the present, it still survives within it; the *new*
age arises in the *old* world, trapped in a veritable spatio-temporal paradox. For Ernst Bloch and Reinhardt Koselleck—who have baptized it
'nonsynchronism'—such conjunction has far-reaching consequences
in the political sphere. And the same applies to literature; to the Joyce–
Kafka generation, to be sure, but not only to that.

Side by side with the novel, in fact—with its average style, homogeneous space, and circumscribed temporal horizon: the solid form of 'the
present'—side by side with the novel, and silently opposed to it, another
great narrative begins to develop in nineteenth-century Europe (and in
between Europe and the world): an epic form, in whose key scene—the
Walpurgisnacht—a Babel of discordant voices points out how precari-
ous is the cohabitation of the past and the future. Kraus, Döblin, Pound,
Mann, Meyrink, Joyce; before them, Melville and Flaubert; before still,
Goethe: as it all begins with the gigantic mosaic of *Faust*, where a man
of modernity must face the medieval and classical past; must learn to
exorcize and conquer them, and finally (but never completely) must
also learn to relinquish them. *Museum der Weltliteratur*, a recent critic
has defined *Faust*; and it's true, Goethe's poem is the perfect text for a
world which has crystallized in its museums a deep ambivalence
towards the past. We should venerate the past as a sacred thing, the
museum tells us—but after having secured it within well-guarded
marble jails;[42] we should acknowledge it as past, yet possibly endow it

---

42 *Museum der Weltliteratur* is the expression used by Heinz Schlaffer in his
study of Goethe's poem (*Faust Zweiter Teil, Die Allegorie des 19, Jahrhunderts*,
Stuttgart 1981, p. 107). On the analogies between the architecture of museums
and that of jails, see the first part of *The Lost Centre*, by Hans Sedlmayr.

with a contemporary meaning as well. As within mythic *bricolage*, or *Faust*'s allegory, in a museum, the signifieds of antiquity become the signifiers of Modernity; face to face with objects torn from their world, the European imagination acquires an extreme, at times irresponsible freedom with regard to historical materials. Would Mona Lisa have acquired her moustache had she not been inside a museum? And indeed, the great modernist myth of origins tells the story of a young painter, unsure of the road to follow, who happens to be near the Trocadéro; he walks inside, and wanders for a while through its rooms crowded with outlandish objects. When Pablo Picasso's stroll is over, Cubism begins, with which everything else begins.

The museum and the *avant-garde*, unsuspectible accomplices in a violent reorganization of the past. But is it simply the past at stake, in nonsynchronism? The great nineteenth-century museums are located in London, Paris, Berlin, and are filled with objects taken from Greece, from the Roman Empire; Mediterranean Europe, taken by force to the north. And then Egypt, Assyria, Persia, India, China . . . As in *Faust*, in the archaeological museum time and space overlap: better, history becomes a trope for geography; the conquest of the past—the conquest of Helen of Greece—a trope for the subjection of the world. And so, at the very hour of its birth, Goethe's cultural dream immediately forces a question upon us. *Weltliteratur*: world literature, human literature? Or the literature of imperialism?

Its capitals, after all, are England and France: the two major colonial powers (and a colonial museum is what the Trocadéro used to be). And then department stores, *marchés aux puces*, panoramas, ads, passages, world fairs; Baedekers, travel agents, catalogues, timetables . . . At the turn of the century, the entire planet is channelled into the Western metropolis (Cosmopolis, as some decide to call it) and the truly epic, world-historical scope of many modernist works is indeed dependent on Europe's world domination.

Unpleasant but true, imperialism plays for modernism the same role played by the French Revolution for the realist novel; it poses the basic problem—how can such a heterogeneous and growing wealth be perceived? how can it be mastered?—addressed by *collage*, intertextuality, or the stream of consciousness. Without imperialism, in other words, we would have no modernism; its raw materials would be lacking, and also the challenge that animated many of its inventions. And after all, what are Conrad and Eliot and Pound in search of? Certainly not of the small, cohesive England cherished a few years earlier by Henry James; but of the Merchant Navy, of the City, of the disorderly width of an Empire which is a planetary embodiment of nonsynchronism.

The truth is, for the great generation of exiles Europe is no longer enough; they perceive it as a limit, an obstacle to the intelligence of reality. 'All of Europe had contributed to the making of Kurtz'; yes, but Kurtz's truth, and with him Europe's, is down in the jungle, not in Brussels or London. Marlow's audience is still a European one, but the material of his stories belongs to the East, to Africa; and their formal pathos lies in the difficulty of saying in a European language experiences which are European no longer. Pound's poetics, and quite a few of the *Cantos*, are obsessed by the (frustrated) ambition of finding a Western equivalent for ideogrammatic writing. The last word of *The Waste Land* is a Sanskrit term, hieratically repeated three times, but declared untranslatable by Eliot himself; and the poem emphasizes more than once the Eastern roots of European symbols and myths, just as Joyce had accepted, a few years earlier, Victor Bérard's thesis on the Phoenician basis of the *Odyssey*.

Europe has become small again. The world escapes it, the new escapes it. The new? Yes and no. The English exiles and the Surrealists, the *Demoiselles d'Avignon* and the *Sacre du Printemps*; in the early years of the century, the genesis of the new coincides as a rule with the rediscovery of the primitive. And after all, it is the appropriate paradox, to bring to an end the trajectory of European literature. Baroque tragedy tears it away from the classical heritage; the novel roots it solidly in the present; *Faust* even starts playing with materials which had long been venerable. No doubt about it, the break with the past has been successful. *Too* successful, perhaps, as for so many other European attempts? That is what it looks like; and from the falling apart of historical continuity originates that overpowering *need for myth* that characterizes the modernist moment. Myth as depth, order, primordial unity; but also as visionary hallucination, and 'hellish fire under your pot', to quote Mann's Mephisto again. It is the 'bloody barbarism' which supports Adrian Leverkühn's 'bloodless intellectualism'; the explosive compression of opposites that embodies the greatness (and the ambiguity) of so many *avant-gardes*—and bears the mark of a Europe wavering between anarchy and dictatorship.

That such an extreme tension would not last long, is hardly surprising. Yet that this phase would also be the last creative drive of European literature—this was a surprise for everybody. But too many tendencies, and too deep, were simultaneously at work as the twentieth century moved on: military devastations, limited political sovereignty, migration of economic hegemony towards the United States, and then the Pacific; so many blows for the symbolic universe of the European nation state. In the cultural field, the new media, and the triumph of sound and image over the written word. And finally, the *coup de grâce* of other literatures, from other continents, still capable of that narrative invention which modernism had stifled, at the cost of a long-standing unpopularity. Face to face with so many difficulties, European literature has stalled: finding itself—for the first time in modern history—an importer of those formal novelties that it is no longer capable of producing. In fact, the very autonomy of Europe is now in doubt, reshuffled as its culture is by the world network that has replaced it. For some of the major European literatures, inter-continental, extra-European exchanges have quickly become the most important ones;[43] as for intra-European relationships, a continent that falls in love with Milan Kundera deserves to end like Atlantis. There is not much more to say, the conditions which have granted European literature its greatness have run their course, and only a miracle could reverse the trend. But Europe has probably already had more than its rightful share of miracles.

---

43   This is certainly the case for the Spanish and Portuguese literatures of Latin America, and for literatures in English from Asia and Africa (not to speak of America and Australia); francophone African literatures may soon play the same role.

Conjectures on World Literature

'Conjectures', too, was an occasional piece, like 'Modern European Literature' before it. At Columbia, the department of English and Comparative Literature was re-thinking its structure, and I had proposed to detach Comparative Literature from English; as a series of gloomy departmental confrontations got under way, the Italian Academy asked me to organize a small conference: four papers, of which mine would be one. It seemed like a good opportunity to bring disagreements into the open.

The discussion was on comparative literature; writing on world *literature instead was, at the time, a somewhat polemical choice—and problematic, too: I remember considering the title 'World Literature?', with a question mark at the end, to signal my perplexity about a concept no one seemed to use any more. Pascale Casanova's* Republique mondiale des lettres, *which was about to be published while I was writing 'Conjectures', helped change this state of affairs; but back then, people were, at a minimum, sceptical (my colleagues at Columbia, for instance, refused to use the words 'World Literature' for the name of the new department). But I had found a strong conceptual model in Wallerstein's world-systems theory, and went ahead just the same.*

Wallerstein's tripartition of core, periphery, and semi-periphery appealed to me because it explained a number of empirical findings I had slowly gathered in the course of the 1990s: France's continental centrality, so often mentioned in the essay on European literature; the peculiar productivity of the semi-periphery, analyzed in Modern Epic; *the unevenness of narrative markets of the* Atlas of the European Novel—*all these, and more, strongly corroborated Wallerstein's model. Besides resting solidly on facts, the theory also highlighted the systemic constraints under which national literatures had to develop: in a starkly realistic reversal of the creative ecosystem of 'Modern European Literature', world-systems theory showed the power of core literatures to overdetermine, and in fact distort, the development of most national cultures.*

Although based entirely on the work of Marxist thinkers—Jameson, Schwarz, Miyoshi, Mukherjee, and of course Wallerstein himself— and backed by quite a lot of historical evidence (or at least: a lot, given the parameters of literary history), 'Conjectures' provoked heated reactions on the left, to which I replied, three years later, in 'More Conjectures'. By an odd twist of fate, this first wave of critiques was followed by an even more violent one—this time, equanimously from the left and the right—aimed at the idea of 'distant reading'. That fatal formula had been a late addition to the paper, where it was initially specified, in an allusion to the basic procedure of quantitative history, by the words 'serial reading'. Then, somehow, 'serial' disappeared, and 'distant' remained. Partly, it was meant as a joke; a moment of relief in a rather relentless argument. But no one seems to have taken it as a joke, and they were probably right.

'Nowadays, national literature doesn't mean much: the age of world literature is beginning, and everybody should contribute to hasten its advent.' This was Goethe, of course, talking to Eckermann in 1827; and these are Marx and Engels, twenty years later, in 1848:

'National one-sidedness and narrow-mindedness become more and more impossible, and from the many national and local literatures, a world literature arises.' *Weltliteratur*: this is what Goethe and Marx have in mind. Not 'comparative', but world literature: the Chinese novel that Goethe was reading at the time of that exchange, or the bourgeoisie of the *Manifesto*, which has 'given a cosmopolitan character to production and consumption in every country'. Well, let me put it very simply: comparative literature has not lived up to these beginnings. It's been a much more modest intellectual enterprise, fundamentally limited to western Europe, and mostly revolving around the river Rhine (German philologists working on French literature). Not much more.

This is my own intellectual formation, and scientific work always has limits. But limits change, and I think it's time we returned to that old ambition of *Weltliteratur*: after all, the literature around us is now unmistakably a planetary system. The question is not really *what* we should do—the question is *how*. What does it mean, studying world literature? How do we do it? I work on west European narrative between 1790 and 1930, and already feel like a charlatan outside of Britain or France. World literature?

Many people have read more and better than I have, of course, but still, we are talking of hundreds of languages and literatures here. Reading 'more' seems hardly to be the solution. Especially because we've just started rediscovering what Margaret Cohen calls the 'great unread'. 'I work on west European narrative, etc. . . .' Not really, I work on its canonical fraction, which is not even 1 per cent of published literature. And again, some people have read more, but the point is that there are thirty thousand nineteenth-century British novels out there, forty, fifty, sixty thousand—no one really knows, no one has read them, no one ever will. And then there are French novels, Chinese, Argentinian, American . . .

LIBRARY, UNIVERSITY OF CHESTER

Reading 'more' is always a good thing, but not the solution.[1]

Perhaps it's too much, tackling the world and the unread at the same time. But I actually think that it's our greatest chance, because the sheer enormity of the task makes it clear that world literature cannot be literature, bigger; what we are already doing, just more of it. It has to be different. The *categories* have to be different. 'It is not the "actual" interconnection of "things"', Max Weber wrote, 'but the *conceptual* interconnection of *problems* which defines the scope of the various sciences. A new "science" emerges where a new problem is pursued by a new method.'[2] That's the point: world literature is not an object, it's a *problem*, and a problem that asks for a new critical method: and no one has ever found a method by just reading more texts. That's not how theories come into being; they need a leap, a wager—a hypothesis, to get started.

WORLD LITERATURE: ONE AND UNEQUAL

I will borrow this initial hypothesis from the world-systems school of economic history, for which international capitalism is a system that is simultaneously *one*, and *unequal*: with a core, and a periphery (and a semi-periphery) that are bound together in a relationship of growing inequality. One, and unequal: *one* literature (*Weltliteratur*, singular, as in Goethe and Marx), or perhaps, better, one world literary system (of inter-related literatures); but a system which is different from what Goethe and Marx had hoped for, because it's profoundly unequal. 'Foreign debt is as inevitable in Brazilian letters as in any other field', writes Roberto Schwarz in a splendid essay on 'The Importing of the Novel to Brazil': 'it's not simply an easily

---

1   I address the problem of the great unread in 'The Slaughterhouse of Literature', in this volume.

2   Max Weber, 'Objectivity in Social Science and Social Policy', in *The Methodology of the Social Sciences*, New York 1949 (1904), p. 68.

dispensable part of the work in which it appears, but a complex feature of it';[3] and Itamar Even-Zohar, reflecting on Hebrew literature: 'Interference [is] a relationship between literatures, whereby a . . . source literature may become a source of direct or indirect loans [*Importing* of the novel, direct and indirect loans, foreign debt: see how economic metaphors have been subterraneously at work in literary history]—a source of loans for . . . a target literature . . . *There is no symmetry in literary interference. A target literature is, more often than not, interfered with by a source literature which completely ignores it.*'[4]

This is what one and unequal means: the destiny of a culture (usually a culture of the periphery, as Montserrat Iglesias Santos has specified)[5] is intersected and altered by another culture (from the core) that 'completely ignores it'. A familiar scenario, this asymmetry in international power—and later I will say more about Schwarz's 'foreign debt' as a complex literary feature. Right now, let me spell out the consequences of taking an explanatory matrix from social history and applying it to literary history.

DISTANT READING

Writing about comparative social history, Marc Bloch once coined a lovely 'slogan', as he himself called it: 'years of analysis for a day of synthesis';[6] and if you read Braudel or Wallerstein

---

3 Roberto Schwarz, 'The Importing of the Novel to Brazil and Its Contradictions in the Work of Roberto Alencar' (1977), in *Misplaced Ideas*, London 1992, p. 50.

4 Itamar Even-Zohar, 'Laws of Literary Interference', in *Poetics Today*, 1990, pp. 54, 62.

5 Montserrat Iglesias Santos, 'El sistema literario: teoría empírica y teoría de los polisistemas', in Darío Villanueva (ed.), *Avances en teoría de la literatura*, Santiago de Compostela 1994, p. 339: 'It is important to emphasize that interferences occur most often at the periphery of the system.'

6 Marc Bloch, 'Pour une histoire comparée des sociétés européennes', *Revue de synthèse historique*, 1928.

you immediately see what Bloch had in mind. The text which is strictly Wallerstein's, his 'day of synthesis', occupies one-third of a page, one-quarter, maybe half; the rest are quotations (1,400, in the first volume of *The Modern World-System*). Years of analysis; other people's analysis, which Wallerstein's page synthesizes into a system.

Now, if we take this model seriously, the study of world literature will somehow have to reproduce this 'page'—which is to say: this relationship between analysis and synthesis—for the literary field. But in that case, literary history will quickly become very different from what it is now: it will become 'second hand': a patchwork of other people's research, *without a single direct textual reading*. Still ambitious, and actually even more so than before (world literature!); but the ambition is now directly proportional *to the distance from the text*: the more ambitious the project, the greater must the distance be.

The United States is the country of close reading, so I don't expect this idea to be particularly popular. But the trouble with close reading (in all of its incarnations, from the new criticism to deconstruction) is that it necessarily depends on an extremely small canon. This may have become an unconscious and invisible premise by now, but it is an iron one nonetheless: you invest so much in individual texts *only* if you think that very few of them really matter. Otherwise, it doesn't make sense. And if you want to look beyond the canon (and of course, world literature will do so: it would be absurd if it didn't!), close reading will not do it. It's not designed to do it, it's designed to do the opposite. At bottom, it's a theological exercise—very solemn treatment of very few texts taken very seriously—whereas what we really need is a little pact with the devil: we know how to read texts, now let's learn how *not* to read them. Distant reading: where distance, let me repeat it, *is a condition of knowledge*: it allows you to focus on units that are much smaller or much larger than the text: devices, themes, tropes—or genres and systems. And if, between the very small and the very large, the text itself disappears, well, it is one of those cases when one can justifiably say, Less is more. If we want to understand the system in its entirety, we must accept losing something. We always pay a price for theoretical knowledge: reality is infinitely rich; concepts are abstract, are poor. But it's precisely this 'poverty' that makes it possible to handle them, and therefore to know. This is why less is actually more.[7]

THE WESTERN EUROPEAN NOVEL: RULE OR EXCEPTION?

Let me give you an example of the conjunction of distant reading and world literature. An example, not a model; and of course my example, based on the field I know (elsewhere, things may be very different). A few years ago, introducing Kojin Karatani's *Origins of Modern Japanese Literature*, Fredric Jameson noticed that in the take-off of the modern Japanese novel, 'the raw material of Japanese social experience and the abstract formal patterns of Western novel construction cannot always be welded together seamlessly'; and he referred in this respect to Masao Miyoshi's *Accomplices of Silence*, and Meenakshi Mukherjee's *Realism and Reality* (a study of the early Indian novel).[8] And it's true, these books return quite often to the complicated 'problems' (Mukherjee's term) arising from the encounter of Western form and Japanese or Indian reality.

Now, that the same configuration should occur in such different cultures as India and Japan—this was curious; and it became even

---

7 Or to quote Weber again: 'concepts are primarily analytical instruments for the intellectual mastery of empirical data'. ('Objectivity in Social Science and Social Policy', p. 106.) Inevitably, the larger the field one wants to study, the greater the need for abstract 'instruments' capable of mastering empirical reality.

8 Fredric Jameson, 'In the Mirror of Alternate Modernities', in Karatani Kojin, *Origins of Modern Japanese Literature*, Durham–London 1993, p. xiii.

more curious when I realized that Roberto Schwarz had independently discovered very much the same pattern in Brazil. So, eventually, I started using these pieces of evidence to reflect on the relationship between markets and forms; and then, without really knowing what I was doing, began to treat Jameson's insight as if it were—one should always be cautious with these claims, but there is really no other way to say it—as if it were a *law of literary evolution*: in cultures that belong to the periphery of the literary system (which means: almost all cultures, inside and outside Europe), the modern novel first arises not as an autonomous development but as a compromise between a western formal influence (usually French or English) and local materials.

This first idea expanded into a little cluster of laws,[9] and it was all very interesting, but . . . it was still just an idea; a conjecture that had to be tested, possibly on a large scale, and so I decided to follow the wave of diffusion of the modern novel (roughly: from 1750 to 1950) in the pages of literary history. Gasperetti and Goscilo on late-eighteenth-century Eastern Europe;[10] Toschi and Martí-López on early-nineteenth-century Southern Europe;[11] Franco and

---

9 I have begun to sketch them out in the last chapter of the *Atlas of the European Novel 1800–1900* (London 1998), and this is more or less how they sound: second, the formal compromise is usually prepared by a massive wave of west European translations; third, the compromise itself is generally unstable (Miyoshi has a great image for this: the 'impossible programme' of Japanese novels); but fourth, in those rare instances when the impossible programme succeeds, we have genuine formal revolutions.

10 'Given the history of its formative stage, it is no surprise that the early Russian novel contains a host of conventions popularized in French and British literature', writes David Gasperetti in *The Rise of the Russian Novel* (DeKalb 1998, p. 5). And Helena Goscilo, in her 'Introduction' to Krasicki's *Adventures of Mr Nicholas Wisdom*: '*The Adventures* is read most fruitfully in the context of the West European literature on which it drew heavily for inspiration.' (Ignacy Krasicki, *The Adventures of Mr Nicholas Wisdom*, Evanston 1992, p. xv.)

11 'There was a demand for foreign products, and production had to comply', explains Luca Toschi, speaking of the Italian narrative market around

Sommer on mid-century Latin America;[12] Frieden on the Yiddish novels of the 1860s;[13] Moosa, Said and Allen on the Arabic novels of the 1870s;[14] Evin and Parla on the Turkish novels of the same years;[15] Anderson on the Filipino *Noli Me Tangere*, of 1887; Zhao

---

1800 ('Alle origini della narrativa di romanzo in Italia', in Massimo Saltafuso [ed.], *Il viaggio del narrare*, Florence 1989, p. 19). A generation later, in Spain, 'readers are not interested in the originality of the Spanish novel; their only desire is that it would adhere to those foreign models with which they have become familiar': and so, concludes Elisa Martí-López, one may well say that between 1800 and 1850 'the Spanish novel is being written in France' (Elisa Martí-López, 'La orfandad de la novela española: política editorial y creación literaria a mediados del siglo XIX', *Bulletin Hispanique*, 1997).

12   'Obviously, lofty ambitions were not enough. All too often the nineteenth-century Spanish-American novel is clumsy and inept, with a plot derived at second hand from the contemporary European Romantic novel.' (Jean Franco, *Spanish-American Literature*, Cambridge 1969, p. 56.) 'If heroes and heroines in mid-nineteenth century Latin American novels were passionately desiring one another across traditional lines . . . those passions might not have prospered a generation earlier. In fact, modernizing lovers were learning how to dream their erotic fantasies by reading the European romances they hoped to realize.' (Doris Sommer, *Foundational Fictions: The National Romances of Latin America*, Berkeley–Los Angeles 1991, pp. 31–2.)

13   'Yiddish writers parodied—appropriated, incorporated, and modified—diverse elements from European novels and stories.' (Ken Frieden, *Classic Yiddish Fiction*, Albany 1995, p. x.)

14   Matti Moosa quotes the novelist Yahya Haqqi: 'there is no harm in admitting that the modern story came to us from the West. Those who laid down its foundations were persons influenced by European literature, particularly French literature. Although masterpieces of English literature were translated into Arabic, French literature was the fountain of our story.' (Matti Moosa, *The Origins of Modern Arabic Fiction*, 2nd edn, 1997 [1970], p. 93.) For Edward Said, 'at some point writers in Arabic became aware of European novels and began to write works like them.' (Edward Said, *Beginnings*, New York 1985 [1975], p. 81.) And Roger Allen: 'In more literary terms, increasing contacts with Western literatures led to translations of works of European fiction into Arabic, followed by their adaptation and imitation, and culminating in the appearance of an indigenous tradition of modern fiction in Arabic.' (Roger Allen, *The Arabic Novel*, Syracuse 1995, p. 12.)

15   'The first novels in Turkey were written by members of the new intelligentsia, trained in government service and well-exposed to French

and Wang on turn-of-the-century Qing fiction;[16] Obiechina, Irele and Quayson on West African novels between the 1920s and the 1950s[17] (plus of course Karatani, Miyoshi, Mukherjee, Even-Zohar and Schwarz). Four continents, 200 years, over twenty independent critical studies, and they all agreed: when a culture starts moving towards the modern novel, it's *always* as a compromise between foreign form and local materials. Jameson's 'law' had passed the

---

literature', writes Ahmet O. Evin (*Origins and Development of the Turkish Novel*, Minneapolis 1983, p. 10); and Jale Parla: 'the early Turkish novelists combined the traditional narrative forms with the examples of the western novel' ('Desiring Tellers, Fugitive Tales: Don Quixote Rides Again, This Time in Istanbul').

16   'The narrative dislocation of the sequential order of events is perhaps the most outstanding impression late Qing writers received when they read or translated Western fiction. At first, they tried to tidy up the sequence of the events back into their pre-narrated order. When such tidying was not feasible during translation, an apologetic note would be inserted . . . Paradoxically, when he alters rather than follows the original, the translator does not feel it necessary to add an apologetic note.' (Henry Y. H. Zhao, *The Uneasy Narrator: Chinese Fiction from the Traditional to the Modern*, Oxford 1995, p. 150.) 'Late Qing writers enthusiastically renewed their heritage with the help of foreign models', writes David Der-wei Wang: 'I see the late Qing as the beginning of the Chinese literary "modern" because writers' pursuit of novelty was no longer contained within indigenously defined barriers but was inextricably defined by the multilingual, crosscultural trafficking of ideas, technologies, and powers in the wake of nineteenth-century Western expansionism.' (*Fin-de-siècle Splendor: Repressed Modernities of Late Qing Fiction, 1849–1911*, Stanford 1997, pp. 5, 19.)

17   'One essential factor shaping West African novels by indigenous writers was the fact that they appeared after the novels on Africa written by non-Africans . . . the foreign novels embody elements which indigenous writers had to react against when they set out to write.' (Emmanuel Obiechina, *Culture, Tradition and Society in the West African Novel*, Cambridge 1975, p. 17.) 'The first Dahomean novel, *Doguicimi* . . . is interesting as an experiment in recasting the oral literature of Africa within the form of a French novel.' (Abiola Irele, *The African Experience in Literature and Ideology*, Bloomington 1990, p. 147.) 'It was the rationality of realism that seemed adequate to the task of forging a national identity at the conjuncture of global realities . . . the rationalism of realism dispersed in texts as varied as newspapers, Onitsha market literature, and in the earliest titles of the African Writers Series that dominated the discourses of the period.' (Ato Quayson, *Strategic Transformations in Nigerian Writing*, Bloomington 1997, p. 162.)

test—the first test, anyway.[18][19] And actually more than that: it had completely reversed the received historical explanation of these matters: because if the compromise between the foreign and the local is so ubiquitous, then those independent paths that are usually taken to be the rule of the rise of the novel (the Spanish, the French, and especially the British case)—*well, they're not the rule at all, they're the exception*. They come first, yes, but they're not at all typical. The 'typical' rise of the novel is Krasicki, Kemal, Rizal, Maran—not Defoe.

EXPERIMENTS WITH HISTORY

See the beauty of distant reading plus world literature: they go against the grain of national historiography. And they do so in the form of *an experiment*. You define a unit of analysis (like here, the formal compromise),[20] and then follow its metamorphoses in a vari-

---

18   In the seminar where I first presented this 'second-hand' criticism, Sarah Golstein asked a very good, Candide-like question: You decide to rely on another critic. Fine. But what if he's wrong? My reply: If he's wrong, you are wrong too, and you soon know, because you don't find any corroboration—you don't find Goscilo, Martí-López, Sommer, Evin, Zhao, Irele . . . And it's not just that you don't find positive corroboration; sooner or later you find all sorts of facts you cannot explain, and your hypothesis is falsified, in Popper's famous formulation, and you must throw it away. Fortunately, this hasn't been the case so far, and Jameson's insight still stands.

19   OK, I confess, in order to test the conjecture I actually did read some of these 'first novels' in the end (Krasicki's *Adventures of Mr Nicholas Wisdom*, Abramowitsch's *Little Man*, Rizal's *Noli Me Tangere*, Futabatei's *Ukigumo*, René Maran's *Batouala*, Paul Hazoumé's *Doguicimi*). This kind of 'reading', however, no longer produces interpretations but merely *tests* them: it's not the beginning of the critical enterprise, but its appendix. And then, here you don't really read the *text* anymore, but rather through the text, looking for your unit of analysis. The task is constrained from the start; it's a reading without freedom.

20   For practical purposes, the larger the geographical space one wants to study, the smaller should the unit of analysis be: a concept (in our case), a device, a trope, a limited narrative unit—something like this. In a follow-up paper, I hope to sketch out the diffusion of stylistic 'seriousness' (Auerbach's keyword in *Mimesis*) in nineteenth- and twentieth-century novels.

ety of environments[21]—until, ideally, *all* of literary history becomes a long chain of related experiments: a 'dialogue between fact and fancy', as Peter Medawar calls it: 'between what could be true, and what is in fact the case'.[22] Apt words for this research, in the course of which, as I was reading my fellow historians, it became clear that the encounter of Western forms and local reality did indeed produce everywhere a structural compromise—as the law predicted—but also, that the compromise itself was taking rather different forms. At times, especially in the second half of the nineteenth century and in Asia, it tended to be very unstable:[23] an 'impossible programme',

---

21   How to set up a reliable sample—that is to say, what series of national literatures and individual novels provide a satisfactory test of a theory's predictions—is of course quite a complex issue. In this preliminary sketch, my sample (and its justification) leave much to be desired.

22   Scientific research 'begins as a story about a Possible World', Medawar goes on, 'and ends by being, as nearly as we can make it, a story about real life'. His words are quoted by James Bird in *The Changing World of Geography*, Oxford 1993, p. 5. Bird himself offers a very elegant version of the experimental model.

23   Aside from Miyoshi and Karatani (for Japan), Mukherjee (for India), and Schwarz (for Brazil), the compositional paradoxes and the instability of the formal compromise are often mentioned in the literature on the Turkish, Chinese and Arabic novel. Discussing Namik Kemal's *Intibah*, Ahmet Evin points out how 'the merger of the two themes, one based on the traditional family life and the other on the yearnings of a prostitute, constitute the first attempt in Turkish fiction to achieve a type of psychological dimension observed in European novels within a thematic framework based on Turkish life. *However, due both to the incompatibility of the themes and to the difference in the degree of emphasis placed on each, the unity of the novel is blemished. The structural defects of* Intibah *are symptomatic of the differences between the methodology and concerns of the Turkish literary tradition on the one hand and those of the European novel on the other.*' (Evin, *Origins and Development*, p. 68; my emphasis.) Jale Parla's evaluation of the Tanzimat period sounds a similar note: 'behind the inclination towards renovation stood a dominant and dominating Ottoman ideology that recast the new ideas into a mould fit for the Ottoman society. The mould, however, was supposed to hold two different epistemologies that rested on irreconcilable axioms. *It was inevitable that this mould would crack and literature, in one way or another, reflects the cracks.*' ('Desiring Tellers, Fugitive Tales', my emphasis.) In his discussion of the 1913 novel *Zaynab*, by Husayn Haykal, Roger Allen echoes Schwarz and Mukherjee (*'it is all too easy to point to the problems of psychological fallacy here*, as

as Miyoshi says of Japan.[24] At other times it was not so: at the beginning and at the end of the wave, for instance (Poland, Italy and

---

Hamid, the student in Cairo acquainted with Western works on liberty and justice such as those of John Stuart Mill and Herbert Spencer, proceeds to discuss the question of marriage in Egyptian society on such a lofty plane with his parents, who have always lived deep in the Egyptian countryside': *The Arabic Novel*, p. 34; my emphasis). Henry Zhao emphasizes from his very title—*The Uneasy Narrator*: and see the splendid discussion of uneasiness that opens the book—the complications generated by the encounter of Western plots and Chinese narrative: 'A salient feature of late Qing fiction', he writes, 'is the greater frequency of narrative intrusions than in any previous period of Chinese vernacular fiction . . . The huge amount of directions trying to explain the newly adopted techniques betrays the narrator's uneasiness about the instability of his status . . . the narrator feels the threat of interpretive diversification . . . moral commentaries become more tendentious to make the judgments unequivocal', and at times the drift towards narratorial overkill is so overpowering that a writer may sacrifice narrative suspense 'to show that he is morally impeccable' (*Uneasy Narrator*, pp. 69–71).

24   In some cases, even *translations* of European novels went through all sorts of incredible somersaults. In Japan, in 1880, Tsubouchi's translation of *The Bride of Lammermoor* appeared under the title *Shumpu jowa* ('Spring Breeze Love Story'), and Tsubouchi himself 'was not beyond excising the original text when the material proved inappropriate for his audience, or converting Scott's imagery into expressions corresponding more closely to the language of traditional Japanese literature' (Marleigh Grayer Ryan, 'Commentary' to Futabatei Shimei's *Ukigumo*, New York 1967, pp. 41–2). In the Arabic world, writes Matti Moosa, 'in many instances the translators of Western fiction took extensive and sometimes unwarranted liberties with the original text of a work. Yaqub Sarruf not only changed the title of Scott's *Talisman* to *Qalb al-Asad wa Salah al-Din* ['The Lion Heart and Saladin'], but also admitted that he had taken the liberty of omitting, adding, and changing parts of this romance to suit what he believed to be his audience's taste . . . Other translators changed the titles and the names of the characters and the contents, in order, they claimed, to make the translated work more acceptable to their readers and more consistent with the native literary tradition.' (*Origins of Modern Arabic Fiction*, p. 106.) The same general pattern holds for late Qing literature, where 'translations were almost without exception tampered with . . . the most serious way of tampering was to paraphrase the whole novel to make it a story with Chinese characters and Chinese background . . . Almost all of these translations suffered from abridgement . . . Western novels became sketchy and speedy, and looked more like Chinese traditional fiction.' (Henry Zhao, *Uneasy Narrator*, p. 229.)

Spain at one extreme; and West Africa on the other), historians describe novels that had, certainly, their own problems—but not problems arising from the clash of irreconcilable elements.[25]

I hadn't expected such a spectrum of outcomes, so at first I was taken aback, and only later realized that this was probably the most valuable finding of them all, because it showed that world literature was indeed a system—but a system *of variations*. The system was one, not uniform. The pressure from the Anglo-French core *tried* to make it uniform, but it could never fully erase the reality of difference. (See here, by the way, how the study of world literature is—inevitably—a study of the struggle for symbolic hegemony across the world.) The system was one, not uniform. And, retrospectively, of course it had to be like this: if

---

25   Why this difference? Probably, because in southern Europe the wave of French translations encountered a local reality (and local narrative traditions) that wasn't that different after all, and as a consequence, the composition of foreign form and local material proved easy. In West Africa, the opposite situation: although the novelists themselves had been influenced by Western literature, the wave of translations had been much weaker than elsewhere, and local narrative conventions were for their part extremely different from European ones (just think of orality); as the desire for the 'foreign technology' was relatively bland—and further discouraged, of course, by the anti-colonial politics of the 1950s—local conventions could play their role relatively undisturbed. Obiechina and Quayson emphasize the polemical relationship of early West African novels vis-à-vis European narrative: 'The most noticeable difference between novels by native West Africans and those by non-natives using the West African setting, is the important position which the representation of oral tradition is given by the first, and its almost total absence in the second.' (Emmanuel Obiechina, *Culture, Tradition and Society*, p. 25.) 'Continuity in the literary strategic formation we have identified is best defined in terms of the continuing affirmation of mythopeia rather than of realism for the definition of identity . . . That this derives from a conceptual opposition to what is perceived as a Western form of realism is difficult to doubt. It is even pertinent to note in this regard that in the work of major African writers such as Achebe, Armah, and Ngugi, the movement of their work has been from protocols of realist representation to those of mythopeic experimentation.' (Ato Quayson, *Strategic Transformations*, p. 164.)

after 1750 the novel arises just about everywhere as a compromise between west European patterns and local reality—well, local reality was different in the various places, just as Western influence was also very uneven: much stronger in Southern Europe around 1800, to return to my example, than in West Africa around 1940. The forces in play kept changing, and so did the compromise that resulted from their interaction. And this, incidentally, opens a fantastic field of inquiry for comparative morphology (the systematic study of how forms vary in space and time, which is also the only reason to keep the adjective 'comparative' in comparative literature): but comparative morphology is a complex issue, which deserves its own paper.

Forms as Abstracts of Social Relationships

Let me now add a few words on that term 'compromise'—by which I mean something a little different from what Jameson had in mind in his introduction to Karatani. For him, the relationship is fundamentally a binary one: 'the abstract formal patterns of Western novel construction' and 'the raw material of Japanese social experience': form and content, basically.[26] For me, it's more of a triangle: foreign form, local material—*and local form*. Simplifying somewhat: foreign *plot*; local *characters*; and then, local *narrative voice*: and it's precisely in this third dimension that these novels seem to be most unstable—most uneasy, as Zhao says of the late Qing

---

26 The same point is made in a great article by António Cándido: 'We [Latin American literatures] never create original expressive forms or basic expressive techniques, in the sense that we mean by romanticism, on the level of literary movements; the psychological novel, on the level of genres; free indirect style, on that of writing . . . the various nativisms never rejected the use of the imported literary *forms* . . . what was demanded was the choice of new *themes*, of different *sentiments*.' ('Literature and Underdevelopment', in César Fernández Moreno, Julio Ortega, and Ivan A. Shulman (eds), *Latin America in Its Literature*, New York 1980, pp. 272–3.)

narrator. Which makes sense: the narrator is the pole of comment, of explanation, of evaluation, and when foreign 'formal patterns' (or actual foreign presence, for that matter) make characters behave in strange ways (like Bunzo, or Ibarra, or Brás Cubas), then of course comment becomes uneasy—garrulous, erratic, rudderless.

'Interferences', Even-Zohar calls them: powerful literatures making life hard for the others—making *structure* hard. And Schwarz: 'a part of the original historical conditions reappears as a sociological form . . . In this sense, forms are the abstract of specific social relationships.'[27] Yes, and in our case the historical conditions reappear as a sort of 'crack' in the form; as a faultline running between story and discourse, world and worldview: the world goes in the strange direction dictated by an outside power; the worldview tries to make sense of it, and is thrown off balance all the time. Like Rizal's voice (oscillating between Catholic melodrama and Enlightenment sarcasm),[28] or Futabatei's (caught between Bunzo's 'Russian' behaviour, and the Japanese audience inscribed in the text), or Zhao's hypertrophic narrator, who has completely lost control of the plot, but still tries to dominate it at all costs. This is what Schwarz meant with that 'foreign debt' that becomes a 'complex feature' of the text: the foreign presence 'interferes' with the very *utterance* of the novel.[29] The one-and-unequal literary

---

27   'The Importing of the Novel to Brazil', p. 53.

28   Rizal's solution, or lack thereof, is probably also related to his extraordinarily wide social spectrum (*Noli Me Tangere*, among other things, is the text that inspired Benedict Anderson to link the novel and the nation state): in a nation with no independence, an ill-defined ruling class, no common language and hundreds of disparate characters, it's hard to speak 'for the whole', and the narrator's voice cracks under the effort.

29   In a few lucky cases, the structural weakness may turn into a strength, as in Schwarz's interpretation of Machado, where the 'volatility' of the narrator becomes 'the stylization of the behaviour of the Brazilian ruling class': not a flaw any longer, but the very point of the novel: 'Everything in Machado de Assis's novels is coloured by the *volatility*—used and abused in different degrees—of

system is not just an external network here, it doesn't remain *outside* the text: it's embedded well into its form.

TREES, WAVES AND CULTURAL HISTORY

Forms are the abstract of social relationships: so, formal analysis is in its own modest way an analysis of power. (That's why comparative morphology is such a fascinating field: studying how forms vary, you discover how symbolic *power* varies from place to place.) And indeed, sociological formalism has always been my interpretive method, and I think that it's particularly appropriate for world literature . . . But, unfortunately, at this point I must stop, because my competence stops. Once it became clear that the key variable of the experiment was the narrator's voice, well, a genuine formal analysis was off limits for me, because it required a linguistic competence that I couldn't even dream of (French, English, Spanish, Russian, Japanese, Chinese and Portuguese, just for the core of the argument). And probably, no matter what the object of analysis is, there will always be a point where the study of world literature must yield to the specialist of the national literature, in a sort of cosmic and inevitable division of labour. Inevitable not just for practical reasons, but for theoretical ones. This is a large issue, but let me at least sketch its outline.

When historians have analyzed culture on a world scale (or on a large scale anyway), they have tended to use two basic cognitive metaphors: the tree and the wave. The tree, the phylogenetic tree

---

their narrators. The critics usually look at it from the point of view of literary technique or of the author's humour. There are great advantages in seeing it as the stylization of the behaviour of the Brazilian ruling class. Instead of seeking disinterestedness, and the confidence provided by impartiality, Machado's narrator shows off his impudence, in a gamut which runs from cheap gibes, to literary exhibitionism, and even to critical acts.' (Roberto Schwarz, 'The Poor Old Woman and Her Portraitist' [1983], in *Misplaced Ideas*, p. 94.)

derived from Darwin, was the tool of comparative philology: language families branching off from each other—Slavo-Germanic from Aryan-Greco-Italo-Celtic, then Balto-Slavic from Germanic, then Lithuanian from Slavic. And this kind of tree allowed comparative philology to solve that great puzzle which was also perhaps the first world-system of culture: Indo-European: a family of languages spreading from India to Ireland (and perhaps not just languages, a common cultural repertoire, too: but here the evidence is notoriously shakier). The other metaphor, the wave, was also used in historical linguistics (as in Schmidt's 'wave hypothesis', which explained certain overlaps among languages), but it played a role in many other fields as well: the study of technological diffusion, for instance, or the fantastic interdisciplinary theory of the 'wave of advance' by Cavalli-Sforza and Ammerman (a geneticist and an archaeologist), which explains how agriculture spread from the fertile crescent in the Middle East towards the north-west and then throughout Europe.

Now, trees and waves are both metaphors—but except for this, they have absolutely nothing in common. The tree describes the passage from unity to diversity: one tree, with many branches: from Indo-European, to dozens of different languages. The wave is the opposite: it observes uniformity engulfing an initial diversity: Hollywood films conquering one market after another (or English swallowing language after language). Trees need geographical *discontinuity* (in order to branch off from each other, languages must first be separated in space, just like animal species); waves dislike barriers, and thrive on geographical *continuity* (from the viewpoint of a wave, the ideal world is a pond). Trees and branches are what nation states cling to; waves are what markets do. And so on. Nothing in common, between the two metaphors. But—*they both work*. Cultural history is made of trees *and* waves—the wave of agricultural advance supporting the tree of Indo-European languages, which is then swept by new waves of linguistic and cultural contact . . . And as world culture oscillates between the two mechanisms, its products are inevitably composite ones. Compromises, as in Jameson's law. That's why the law works: because it intuitively captures the intersection of the two mechanisms. Think of the modern novel: certainly a wave (and I've actually called it a wave a few times)—but a wave that runs into the branches of local traditions,[30] and is always significantly transformed by them.

This, then, is the basis for the division of labour between national and world literature: national literature, for people who see trees; world literature, for people who see waves. Division of labour . . . and challenge; because both metaphors work, yes, but that doesn't mean that they work equally well. The products of cultural history are always composite ones: but which is the dominant mechanism in their composition? The internal, or the external one? The nation or the world? The tree or the wave? There is no way to settle this controversy once and for all—fortunately: because comparatists need controversy. They have always been too shy in the presence of national literatures, too diplomatic: as if one had English, American, German literature—and then, next door, a sort of little parallel universe where comparatists studied a second set of literatures, trying not to disturb the first set. No; the universe is the same, the literatures are the same, we just look at them from a different viewpoint; and you become a comparatist for a very simple reason: *because you are convinced that that viewpoint is better.* It has greater explanatory power; it's conceptually more elegant; it avoids that ugly 'one-sidedness and narrow-mindedness'; whatever. The point is that there is no other justification for the study of world

30 '*Grafting* processes', Miyoshi calls them; Schwarz speaks of 'the *implantation* of the novel, and of its realist *strand* in particular', and Wang of '*transplanting* Western narrative typologies'. And indeed, Belinsky had already described Russian literature as 'a *transplanted* rather than indigenous growth' in 1843.

literature (and for the existence of departments of comparative literature) but this: to be a thorn in the side, a permanent intellectual challenge to national literatures—especially the local literature. If comparative literature is not this, it's nothing. Nothing. 'Don't delude yourself', writes Stendhal of his favourite character: 'for you, there is no middle road.' The same is true for us.

The Slaughterhouse of Literature

For a dozen years—from the essay 'On Literary Evolution', in 1987, through the Appendix to The Way of the World *(1990), 'Modern European Literature' (1992), the book* Modern Epic *(1996), and this essay—evolutionary theory was unquestionably the most important single influence on my work. Initially, it offered mostly a way to think about very large systems, like the European archipelago of 'Modern European Literature'; later, in* Modern Epic, *it helped me analyze small-scale mechanisms, like the mutations of the stream of conscious-ness, or the 'refunctionalization' of formal devices. 'Slaughterhouse' is a further, more detailed study of formal mutation and cultural selection, which began as part of a graduate seminar at Columbia. We started with a sample of late-nineteenth-century detective stories; with a well-defined formal trait (clues); and with the hypothesis that the destiny of individual stories would hinge on the handling of this formal trait. Except for Conan Doyle (about whom, in any case, what I thought I knew turned out to be wrong), I had no idea whether clues would be present or not in the stories we were going to read: had they been, then they clearly couldn't be the crucial survival trait; otherwise, perhaps we had the beginning of an explanation. And off we went.*

The findings are reported in the pages that follow, and I won't anticipate them here; but this I will say: they were *findings. And this was new. Up to this point, even in essays I had devoted a lot of work to (like the first two of this collection) I had never set out to find 'new facts'; the facts were known; what was missing was their explanation. Here, it was the other way around: the evolutionary model was a given, and I was looking for data that would support, or challenge, its application to literature. In the article I repeatedly describe this as an 'experiment'—which, in the strict sense of the word, it wasn't. But it was an example of that 'falsifiable criticism' that I had envisaged in my first theoretical essay—the 1983 introduction to* Signs Taken for Wonders—*and that now, almost twenty years later, I had finally found a way to realize.*

Finding clear, hard facts that contradicted my hypotheses, and forced me to change them, was truly a new beginning: exhausting—and incredibly exciting. It felt like the entire history of literature could be rewritten in a new vein; whence, among other things, the promise of a follow-up study on 'The Rivals of Jane Austen'—in a gesture that would become a leitmotiv *of the essays that follow, reaching its apex in 'Style, Inc.', where I promise two such studies, plus a third one in a later exchange with Katie Trumpener. But the radical re-thinking of literary history that seemed around the corner produced such a snowball-effect that the appeal of the new experiment punctually eclipsed the sober duty of replicating the old one; so that, in conclusion, not a single follow-up was ever written.[1] Not a responsible behaviour; but I just couldn't help it.*

Where I did act responsibly was in the amount of reading I did for the essay: all those forgotten detective stories that I chart in the text. But

---

1   I had actually done a lot of preparatory work on Austen's rivals, but it all came to nothing because, at the time, I had no idea how to analyze the simultaneous variation of more than one formal trait. Eventually, in a collective study entitled 'Quantitative Formalism', Sarah Allison, Ryan Heuser, Matthew Jockers, Michael Witmore and I did apply multivariate analysis—in which several variables are considered simultaneously—to the study of novelistic genres; see *Pamphlet 1* of the Stanford Literary Lab, at litlab.stanford.edu; now also in *n+1*, 13 (2012).

was it still reading, what I was doing? I doubt it: I read 'through' those stories looking for clues, and (almost) nothing else; it felt very different from the reading I used to know. It was more like what Jonathan Arac described, in the controversy around 'Conjectures', as a 'formalism without close reading'; a nice formulation, of which 'Slaughterhouse' was perhaps the first clear example: identifying a discrete formal trait, and then following its metamorphoses through a whole series of texts. The 'Quantitative Formalism' that gave its title to the first pamphlet of the Literary Lab had not yet occurred to me; but, after 'Slaughterhouse', it was really just a matter of time.

THE SLAUGHTER

Let me begin with a few titles: *Arabian Tales, Aylmers, Annaline, Alicia de Lacey, Albigenses, Augustus and Adelina, Albert, Adventures of a Guinea, Abbess of Valiera, Ariel, Almacks, Adventures of Seven Shillings, Abbess, Arlington, Adelaide, Aretas, Abdallah the Moor, Anne Grey, Andrew the Savoyard, Agatha, Agnes de Monsfoldt, Anastasius, Anzoletto Ladoski, Arabian Nights, Adventures of a French Sarjeant, Adventures of Bamfylde Moore Carew, A Commissioner, Avondale Priory, Abduction, Accusing Spirit, Arward the Red Chieftain, Agnes de Courcy, An Old Friend, Annals of the Parish, Alice Grey, Astrologer, An Old Family Legend, Anna, Banditt's Bride, Bridal of Donnamore, Borderers, Beggar Girl . . .*

It was the first page of an 1845 catalogue: Columbell's circulating library, in Derby: a small collection, of the kind that wanted only successful books. But today, only a couple of titles still ring familiar. The others, nothing. Gone. The history of the world is the slaughterhouse of the world, reads a famous Hegelian aphorism;

and of literature. The majority of books disappear forever—and 'majority' actually misses the point: if we set today's canon of nineteenth-century British novels at two hundred titles (which is a very high figure), they would still be only about *0.5 per cent* of all published novels.

And the other 99.5 per cent? This is the question behind this article, and behind the larger idea of literary history that is now taking shape in the work of several critics—most recently Sylvie Thorel-Cailleteau, Katie Trumpener, and Margaret Cohen. The difference is that, for me, the aim is not so much a change in the canon—the discovery of precursors to the canon or alternatives to it, to be restored to a prominent position—as a change in how we look at *all* of literary history: canonical and noncanonical: together.[2] To do so, I focus on what I call *rivals*: contemporaries who write more or less like

---

2 For the precursor thesis, which is quite widespread, see, e.g., Margaret Doody, 'George Eliot and the Eighteenth-Century Novel', *Nineteenth-Century Fiction* 35 (1980), pp. 267–8: 'The period between the death of Richardson and the appearance of the novels of Scott and Austen . . . sees the development of the paradigm for women's fiction of the nineteenth century—*something hardly less than the paradigm of the nineteenth-century novel itself*' (my emphasis). Trumpener follows in part the precursor model (as in her discussion of national tales and historical novels) and in part the alternative model (as in the concluding paragraph of her book: 'What a geopoliticized investigation of romantic fiction reveals is not only Scott's centrality in establishing a novel of imperial expansion but also *how differently some of Scott's contemporaries imagined a critical, cosmopolitan fiction of empire*' [*Bardic Nationalism: The Romantic Novel and the British Empire*, Princeton, NJ, 1997), p. 291; my emphasis]). Cohen's opening chapter, 'Reconstructing the Literary Field', is the most resolute statement I know of the alternative thesis: 'From my literary excavation, Balzac and Stendhal will emerge as literary producers among other producers, seeking a niche in a generic market . . . Balzac and Stendhal made their bids for their market shares in a hostile takeover of the dominant practice of the novel when both started writing: sentimental works by women writers. And they competed with writers challenging the prestige of sentimentality with other codes which contemporaries found equally if not more compelling' (*The Sentimental Education of the Novel*, Princeton, NJ, 1999], p. 6).

canonical authors (in my case, more or less like Arthur Conan Doyle), but not quite, and who interest me because, from what I have seen of that forgotten 99 per cent, they seem to be the largest contingent of the 'great unread', as Cohen calls it. And that's really my hope, as I have said: to come up with a new sense of the literary field as a whole.[3]

But of course, there is a problem here. Knowing two hundred novels is already difficult. *Twenty thousand?* How can we do it, what does 'knowledge' mean, in this new scenario? One thing for sure: it cannot mean the very close reading of very few texts—secularized theology, really ('canon'!)—that has radiated from the cheerful town of New Haven over the whole field of literary studies. A larger literary history requires other skills: sampling; statistics; work with series, titles, concordances, incipits—and perhaps also the 'trees' that I discuss in this essay. But first, a brief premise.

THE SCHOOL AND THE MARKET

The slaughter of literature. And the butchers—readers: who read novel A (but not B, C, D, E, F, G, H . . .) and so keep A 'alive' into the next generation, when other readers may keep it alive into the following one, and so on until eventually A becomes canonized. Readers, not professors, make canons: academic decisions are mere echoes of a process that unfolds fundamentally outside the school: reluctant rubber-stamping, not much more. Conan Doyle is a perfect case in point: *socially* supercanonical right away, but *academically* canonical only a hundred years later. And the same happened to Cervantes, Defoe, Austen, Balzac, Tolstoy . . . [4]

---

3   As the rest of this essay makes clear, I don't really believe that professors can change the canon. Even if they could—and even if, say, ten, twenty, fifty, a hundred, or two hundred novels were added to the nineteenth-century canon—it would be a dramatic change *for the canon*, yes, but not for the question I address here. Reducing the unreads from 99.5 to 99.0 per cent is no change at all.

4   My model of canon formation is based on novels for the simple reason

A space outside the school, where the canon is selected: the market. Readers read A and so keep it alive; better, they *buy* A, inducing its publishers to keep it in print until another generation shows up, and so on. A concrete example can be found in James Raven's excellent study of British publishing between 1750 and 1770: if one looks at the table of 'the most popular novelists by editions printed 1750–1769', it's quite clear that the interplay of readers and publishers in the marketplace had completely shaped the canon of the eighteenth-century novel many generations before any academic ever dreamed of teaching a course on the novel: on that list of editions, Sterne is first, Fielding second, Smollett fourth, Defoe fifth, Richardson sixth, Voltaire eleventh, Goldsmith fifteenth, Cervantes seventeenth, and Rousseau nineteenth. They are all there.[5]

---

that they have been the most widespread literary form of the past two or three centuries and are therefore crucial to any social account of literature (which is the point of the canon controversy, or should be). Given what I have just said, John Guillory's focus on poetry in *Cultural Capital: The Problem of Literary Canon Formation* (Chicago 1993) strikes me as very odd; it makes of his book a Janus-like creature, always right in its specific analyses but wrong in its general claims. Yes, the academic canon was indeed the one he describes, but the (more significant) social canon was different and completely unrelated to it. Similarly, the rise to prominence of metaphysical poetry was indeed a significant change within the academy, but outside the academy it was no change at all, because lyric poetry had already virtually lost its social function (for Walter Benjamin, this happened sometime between Heine and Baudelaire, eighty years before the New Critical canon). English professors could do with poetry whatever they wanted, *because it did not matter.* In the near future, who knows, the same may happen to novels. Right now, Jane Austen is canonical and Amelie Opie is not, because millions of readers keep reading Austen for their own pleasure; but nothing lasts forever, and when readers no longer enjoy her books (they have seen the movies, anyway), a dozen English professors will suddenly have the power to get rid of *Persuasion* and replace it with *Adeline Mowbray.* Far from being a socially significant act, however, that change in the (academic) canon will prove only that nineteenth-century novels have become irrelevant.

5   See James Raven, *British Fiction, 1750–1770: A Chronological Check-List of Prose Fiction Printed in Britain and Ireland* (Newark 1987), pp. 14–17. Let me make clear that, although canonical novels are usually quite successful right away, the key to canonization is not the extent of a book's initial popularity but

THE BLIND CANON-MAKERS

So, the market selects the canon. But how? Two economic theorists, Arthur De Vany and W. David Walls, have constructed a very convincing model for the film industry (a good term of comparison for eighteenth- and nineteenth-century novels):

> Film audiences make hits or flops . . . not by revealing preferences they already have, but by discovering what they like. When they see a movie they like, they make a discovery and they tell their friends about it; reviewers do this too. This information is transmitted to other consumers and demand develops dynamically over time as the audience sequentially discovers and reveals its demand . . . A hit is generated by an information cascade . . . A flop is an information bandwagon too; in this case the cascade kills the film.[6]

A demand that develops 'dynamically' and 'sequentially': what this means is that 'the probability that a given customer selects a particular movie is proportional to the fraction of all the previous moviegoers who selected that movie'. It's the feedback loop of 'increasing returns', where 'past successes are leveraged into future successes' until, in the end, 'just 20% of the films earn 80% of box office revenues'.[7] Twenty per cent, eighty per cent: what an interesting process. The starting point is thoroughly *poli*centric

---

its steady survival from one generation to the next. As for the exceptions to this model, they are neither as common nor as striking as the critical legend would have it. *The Red and the Black*, supposedly ignored by nineteenth-century readers, went through at least seventeen French editions between 1830 and 1900; *Moby-Dick*, another favourite counterexample, went through at least thirteen English and American editions between 1851 and 1900. Not bad.

6   Arthur De Vany and W. David Walls, 'Bose-Einstein Dynamics and Adaptive Contracting in the Motion Picture Industry', *Economic Journal*, November 1996, p. 1493.

7   Ibid., pp. 1501, 1505.

(thousands of independent moviegoers, without hidden puppeteers of any sort)—but the result is extraordinarily *centralized*. And the centralization of the literary market is exactly the same as for films. After all, this is precisely how the canon is formed: very few books, occupying a very large space. This is what the canon *is*.

As more readers select Conan Doyle over L. T. Meade and Grant Allen, more readers are likely to select Conan Doyle again in the future, until he ends up occupying 80, 90, 99.9 per cent of the market for nineteenth-century detective fiction. But why is Conan Doyle selected in the first place? Why him, and not others? Here the economic model has a blind spot: the event that starts the 'information cascade' is unknowable. It's there, it *has* to be there, or the market wouldn't behave as it does, but it can't be explained. Moviegoers 'discover what they like', but we never discover *why* they like it. They're the blind canon-makers, as it were.

Now, this is understandable for economic theory, which is not supposed to analyze aesthetic taste. But literary history is, and my thesis here is that what makes readers 'like' this or that book is— form. Walter Benjamin, *Central Park*:

> Baudelaire's conduct in the literary market: Baudelaire was, through his deep experience of the nature of the commodity, enabled, or perhaps forced, to acknowledge the market as an objective . . . He devalued certain poetic freedoms of the romantics by means of his classical use of the Alexandrine, and classical poetics by means of those *caesurae* and blanks within the classical verse itself. In short, his poems contain certain specific precautions for the eradication of their competitors.[8]

---

8 Walter Benjamin, 'Central Park' (1937–38), *New German Critique* 34 (1985), p. 37.

Formal choices that try to 'eradicate' their competitors. Devices—
in the market: this is the idea. Formalism, and literary history.

FIRST EXPERIMENT

So, I started working on two groups of texts: the rivals of Austen
and the rivals of Conan Doyle. But here I will limit myself to the
latter, because detective stories have the advantage of being a very
simple genre (the ideal first step in a long-term investigation), and
because they possess a 'specific device' of exceptional visibility and
appeal: clues.[9] I brought to my graduate seminar about twenty

---

9   On the significance of clues see Victor Shklovsky, 'Sherlock Holmes and
the Mystery Story', in *Theory of Prose*, trans. Benjamin Sher (Elmwood Park, IL
1990); Siegfried Kracauer, *Der Detektiv-Roman: Ein philosophischer Traktat*, vol.
I of *Schriften* (Frankfurt am Main 1971); Theodor Reik, 'The Unknown
Murderer', in *The Compulsion to Confess: On the Psychoanalysis of Crime and
Punishment* (New York 1959); Ernst Bloch, 'A Philosophical View of the
Detective Novel', in *The Utopian Function of Art and Literature: Selected Essays*,
trans. Jack Zipes and Frank Mecklenburg (Cambridge, MA 1988); Tzvetan
Todorov, 'The Typology of Detective Fiction', in *The Poetics of Prose*, trans.
Richard Howard (Ithaca, NY 1977); Umberto Eco, 'Horns, Hooves, Insteps:
Some Hypotheses on Three Types of Abduction', in Umberto Eco and Thomas
A. Sebeok, eds, *The Sign of Three: Dupin, Holmes, Peirce* (Bloomington 1983);
and Carlo Ginzburg, 'Clues: Morelli, Freud, and Sherlock Holmes' (1979), also
in *The Sign of Three*, where clues are presented as the veritable origin of
storytelling: 'The hunter may have been the first to 'tell a story' because only
hunters knew how to read a coherent sequence of events from the silent (even
imperceptible) signs left by their prey' (p. 89).
    I speak of clues as a *formal* device because their narrative function (the
encrypted reference to the criminal) remains constant, although their
concrete embodiment changes from story to story (they can be words,
cigarette butts, footprints, smells, noises, and so on). Shklovsky makes the
point with characteristic intelligence: 'One critic has explained the perennial
failure on the part of the state investigator and the eternal victory of Conan
Doyle's private detective by the confrontation existing between private
capital and the public state. I do not know whether Conan Doyle had any
basis for pitting the English state against the English bourgeoisie. Yet I
believe that if these stories were written by a writer living in a proletarian
state, then, though himself a proletarian writer, he would still make use of an

detective stories of Conan Doyle's times; we combed them for clues, and the results are visualized in the tree of Figure 1.[10] Where two things stand out from the very first branching, at the bottom of the figure: first, that quite a few of Conan Doyle's rivals use no clues at all; second, that these writers are all completely forgotten. Form, and the market: if a story lacks a certain device, a negative 'information cascade' is triggered, and the market rejects it. Readers must have 'discovered' clues, which probably explains the second bifurcation, these strange stories where clues *are* present, but have no function, no necessity (in Boothby they are 'planted' on the last page of the story; in 'Race with the Sun', the protagonist figures

---

unsuccessful detective. Most likely, it is the state detective that would be victorious in such a case, while the private detective would no doubt be floundering in vain. In such a hypothetical story Sherlock Holmes would no doubt be working for the state while Lestrade would be engaged in private practice, *but the structure of the story would not change*' (p. 110; my emphasis). The case of Austen's rivals is more complex; it cannot possibly be reduced to just one device, and many other things change as well. I will present the results of this parallel study in a future article.

10   The initial sample included the twelve *Adventures of Sherlock Holmes*, written in 1891 and 1892, and seven stories drawn from *The Rivals of Sherlock Holmes, Further Rivals of Sherlock Holmes*, and *Cosmopolitan Crimes*, all edited by Hugh Greene between 1970 and 1974: Catherine L. Pirkis's 'Redhill Sisterhood' (1894); Guy Boothby's 'Duchess of Wiltshire's Diamonds' (1897); L. T. Meade and Clifford Halifax's 'Race with the Sun' (1897); M. M. Bodkin's 'How He Cut His Stick' (1900); Clifford Ashdown's 'Assyrian Rejuvenator' (1902); Palle Rosenkranz's 'Sensible Course of Action' (1909); and Balduin Groller's 'Anonymous Letters' (1910). A little later (when a student suggested that perhaps Conan Doyle's success depended on the prestige of the *Strand*) I added a couple of stories published in the same magazine, Huan Mee's 'In Masquerade' (1894) and Alice Williamson's 'Robbery at Foxborough' (1894). Again, this was an initial sample, designed to get started; later I put together a more reliable series. Incidentally, Greene's three volumes were immediately reissued by Penguin, became a BBC series—and then disappeared; they have been out of print for many years, with no sign of a further resurrection. A similar destiny has befallen most women's novels reissued after 1970 by independent and mainstream presses. Changing the academic canon may be relatively easy, but changing the social canon is another story.

them out, then forgets and almost gets killed). A bizarre arrangement, which must have come into being more or less like this: some writers sensed that these curious little details were really popular, so they decided to use them—but they didn't really understand *why* clues were popular, so they used them in the wrong way. And it didn't work very well.

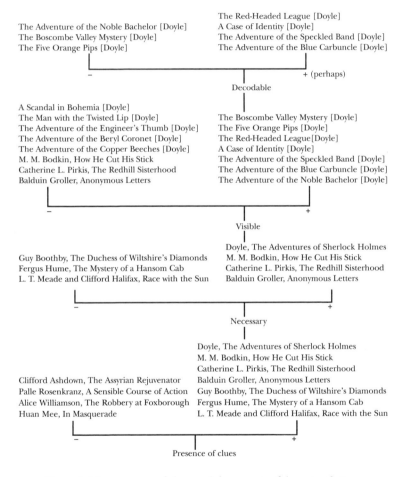

Figure 1: The presence of clues and the genesis of detective fiction

Third bifurcation; clues are present, they have a function, but are not visible: the detective mentions them in his explanation, but we have never really 'seen' them in the course of the story. Here we lose the last rivals (which was exactly what I had expected)—but we also lose half of the *Adventures of Sherlock Holmes*, which I hadn't expected at all. And at the next bifurcation (clues must be decodable by the reader: soon to be the First Commandment of detective fiction) things get even stranger. It's not always easy to decide whether a clue is decodable or not, of course, but still, even being generous, there are decodable clues in no more than four of the *Adventures* (and being strict, in none).[11]

When we first looked at these results in the seminar, we found them hard to believe. Conan Doyle is so often right—and then loses his touch at the very end? He finds the epoch-making device but does not work it out? It didn't make sense; the tree had to be wrong. But the tree was right—in the forty-odd stories Conan Doyle wrote after the *Adventures*, one finds exactly the same oscillations—and it actually highlighted an important Darwinian feature of literary history: in times of morphological change, like the 1890s for detective fiction, the individual writer behaves exactly like the genre as a whole: *tentatively*. During a paradigm shift no one knows what will work and what won't; not Ashdown, not Pirkis, and not Conan Doyle; he proceeds by trial and error, making fewer errors early on, when the problems are simpler—and more errors later, when they are more complex. It makes perfect sense. And as for finding a great device and not recognizing it, the same thing happened to Dujardin, in the same years, with the stream of consciousness: he found it, and he immediately lost it. And the reason that he and Conan Doyle didn't recognize

---

11 For instance, 'The Adventure of the Speckled Band', usually seen as a splendid cluster of clues, has been repeatedly criticized by articles pointing out that snakes do not drink milk, cannot hear whistles, cannot crawl up and down bell cords, and so on.

their discoveries is simple: *they were not looking for them*. They found them by chance, and never really understood *what* they had found.

What I mean by 'chance' here, let me open a brief parenthesis, is that Conan Doyle stumbled upon clues while he was working at something completely different, which was the myth of Sherlock Holmes. Think of the opening scenes of the *Adventures*, when Holmes 'reads' a whole life from the signs on the body of his client: this is what Conan Doyle wants from clues: a support for Holmes's omniscience. They are a function of Holmes, an attribute, like coke and the violin. Then Conan Doyle starts 'playing' with clues and eventually turns them from a mere ornament into a puzzle-solving mechanism: he finds a *new use* for them—'refunctionalization', as the Russian formalists called it; 'exaptation', as Gould and Vrba have called it within the Darwinian paradigm. But he is not looking for this new use, and he never fully recognizes it.

And he is not looking for the new use for an interesting reason. Clues begin as attributes of the omniscient detective, I have said, and then turn into details open to the rational scrutiny of all. *But if they are the former, they cannot be the latter*: Holmes as Superman needs unintelligible clues to prove his superiority; decodable clues create a potential parity between him and the reader. The two uses are incompatible: they may coexist for a while, but in the long run they exclude each other. If Conan Doyle keeps 'losing' clues, then, it's because part of him *wants* to lose them: they threaten Holmes's legend. He must choose, and he chooses Holmes.[12]

---

12   But was Conan Doyle really the first to make such a full use of clues? It is a big question, to which I briefly (and by no means conclusively) reply that a glance at some supposed precursors suggests that although clues surface here and there in the nineteenth century, before Conan Doyle they have neither his arresting 'strangeness' ('I could only catch some allusion to a rat' ['The Boscombe Valley Mystery']) nor the structural function of revealing the past to the detective. In Fergus Hume's *Mystery of a Hansom Cab* (1886), for instance, the clue of a

THE TREE

Parenthesis closed, and back to the real protagonist of this essay: the tree of Figure 1. I began using it merely as a sort of shorthand visualization, but after a while realized that it was more than that: it functioned like a cognitive metaphor, which made me quite literally *see* literary history in a new way. First of all, in terms of the forces that shape it. Think about it: what 'raises' this tree, this branching pattern of literary history? Texts? Not really: texts are distributed among the various branches, yes, but the branches themselves are not generated by texts: they are generated by *clues*—by their

---

half-ripped letter is duly reproduced and decoded, but it merely adds a new subplot (while in Wilkie Collins's *Moonstone* [1868] a similar note does nothing at all). In Edward Bulwer-Lytton's *Pelham* (1828) a miniature found at the murder site points clearly towards a certain character—who turns out to be innocent. In Dickens's *Bleak House* (1853) the Holmes-like bravura piece of the reading of clues ('And so your husband is a brickmaker?') is completely unconnected with the mystery, while Detective Bucket relies for his part on witnesses and personal reconnaissance. The most vivid clue in *The Moonstone*—a smear of paint on a nightgown—also points towards the wrong man and is anyhow dwarfed by an absurd story of opium-induced somnambulism, while other clues are thoroughly manipulated by this or that character. Most striking of all, Mary Elizabeth Braddon's *Lady Audley* (1862) uses a genuine legion of clues, but . . . for ethical rather than hermeneutical purposes: they prove that a character has something to hide (and they do it remarkably well) but don't contribute to the solution of the mystery. They are atmosphere; sinister details, signs that something is wrong: not ways to solve the problem. Tellingly, they gravitate towards the beginning of the story, to get it started and capture the reader's attention: then they gradually disappear, and the solution is again reached by different means.

It's the problem with all searches for 'precursors': they are *so* sloppy. They play and play with the device (as a rule, devices don't develop abruptly, out of nothing, but are around for some time, in one form or another), but cannot figure out its unique structural function. That, and that only, is the real formal discovery: sudden, 'punctual': a revelation, the last piece of the puzzle. And of that, all the 'precursors' in the world are incapable: one looks at nineteenth-century clues, and is astonished at *how long it took for two and two to make four*. Mysteries were conceived, clues were imagined—but they were not connected to each other. It's the conservative, *inertial* side of literary history: the resistance to new forms; the effort *not* to change, for as long as possible. In a minute, we will see more of it.

absence, presence, necessity, visibility, etc. The branches are the result of the twists and turns of a *device*, of a unit much *smaller* than the text. Conversely, the branches are also part of something much *larger* than any text, which is the *genre*: the tree of *detective fiction*. Devices and genres: two *formal* units. A very small formal unit and a very large one: these are the forces behind this figure—and behind literary history. Not texts. Texts are real objects—but not objects *of knowledge*. If we want to explain the laws of literary history, we must move to a formal plane that lies beyond them: below or above; the device, or the genre.

And genre also changes, in this new view of history. Usually, we tend to have a rather 'Platonic' idea of genre: an archetype and its many copies (the historical novel as *Waverley* rewritten over and over again; the picaresque as Lazarillo and his siblings). The tree suggests a different image: branches, formal choices, that don't replicate each other but rather move *away* from each other, turning the genre into a wide field of diverging moves. And *wrong* moves, mostly: where nine writers out of ten (and half of the tenth) end up on dead branches. This was my initial question, remember: what happens to the 99.5 per cent of published literature? This: it's caught in a morphological dead end. There are many ways of being alive, writes Richard Dawkins in *The Blind Watchmaker*, but many more ways of being dead . . . many successful books, but infinitely more books that are *not* successful—and this tree shows why.[13]

Wrong moves, good moves. But in what sense 'good'? In terms of the external context, no doubt: the growing scepticism about the reliability of witnesses, and the parallel insistence on 'objective' evidence, must have 'prepared' an audience for clues, and so, too, the intellectual trends mentioned by Ginzburg (attributionism, then psychoanalysis). All true. Still, I suspect that the reason clues were

---

13   Dawkins, *The Blind Watchmaker* (New York 1986).

'discovered' by European audiences was first and foremost an internal one. Detective fiction, writes Todorov, is made of two separate stories (crime and investigation, past and present, *fabula* and *sjuzhet*), and these two stories 'have no point in common'.[14] Well, not quite: clues are precisely that point in common. An incredibly central position, where the past is suddenly in touch with the present; a hinge that joins the two halves together, turning the story into something more than the sum of its parts: a structure. And the tightening up starts a morphological virtuous circle that somehow improves every part of the story: if you are looking for clues, each sentence becomes 'significant', each character 'interesting'; descriptions lose their inertia; all words become sharper, stranger.

A device aimed at the 'eradication of . . . competitors', wrote Benjamin: clues. A device designed to colonize a market niche, forcing other writers to accept it or disappear. In this sense, clues are also what is missing from De Vany and Walls's model: the recognizable origin of the 'information cascade' that decides the shape of the market. A little device—with enormous effects.[15]

---

14   Todorov, 'Typology', p. 44.
15   'When two or more . . . technologies "compete" . . . for a "market" of potential adopters', writes Brian Arthur, 'insignificant events may by chance give one of them an initial advantage in adoptions. This technology may then improve more than the others . . . Thus a technology that by chance gains an early lead in adoptions may eventually "corner the market" of potential adopters, with the other technologies becoming locked out . . . Under increasing returns . . . insignificant circumstances become magnified by positive feedbacks to "tip" the system into the actual outcome "selected". The small events of history become important' ('Competing Technologies, Increasing Returns, and Lock-In by Historical Events', *Economic Journal*, March 1989, pp. 116, 127). Insignificant events, insignificant circumstances: for Arthur, these 'small events of history' are often external to the competing technologies and therefore may end up rewarding the (relatively) *worse* design. In my reconstruction, by contrast, the small event of clues is located inside the given (literary) technology, and contributes to a (relatively) *better* design. Different. Still, it seems to me that Arthur makes two independent claims: first, that under certain conditions small initial differences

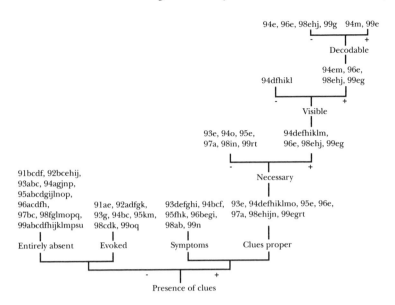

Figure 2: Clues in the Strand magazine, 1891–99

SECOND EXPERIMENT

Forms, markets, trees, branches—much as I liked all these things, they rested on a very narrow and haphazard collection of texts. So I decided to look for a more respectable series, and asked Tara McGann, my research assistant at Columbia, to find all the mystery

---

have growing long-term effects; second, that these differences may be external to the technologies themselves. (An 'external' explanation, in our case, would sound something like this: 'Doyle was selected not because of how he wrote but because the *Strand* gave him unique visibility.' Plausible, but false: in the 1890s the *Strand* published over a hundred different detective stories.) The present essay entirely corroborates the first claim and follows a different path regarding the second, but if I understand Arthur's point, whether differences are internal or external (and whether the prevailing technology is better or not) is a matter not of principle but of *fact*, which must be settled case by case on the basis of historical evidence. After all, if it is perverse to believe that the market always rewards the better solution, it is just as perverse to believe that it always rewards the worse one!

stories published in the *Strand* during the first Holmes decade. The total came to 108 (plus another fifty items or so that sounded like mysteries: 'The Minister's Crime', 'A Mystery of the Atlantic', etc.), and—it took time. But I have read them all, and Figure 2 visualizes the results.[16]

Mixed results. On the one hand, the right side of the figure closely resembles the first tree; on the other, the genre looks more complicated, more bush-like. Down at the bottom there are two large new branches: stories in which clues are not actually present but are evoked by the characters ('If only we had a clue!' 'Did you find any clues?') and others in which they are present, but in the skewed form of medical symptoms. The first group is curious, is like a window on the initial stages of a new device: the trick has become visible, recognizable, it has a name, everybody wants it and talks about it . . . but talking about a device is not the same as actually 'doing' it, and this naive verbal *escamotage* never works too well.

The stories in the second group ('symptoms') are interesting in another way: they don't pretend to have clues but try to replace them with something else. And symptoms, of course, are the very origin of clues: they are the 'small details' of medical semiosis whose significance was pointed out to young Conan Doyle by Joseph Bell, the Edinburgh professor of medicine who was the model for Holmes. Basically, then, these stories are replaying the film backwards; and it's reasonable, this regrounding of clues in their original intellectual humus. But there is a problem: 'clues are seldom coded, and their interpretation is frequently a matter of complex inference', writes Umberto Eco, 'which makes criminal novels more interesting than the detection of pneumonia'.[17]

---

16   The tree charts the stories according to their publication dates (1894c, 1891a, etc.); as the detailed bibliography would be almost as long as the essay itself, however, it is omitted here.

17   Umberto Eco, *A Theory of Semiotics* (London 1977), p. 224. Eco makes a similar point in 'Horns, Hooves, Insteps', pp. 211–12.

Precisely. And just as clues are usually more interesting than symptoms, Holmes's cases are more interesting than the *Stories from the Diary of a Doctor* or the *Adventures of a Man of Science*—and much more successful.

TRENDS

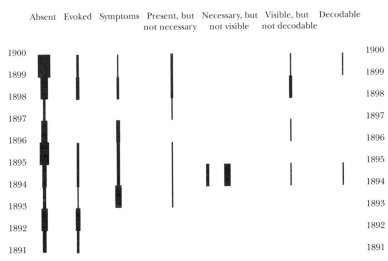

| Absent | Evoked | Symptoms | Present, but not necessary | Necessary, but not visible | Visible, but not decodable | Decodable |

Figure 3

From the morphology of the second sample, to its temporal distribution: Figure 3, which shows how the various branches become more crowded over time (thicker line), or less crowded (thinner line), or disappear altogether. This kind of visualization helps to see historical trends—and 'symptoms', for instance, do indeed look stronger early on and then seem to peter out, after they lose their competition with clues. And it makes sense, in evolutionary terms. But on the other hand, if you look at the far left and far right of the diagram, you find something that does *not* make sense at all. Stories completely without clues and stories with fully formed ones: here trends should be at their sharpest: a clear drop, a clear rise. But nothing of the sort. Mysteries with decodable clues don't gain ground, and mysteries without clues don't lose it (if anything, they become more frequent!).[18]

This is fascinating, because it goes so stubbornly against common sense. And not just my own Darwinian sense: when I presented the tree at the School for Theory and Criticism, at Dartmouth (not a very Darwinian environment), I received endless objections—but no one challenged the idea that stories without clues were doomed, and those with clues would become more frequent. That an epoch-making device should be widely imitated *makes so much sense*. And it does. But it doesn't happen.

Why not? I can think of two possibilities. The first is that Conan Doyle's rivals are still exploring alternatives: in 1899, for instance, 'Hilda Wade' tries to replace the study of clues with that of personality and the investigation of the past with the prediction of the future.[19] Very courageous idea—but a little weird. Between 1896 and 1899 there are also four series unified by the figure of the villain (*An African Millionaire*, *The Brotherhood of the Seven Kings*, *Hilda Wade*, and *Stories of the Sanctuary Club*), which is a very popular choice in the 1890s (Dracula, Svengali, Moriarty, Dr Nikolas . . .) and also a remote source of detective fiction, *Kriminalliteratur*. This is why we don't find more clues, then: the competition is still on: Conan Doyle's rivals are still hoping to find something better. They won't, but they're still trying.

---

18   Of the two stories with decodable clues, the one from 1894 ('Martin Hewitt, Investigator: The Affair of the Tortoise') is at least as dubious as Conan Doyle's 'Speckled Band', while the other ('Stories of the Sanctuary Club. The Death Chair', by L. T. Meade and Robert Eustace) gives the reader a big help with its telltale title (the death chair is a catapult that throws people hundreds of feet up in the air and into a neighbouring park).

19   'The police . . . are at best but bungling materialists. They require a *clue*. What need of a *clue* if you can interpret character?' ('Hilda Wade. IV. The Episode of the Man Who Would Not Commit Suicide', by Grant Allen).

Second possibility (which does not exclude the previous one): in 1891, when clues showed up, these writers were all already formed, and they simply couldn't change their writing style— even Conan Doyle never really learned how to use the new device. For clues to really take root, then, a new generation was needed (Agatha Christie and company) that would *begin* to write within the new paradigm. It's a good instance of the rigidity of literary evolution: you only learn once; then you are stuck. You learn, so it's culture, not nature: but it's a culture which is as unyielding as DNA. And the consequence of this is that literary changes don't occur slowly, piling up one small improvement upon another: they are abrupt, structural, and leave very little room for transitional forms. This was a striking result of this research: the *absence* of intermediate steps. A jump—Conan Doyle. Another jump—Christie. End of the story. The rest are steps *to the side*, not forward.

These two explanations are both 'tactical'—confined to the 1890s—and neither one questions the final triumph of clues: the fact that ten years later, or twenty, clues would be everywhere, and stories without them dead. But what if these expectations were wrong? What if the pattern of Figure 3 were not limited to the 1890s but returned in the 1910s, or the 1930s? Let me be clear: I have no data for this hypothesis (and someone else will have to do the reading this time), but it's an intriguing possibility, worthy of being formulated at least. So, here is Todorov on detective fiction:

> Two entirely different forms of [narrative] interest exist. The first can be called *curiosity*: it proceeds from effect to cause: starting from a certain effect (a corpse and certain clues) we must find its cause (the culprit and his motive). The second form is *suspense*, and here the move is from cause to effect: we are first shown the causes, the initial *données* (gangsters preparing a heist), and our interest is

sustained by the expectation of what will happen, that is, certain effects (corpses, crimes, fights).[20]

Curiosity, and suspense; detection, and adventure; a backward-looking narrative logic, and a forward-looking one. But the symmetry is misleading, because adventure stories are not just one narrative choice among many, but the most powerful form of story-telling from the beginning of time until today. Having challenged their appeal by enforcing a veritable *rationalization of adventure*—a Weberian universe, where not only have all the most exciting events already happened when the story begins, but they can only be re-experienced under strict logical constraints—having thus disenchanted the fictional world was the great achievement of clues. But the attempt could only succeed up to a point. Strong enough to branch off into a new genre, with its own market niche, clues could not really defeat the forces of cultural *longue durée*, which have returned to occupy bookstalls and movie screens around the world.[21]

---

20   Todorov, 'Typology', p. 47.

21   In the detective stories of the 1890s the resistance to Conan Doyle's rationalization of fiction takes many forms, my personal favourites being 'A Thing that Glistened' (by Frank R. Stockton), 'The Case of Roger Carboyne' (by H. Greenhough Smith), 'A Work of Accusation' (by Harry How), 'The Man Who Smiled' (by L. T. Meade and Clifford Halifax, from *The Adventures of a Man of Science*), and 'The Star-Shaped Marks' (also by Meade and Halifax, from *The Brotherhood of the Seven Kings*). In 'A Thing that Glistened' a deep-sea diver who is trying to recover a stolen bracelet is attacked by a shark, which swallows his underwater lamp; struck by the idea that 'this creature has a liking for shiny things', the diver cuts the shark open and finds not the bracelet but a bottle, filled with phosphorescent oil, containing a cylinder with the confession of a murder for which his innocent brother is about to be executed. In 'The Case of Roger Carboyne', the mystery of a mountain climber's death is solved when an 'aeronaut' confesses to having inadvertently fished him up with the anchor of his balloon and then dropped him. In 'A Work of Accusation' a somnambulist artist paints the face of the man he has murdered, then has a heart attack. The man who smiled is a civil servant who, as a consequence of 'a shock', laughs in such a way that he literally drives people crazy; when he is almost eaten alive by a tiger, the countershock cures him. Finally, in 'The Star-Shaped Marks' a group of

It's the formidable stability of narrative morphology; *histoire immo-bile*, in Fernand Braudel's great oxymoron.

THE THREE HISTORIES

I have insisted on the role of form in the marketplace. But in *history?* Is there a temporal frame, a historical 'tempo', that is unique to forms? Here is Braudel on the *longue durée*:

> From the recent experiments and efforts of history, an increasingly clear idea has emerged . . . of the multiplicity of time . . .
>
> Traditional history, with its concern for the short time span, for the individual and the event, has long accustomed us to the head-long, dramatic, breathless rush of its narrative.
>
> The new economic and social history puts cyclical movement in the forefront of its research and is committed to that time span . . . an account of conjunctures which lays open large sections of the past, ten, twenty, fifty years at a stretch ready for examination.
>
> Far beyond this second account we find a history capable of traversing even greater distances, a history to be measured in centuries this time: the history of the long, even of the very long time span, of the *longue durée*.[22]

Event, cycle, structure ('for good or ill, this word dominates the problems of the *longue durée*'[23]): as a rule, every literary text comprises all three of Braudel's histories. Some elements are

---

murderers set up an X-ray machine in the building next door and bombard the victim with radiation through the bedroom wall.

As this short list shows, many writers tried to outdo Conan Doyle by abandoning logic altogether and reintroducing the marvellous—what may be true but is not believable, as Aristotle's *Poetics* would have put it.

22   Braudel, 'History and the Social Sciences: The Longue Durée', in *On History*, trans. Sarah Matthews (Chicago 1980), p. 27.

23   Ibid., p. 33.

entwined with contemporary events; others, with a span of decades; others still, with a duration of centuries. Take *Jane Eyre*: Jane's threat to keep Rochester prisoner 'till you have signed a charter' points to recent (British) political events; the *Bildungsroman* structure, to the previous (western European) half century; and the Cinderella plot, to a (worldwide) *longue durée*. But the really interesting thing is that Braudel's (spatio-)temporal layers are active not just in different textual locations (which is obvious), but in locations that are *different in nature*: the first layer usually points to what is *unique* to the given text, while the other two point to what is *repeatable*: what it shares with some (the *Bildungsroman*) or even ('Cinderella') with many other texts.

Here form comes in. Because form is precisely *the repeatable element of literature*: what returns fundamentally unchanged over many cases and many years.[24] This, then, is what formalism can do for literary history: teach it to smile at the colourful anecdote beloved by New Historicists—'the most capricious and the most delusive

---

24 Tentatively, large genres like tragedy, or the fairy tale, or even the novel, seem rooted in the *longue durée*, while 'subgenres' (the gothic, the silver-fork school, the *Bildungsroman*, the nautical tale, the industrial novel, etc.) thrive for shorter periods (thirty to fifty years, empirical findings suggest). The same seems true of devices: some of them belong definitely to the *longue durée* (agnition, parallelism), while others are active for a few generations and then dwindle away (free indirect style, clues).

Let me add that, whereas the idea of a literary *longue durée* is not hard to grasp, that of a literary 'cycle' seems much more dubious: although the time span of many subgenres is roughly the same as that indicated by Braudel, the defining feature of the economic cycle (the ebb and flow of expansion and contraction) is nowhere to be seen. If literary historians are to make use of multiple temporal frames, then, they will have to reconceptualize their relationship. Similar reflections occur in one of the rare pieces of literary criticism to take Braudel's model seriously: Fredric Jameson, 'Radicalizing Radical Shakespeare: The Permanent Revolution in Shakespeare Studies', in Ivo Kamps, ed., *Materialist Shakespeare: A History* (London 1995).

level of all'[25]—and to recognize instead the *regularity* of the literary field. Its patterns, its slowness. Formalism and literary history; or, literature repeats itself.

THE GREAT UNREAD

The main lines of this argument had already been drawn when a Columbia graduate student, Jessica Brent, raised a very intelligent objection. The tree, fine: a good way of 'seeing' a larger literary history. Clues, fine: they offer a good general sense of the genre. And no objection to the idea that Conan Doyle's narrative structure may be better designed than that of his rivals (although of course one could argue forever on that 'better'). But if this approach is generalized as *the* method for the study of noncanonical literature (as I was certainly inclined to do), then there is a problem: if we search the archive for one device only, and no matter how significant it may be, all we will find are inferior versions of the device, *because that's really all we are looking for.* No matter what our intentions may be, the research project is a tautological one: it is so focused on a canonized device (and canonized for a good reason, but that's not the point) that in the noncanonical universe it can only discover . . . the absence of the device, that is, of the canon. True, but trivial.

Jessica Brent was right, period, so all I can do is explain how my mistake came about. Face to face with the forgotten 99.5 per cent of literature, and perplexed by its size, I couldn't simply 'start reading': I had to read in the light *of something*—and I chose the 0.5 per cent that had been canonized. 'Irreplaceable advantages' of historians, writes Braudel with his characteristic euphoria:

---

25 Braudel, 'History and the Social Sciences', p. 28.

Of all the forces in play, we know which will prevail, we can make
out beforehand the important events, 'those that will bear fruit', to
whom the future will finally be delivered. What an immense privilege! From amongst all the jumbled facts of our present lives, who
could distinguish equally surely the lasting from the ephemeral?[26]

What an immense privilege . . . sometimes. With Conan Doyle's
rivals, who are basically a duller version of the 'lasting' phenomenon, yes. But in other cases the privilege may well become blindness.
When an entire genre disappears, for instance—as in Margaret
Cohen's work on French sentimental novels—the method I have
sketched would be an *obstacle* to knowledge.[27] The same is true of
the 'lost best-sellers' of Victorian Britain: idiosyncratic works,
whose staggering short-term success (and long-term failure)
requires an explanation in its own terms. And so too for those 'crazy
devices' that one encounters here and there in the archive: stylistic
clusters or plot sequences that are so weird that they can't be replicas of other texts, but something else altogether.

My final guess, then, is that in the great unread we will find many
different kinds of creatures, of which my 'rivals' are only one
instance. This is why the tree is useful: it is a way to 'open up' literary history, showing how the course selected by European audiences
(Conan Doyle, the canon) is only *one* of the many coexisting
branches that could *also* have been chosen (and weren't). What the
tree says is that literary history *could be different from what it is.*
Different: not necessarily better. And there are strong reasons for

---

26   Braudel, 'The Situation of History in 1950', in *On History*, pp. 16–17.
27   'The great challenge confronting any excavation [of the literary
archive] is to denaturalize expectations and take forgotten literature on its own
terms', writes Cohen in her introduction. 'Without understanding that forgotten
works are shaped by a coherent, if now lost, aesthetic, one simply dismisses them
as uninteresting or inferior in terms of the aesthetic(s) which have won out'
(*Sentimental Education of the Novel*, p. 21).

its being what it is; most of my article tries precisely to explain why Conan Doyle's selection makes sense. But 'explaining' means organizing the evidence we have so as to account for a given result: it doesn't mean maintaining that that result was inevitable. That's not history; that's theodicy. Inevitable was *the tree*, not the success of this or that branch: in fact, we have seen how *unlikely* the branch of clues was in the 1890s.

Inevitable was the tree; many branches, different—and for the most part still completely unknown. Fantastic opportunity, this uncharted expanse of literature; with room for the most varied approaches, and for a truly *collective* effort, like literary history has never seen. Great chance, great challenge (what will knowledge indeed mean, if our archive becomes ten times larger, or a hundred), which calls for a maximum of methodological boldness: since no one knows what knowledge will mean in literary studies ten years from now, our best chance lies in the radical diversity of intellectual positions, and in their completely candid, outspoken competition. Anarchy. Not diplomacy, not compromises, not winks at every powerful academic lobby, not taboos. Anarchy. Or as Arnold Schoenberg once wonderfully put it: the middle road is the only one that does not lead to Rome.[28]

---

28   The reader who has made it this far probably knows that the conjunction of formalism and literary history has been a constant (perhaps *the* constant) of my work, from the essays 'The Soul and the Harpy' and 'On Literary Evolution' (in *Signs Taken for Wonders: Essays in the Sociology of Literary Forms*, 3rd edn [London 1997]) to the introductory chapters to *The Way of the World: The Bildungsroman in European Culture* (London 1987) and *Modern Epic: The World-System from Goethe to García Márquez* (London 1996) and the six 'Theoretical Interludes' of *Atlas of the European Novel, 1800–1900* (London 1998). In these books I discuss extensively the relationship between form and ideology, which I could not address here for reasons of space.

Planet Hollywood

Working at the last chapter of the Atlas of the European Novel, *on the markets for novels in nineteenth-century Europe, I had discovered the truth of Haldane's famous dictum that 'size is never just size': small national markets were not the scaled-down replicas of large ones, but different structures, where 'strong' forms occupied more and more space, while 'weak' ones tended to disappear altogether, thus drastically reducing the spectrum of possible choices. A quick look at Manhattan video-stores—which had been part of a graduate seminar at Columbia, and was later published in* New Left Review[1]*—had found the same correlation between size (of the store) and diversity (of film genres available), and 'Planet Hollywood' continued this line of research, combining it with my more recent interest in the international constraints on cultural systems: a sort of 'Conjectures on World Film', as it were, in which Hollywood replaced Paris as the centre of the world.*

American box-office hits confirmed the analogy between Hollywood and Paris; but meanwhile, my focus was slowly shifting in another direction. In the Atlas, *where my object of study had been literary markets, I had used novelistic genres in a wholly instrumental way, as the variable*

---

1 'Markets of the Mind', *New Left Review* II/5 (September–October 2000).

whose fluctuations provided an insight into the structure of the various European spaces. 'Planet Hollywood' used the same two variables— film genres, and national markets—but reversed their role: this time, genres were the object of study, and their differential geographical distribution a clue to their cultural meaning. Instead of using morphology to understand geography, the other way around.

'Planet Hollywood' was conceived as a short piece, and its analytical work doesn't go very far. But two particularly skewed spatial patterns—action films, which travelled well in many directions, and comedies, which travelled hardly at all—caught my attention. In the article, I explain these opposite outcomes with, respectively, a heavy reliance on plot (action films), and on language (comedies); which is true, and also, in itself, not much of a discovery: narrative theory has always known that a story is composed of the distinct layers of story and style. What was new, however, was the clarity of the empirical confirmation: plot and style becoming manifestly de-coupled as a result of their movement (or not) in space. And not just 'in space', but at the very large scale of 'Planet Hollywood'; as if only an unusually powerful filtering mechanism could separate these formal traits, and make them perfectly recognizable. It's another fascinating aspect of the 'size is not just size' idea: world literature, not just as a unique object of study in and of itself, but as a sort of 'natural laboratory' for all sorts of theoretical experiments. As a global digital archive is (slowly) coming into being, there is no saying what results we may find.

Some time ago, while working on nineteenth-century literary markets, I was struck by how thoroughly British and French novels managed to streamline European cultural consumption: hundreds of thousands of people reading more or less the same books, and at the same time. This looked so much like the beginning of the culture industry that it suggested a little follow-up experiment—on film markets, this time. I began with the records published in *Variety*, and listed the five most successful American films for every year between 1986 and 1995; then I turned to non-American markets, in order to assess the extent of Hollywood's planetary diffusion. Here, the sources (*Variety International*, *Screen International*, and various related yearbooks) turned out to be extremely patchy, and I decided to map only those countries for which at least two years were fully documented; this made the sample a little more reliable, but unfortunately much more unbalanced: of forty-six countries with 'enough' data, twenty-five are in Europe; Africa is almost entirely absent, as are many Asian and Latin American countries, and the demographic giants of India, China and Russia.

Big blanks. Since, however, some interesting patterns emerge, I am writing these pages anyway. Take them for what they are: initial hypotheses that should be tested against a larger, more precise set of data.

I

Figure 1: the sheer power of Hollywood. In twenty-four countries (the black triangles), American films make up between 75 and 90 per cent of the decade's top hits; in another thirteen (the black stars) the percentage climbs above 90; in five cases it reaches 100. (While spending a year in Berlin, every now and then I checked the top ten hits of the week; always at least nine American films, if not ten.) 'When one talks of cinema', wrote the Brazilian *avant-garde* director Glauber Rocha in the 1960s, 'one talks of American cinema . . . Every discussion of cinema made outside Hollywood must begin with Hollywood.' Indeed

But first, a few words on those nations (the white circles) where Hollywood encounters an obstacle, and falls below 75 per cent of box-office hits. Sweden and Denmark are the core nations of Scandinavia: an area, as a dissertation by Leyvoy Joensen has

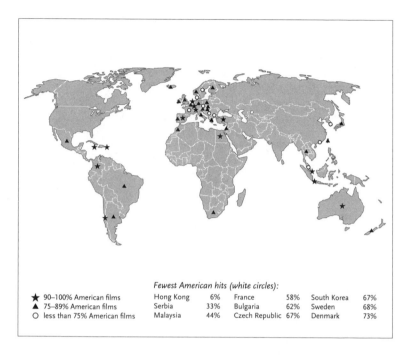

			Fewest American hits (white circles):			
★	90–100% American films	Hong Kong	6%	France	58%	South Korea	67%
▲	75–89% American films	Serbia	33%	Bulgaria	62%	Sweden	68%
○	less than 75% American films	Malaysia	44%	Czech Republic	67%	Denmark	73%

Figure 1: US films as a percentage of top five box-office hits, 1986–95

shown, with a very strong regional identity, where not just Danish or Swedish novels, but Icelandic and Faroese ones had quite a criss-cross circulation. As for the Czech Republic, Serbia and Bulgaria, they are the tip of the—melting—east European iceberg: in the Czech Republic, American films accounted for less than 30 per cent of box-office hits before 1989; afterwards, they reached 76 per cent. And the same trend is visible in Slovakia and Poland (and Estonia, Romania, Slovenia: but their data were too erratic, so they don't appear in the map).

Then, France. Where the story is different; Paris was the Hollywood of the nineteenth century, its novels were read and imitated everywhere— they even invented cinema there! No wonder they hate the other Hollywood, no one likes to give up symbolic hegemony; but no one keeps it by mere force of will either, and although France knows how to protect its own market (which was twice inundated by foreign films, in the 1920s and 1940s, and twice bounced back), there is no question of its competing with Hollywood abroad. Between 1986 and 1995, only four non-American films enjoyed a large international success: *A Fish Called Wanda, Four Weddings and a Funeral, Crocodile Dundee, The Last Emperor*: two British comedies, an Australian comedy, an American–Italian melodrama. None of them was French. In fact, none was any different from the usual Hollywood fare . . .

II

Scandinavia, Eastern Europe, France: all 'residual' sub-systems, which don't threaten Hollywood's hegemony. The true rival is in Asia: Hong Kong. (As I already said, I could not find enough data for the other obvious candidate, India.) In the sample decade, only *Jurassic Park* and *Speed* made it into the Hong Kong list; all other hits were local products. And Hong Kong has also its regional sphere of influence: Malaysia, Taiwan, partly Thailand, probably Pakistan and Bangladesh and China (whose insufficient data don't appear in the map).

Of course, the future of the Hong Kong film industry is not clear: it may be stunted by the incorporation into the People's Republic of China—or the exact opposite: the larger market may be a boost to production and inventiveness. Be that as it may, in the last generation or so (from Bruce Lee to Jackie Chan and beyond) Hong Kong films have very efficiently caught the wake of Hollywood's greatest export staple: the films of action and adventure charted in Figure 2.[2] With its

---

2 This map, and those that follow, will make use of film genres—a controversial point, given that some critics believe in the existence of genres, and others don't. Without getting into the general argument, I will just say that I belong to the first group, even more stubbornly in the case of film: if you look at a newspaper, or walk into a video-store, the reality of film genres literally leaps at you, as each film is being sold *as something*: a comedy, a film noir, science fiction,

many fuzzy internal divisions, but quite clear external borders, this is by far the most successful form both inside the US and abroad (with the exception of Europe, about which more later). South and East Asia are these films' favourite destination: they account for 50 per cent of the decade's hits in Singapore, 55 in South Korea, 65 in Indonesia, 67 in Taiwan and Thailand, 80 in Malaysia (and the sporadic data for Pakistan, India and Bangladesh confirm this pattern).

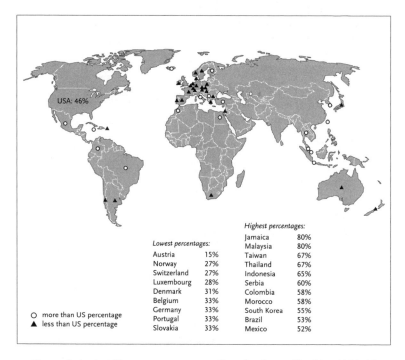

Figure 2: Action films as a percentage of top five box-office hits, 1986–95

---

whatever. Taxonomy here is not a scholastic pastime, it's a product of the film industry itself, which makes it easier to recognize the film, and to buy the ticket. As for the categories I will use, I borrowed them from one section of the film industry itself—video-stores. I chose an independent store in Greenwich Village, a Blockbuster store, and the Theater for the Living Arts catalogue, reduced their (largely coincident) categories to four large ones (Action; Comedies; Children; Dramas), and applied them to my sample.

Behind this diffusion is at work one of the constants of cultural geography: stories travel well—better than other genres, anyway. It was true centuries ago, when Indian and Arab tales crossed the Mediterranean, and transformed European storytelling; it is true today, for these concatenations of striking events and hyperbolic actions (and tomorrow, with videogames: stories that never stand still, where the only thing that matters is what happens next . . .). And stories travel well because they are largely *independent of language*. Within a narrative text, style and plot constitute discrete layers, and the latter can usually be translated (literally: carried across) independently from the former. (A favourite example of narrative theorists used to be, 'one can take a novel, and turn the plot into a ballet': just what happens in so many Hong Kong films.) This relative autonomy of the story-line explains the ease with which action films dispense with words, replacing them with sheer noise (explosions, crashes, gunshots, screams . . .); while this brisk dismissal of language, in turn, facilitates their international diffusion. Significantly enough, in the 1920s American films were already enjoying a worldwide hegemony: what brought it to a halt was the invention of sound, which elevated language into a powerful barrier, supporting the quick take-off of the various national film industries. The abrogation of language in action films is a powerful factor in turning the tide around.

III

Next map: comedies (Figure 3). In the US, they account for 20 per cent of box-office hits; elsewhere they are usually much less successful—look at East Asia, the Mediterranean, or at the percentages indicated in the map. By contrast, even in those countries (the white circles) where Hollywood comedies are relatively more successful, the difference with the US is often insignificant.

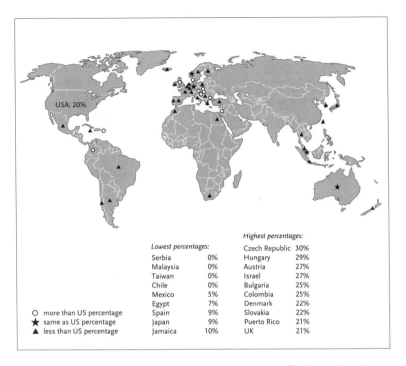

Figure 3: Comedies as a percentage of top five box-office hits, 1986–95

Another rule of cultural geography: relatively speaking, comedies do *not* travel well. Compared to other French genres, the enormously popular comic novel of early-nineteenth-century France, the *roman gai*, had a rather modest European diffusion. In a neat reversal of what we just saw, the main reason for this inertia is almost certainly language: since jokes and many other ingredients of comedy rely heavily on short circuits between signifier and signified, they are weakened by translation—and indeed comic films reached the apex of their world diffusion long ago, before the age of sound. Just as significant as language, however, is the fact that laughter arises out of unspoken assumptions that are buried very deep in a culture's history: and if these are not *your* assumptions, the automatic component so essential to laughter disappears. Which is interesting, we usually associate the national spirit with the sublime (*et pour cause*: unknown soldiers, torn flags, battlefields, martyrs . . .) yet, what makes a nation laugh turns out to be just as distinctive as what makes it cry. If not *more* distinctive, in fact: the same sublime objects reappear relentlessly from one culture to another, whereas the targets of comic aggression seem to be much more idiosyncratic, more variable. All sublime nations resemble each other, we could paraphrase *Anna Karenina*, but when they start laughing, they all do so in their own unique way.

The international weakness of Hollywood comedies, then, has much to do with their being American; or perhaps, better, with their being non-Brazilian, non-Finnish, etc. In many cases—Brazil, Argentina, Mexico, Sweden, Finland, Britain, Australia, Hong Kong—market records suggest a genuine passion for national comedies which becomes spectacular in Italy, where *every* single national hit of the sample decade was a comedy (as would be, a few years later, the biggest Italian success of all times, *Life Is Beautiful*). This fixation—which began in the sixties, and apparently will never end—must have something to do with that mix of aggression and anxiety that psychoanalysis has recognized in laughter, and that is so typical of the emotional cosmos of the *commedia all'italiana*. It's the grimace of a culture structurally unsure about its position in the world: the last of the 'advanced' countries, arrogantly showing its teeth to what is left of the past—or the first of the 'backward' ones, populistically bent on 'decrowning' those placed above it?

IV

Figure 4: children's films. In the US, 25 per cent of box-office hits; in most other countries, much less—at times almost nothing (and I will come to that in a moment). But the American results are arresting in themselves. One in every four box-office hits aimed at children? This seemed so odd that I checked the statistics for the years of my own childhood, and in the pages of *Variety* for 1955 and '56 and '57 I found what I remembered so well: there were so *few* children's films then! A cartoon in the top ten around Christmas—for a couple of weeks, in a couple of places; period. (I say a couple of places because, then, the American market was still so uneven that the top ten changed a lot from town to town; today, the very idea seems quaint.) In the mid-fifties, not a *single* film for children made *Variety*'s top twenty for the year, with the only possible exceptions of *20,000 Leagues Under the Sea* and *Around the World in 80 Days*: both children's films in a very dubious sense (and both drawn from nineteenth-century French novels, by the way).

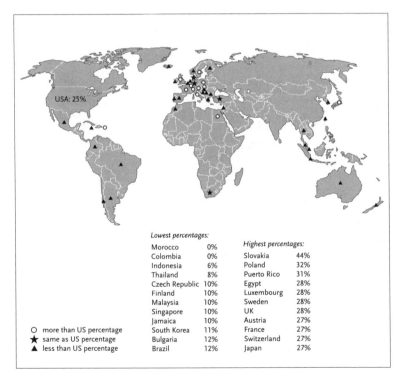

Figure 4: Children's films as a percentage of box-office top five, 1986–95

Today, the top twenty routinely includes four or five children's films, and the reason, I suspect, is quite simple: money. These films are more successful because much more money is spent on children's entertainment. But this extra income is not available everywhere, and the result is the skewed distribution of Figure 4, where the (relative) absence of the genre tends to overlap with the poverty of each given country. The correlation is not perfect, they never are (look at the data for Egypt, or Puerto Rico, or Singapore), but it seems real enough, and, incidentally, it also works *inside* the United States: studying New York video-stores, my students and I discovered that the presence of children's films in Harlem and the Bronx ranged between 3 and 8 per cent; in the Upper West Side and Upper East Side, between 10 and 19 per cent. Three times higher.

'Children's films' is a sloppy definition, of course: it points to the audience, not the film—and to an audience which is moreover quite problematic. Children, after all, don't usually go to the movies by themselves and, as adults must take them, a little generic paradox ensues: whom should the film be for—the adult, or the child? Faced with this problem, the fifties offered either straightforward fairy tales (for the child: *Cinderella*, *Snow White*, even *Fantasia*), or those Jules Verne novels I mentioned earlier (which were much more successful than the fairy tales: another sign of a market directed at the adult). But today the two forms have converged, blending into a hybrid which appeals to children and adults alike: *ET*, *Roger Rabbit*, *Back to the Future*, the various *Star Wars* and *Indiana Jones* movies—these are stories designed for a new human species of savvy children and silly grown-ups (*Homo puerilis*). Their god is Steven Spielberg (and Benigni is his prophet: *Life is Beautiful*— what a childish adult wants a child to know about Auschwitz).

In one film after another (*Jaws*, *Close Encounters*, *Indiana Jones and the Temple of Doom*, *Jurassic Park*; even the uncanny detail of the girl in red, in *Schindler's List*), Spielberg has not only chosen stories in which children and adults are somehow involved together, but where the ambiguities so typical of (adult) life are defused by the (child's) desire for polarization so well described by Bruno Bettelheim. The best example is Schindler himself; this Third Reich shark turned benefactor, who offered an incredible chance to study the contradictions of historical existence. But Spielberg is not interested in understanding complicated things, and in his hands this figure out of Dostoevsky, or Brecht becomes—nothing.

V

So. The diffusion of American comedies is low almost everywhere, children's films tend to prefer wealthy areas, action films South and East Asia . . . Each genre has its favourite space, its different diffusion pattern, and it's precisely this difference that makes cultural geography useful (if all films were evenly distributed everywhere, these maps would be pointless: maps need unevenness, they signify through unevenness). And the unevenness is there because each region of the world functions like a cultural ecosystem: it tends to select one genre—and to reject another. It selects one genre *because* it rejects the other: setting side by side the maps of children's and action films, a striking coincidence emerges between the strength of the latter and the weakness of the former: Colombia, Jamaica, Morocco, Thailand, Malaysia, Indonesia and South Korea are all present in the tables charting the ten countries with most action films and fewest children's films. Same message from Figure 5, which charts the ten countries with the *fewest* action films and most dramas: seven European countries (Portugal, Spain, Switzerland, Austria, Belgium, Luxembourg and Norway) are present in both lists— while five of the remaining six countries are also in Europe.[3]

---

3 'Drama' is not a very good label, I know, it sounds like a passepartout

Fewest adventure films:		Most dramas:	
Austria	15%	Spain	41%
Norway	27%	Belgium	33%
Switzerland	27%	Portugal	33%
Luxembourg	28%	Switzerland	30%
Denmark	31%	Luxembourg	28%
Belgium	33%	Morocco	28%
Germany	33%	Austria	27%
Portugal	33%	Finland	27%
Slovakia	33%	Norway	27%
Spain	34%	Greece	26%

▲ ten countries with fewest adventure films
○ ten countries with most dramas

Figure 5: Countries with fewest adventure films and most dramas

We see here the Darwinian side of cultural geography: forms that *fight for space*. They fight for the limited resources of the market, and if one manages to successfully occupy one space, other forms will encounter all sorts of obstacles. In trying to explain large

---

notion designed to catch all those films that cannot fit elsewhere, but there is one sense in which it is actually appropriate: dramas have a very strong theatrical component (that's probably why they do so well in Europe, where the theatre is still a major cultural presence): the setting is often circumscribed, like the theatre—even, say, in *Forrest Gump*, where the protagonist moves around a lot, but the film is symbolically dominated by his monologue on the bus bench. Like the theatre, 'dramas' focus on language, and on its problems: *Forrest Gump* again, *Ghost, Rain Man, Dances with Wolves* (the last two titles both being translations from a different linguistic universe).

geographical patterns, then, the isolated case is seldom enough: the strength (or weakness) of one form can only be explained by looking at the whole system of variables at play. And with this, I turn to my last point.

VI

The nineteenth century saw a European diffusion of Anglo-French novels; the twentieth century, a planetary diffusion of American film. And the reactions to this centralized global market? Every discussion of cinema made outside Hollywood must begin with Hollywood, said Glauber Rocha. Must it also *end* with Hollywood?

Here, the history of the novel offers an interesting precedent. In his work on Brazilian novels, Roberto Schwarz has shown that the power of metropolitan models has a twofold effect on cultures of the periphery. First of all, it generates a 'disagreement between the form [which is foreign] and the material [which is local]': 'nothing is more Brazilian than these half-baked novels', he goes on, so full of 'dissonance' and 'compositional defects'. 'An impossible programme', says Masao Miyoshi of the modern Japanese novel; and similar things have been independently said just about everywhere.[4] In the case of less powerful literatures, then—which means: almost *all* literatures, inside and outside Europe—the import of foreign novels doesn't just mean that people read a lot of foreign books; it also means that local writers become uncertain of how to write *their own* novels. Market forces shape consumption *and* production too: they exert a pressure on the very form of the novel, giving rise to a genuine morphology of underdevelopment.

---

4 See my 'Conjectures on World Literature', *New Left Review* II/1 (January–February 2000).

But this is not the whole story. Every now and then, one of those 'impossible programmes' *works*. Machado de Assis takes the 'compositional defects' of Brazilian novels, and turns them into an incredibly original narrative style. Elsewhere, the clash with the symbolic power of Western Europe produces major paradigm shifts, like the Russian novels of ideas, or Latin American magical realism (or the slightly different case of the Kafka–Joyce generation). Although these remain *exceptions*, they occur often enough to show a counter-force at work within the world literary system. The morphology of underdevelopment is not without its surprises.

And in film? Here, reversing the tide is probably more difficult, given the stronger economic constraints (production costs, distribution monopolies, dumping practices . . .), but hardly impossible. A critical reconstruction of the history of film, and of its present, will eventually offer an answer. From the viewpoint of method, however, the crucial point is the one made by Christopher Prendergast in his review of Pascale Casanova's *République mondiale des lettres*: when trying to understand the world-system of culture, 'a single, generalizing description misses too much and is destined to do so, if it is offered as *the* description'.[5] This, of course, is just as true for the quantitative evidence I have used as for the study of individual directors, or film genres: the solution lies in multiple layers of description and explanation, linked together by a chain of successfully analyzed 'details' (Prendergast again). God lies in the detail—perhaps. Our understanding of culture certainly does.

---

5 'Negotiating World Literature', *New Left Review* II/8 (March–April 2001).

More Conjectures

'Conjectures on World Literature' received many critiques, and 'More Conjectures' was my attempt to respond to the most interesting ones. But the strongest objection materialized only after my response, in 2007, in a paper by Jêrome David. Here is the key passage:

If an economic system needs the periphery, because it is rich in cheap unskilled labor force, what is the function of its alleged equivalent in a literary world-system? In this regard the periphery has no function in the symbolic economy other than to arbitrate the rivalry between the 'narrative superpowers', through its variable porosity to each. This means, I think, that the interdependence of the economic systemic components is not of the same kind as the relations between the literary ones: the economic core could not exist without the peripheral productive force [but, by contrast] the core of the literary world system does not need the periphery in order to produce anything, because the logic of formal evolution is bound, in Moretti's analysis, to a Kuhnian conception of generic (i.e. paradigmatic) shifts that take place within the core. This is one limitation of the use of the Wallersteinian model in literary history: the economic background of the world-systems hypothesis highlights literary exchanges, but confers on them a misleading systematicity. Rumania, in the nineteenth-century space of the novel, means nothing to English or French writers and readers; it is not even the country of a *cultural raw material (like folktales) that could be transformed at the core with symbolic benefits.*[1]

Let me radicalize David's point. When China banned the import of opium, or the sepoys of the East India Company rose up in arms, Britain went immediately to war, because—had it lost those markets—its entire social structure would have dramatically changed. Had the entire world closed its doors to British novels, however, the history of the English novel would have remained exactly the same. This was the problem that David had brought to light: a fundamental asymmetry in the structure of the literary system—and thus also of literary-historical explanation—whereby the activity of the literary core largely determines developments in the periphery, but the reverse is usually not the case. But if the (literary) periphery is not necessary to the existence of the (literary) core, then only half of Wallerstein's model can be fruitfully applied to literature; and is a half-model still a model—or no model at all? I am not sure; but if it were the latter, as I suspect, then the only response to David's critique would consist in repeating a sentence of 'More Conjectures' that addressed a different set of objections: 'Here things are easy: Parla and Arac are right—and I should have known better.' Those were difficult words to write, at the time; but extremely liberating. Once you have been really proved wrong, the argument is no longer about you; it's about a world of facts that everybody agrees to share (and respect); about hypotheses that have an objectivity of their own, and can be tested, modified, or indeed rejected. A little narcissistic wound is a small price to pay for such progress.

---

1   David's paper, still unpublished, was presented at the conference, 'For a Theory of the Novel in the Twenty-first Century', at the Center for the Study of the Novel, at Stanford. The last sentence in the passage—'it is not even the country of a cultural raw material' etc.—is not entirely accurate, as core cultures do occasionally appropriate products that have been developed elsewhere, in order to re-market them under their own trademark. This, however, does not happen often enough to falsify David's assertion.

In the past year or so, several articles have addressed the issues raised in 'Conjectures on World Literature': Christopher Prendergast, Francesca Orsini, Efraín Kristal and Jonathan Arac in *New Left Review*, Emily Apter and Jale Parla elsewhere.[2] My thanks to all of them; and as I obviously cannot respond to every point in detail, I will focus here on the three main areas of disagreement among us: the (questionable) paradigmatic status of the novel; the relationship between core and periphery, and its consequences for literary form; and the nature of comparative analysis.

I

One must begin somewhere, and 'Conjectures' tried to sketch how the literary world-system works by focusing on the rise of the modern novel: a phenomenon which is easy to isolate, has been studied all the world over, and thus lends itself well to comparative work. I also added that the novel was 'an example, not a model; and of course my example, based on the field I know (elsewhere, things may be very different)'. Elsewhere things are different indeed: 'If the novel can be seen as heavily freighted with the political, this is not patently the case for other literary genres. Drama seems to travel less anxiously . . . How might the . . . construct work with

---

2 'Conjectures on World Literature', *New Left Review* II/1 (January–February 2000); Christopher Prendergast, 'Negotiating World Literature', *New Left Review* II/8 (March–April 2001); Francesca Orsini, 'Maps of Indian Writing', *New Left Review* II/13 (January–February 2002); Efraín Kristal, '"Considering Coldly . . . ": A Response to Franco Moretti', *New Left Review* II/15 (May–June 2002); Jonathan Arac, 'Anglo-Globalism?' *New Left Review* II/16 (July–August 2002); Emily Apter, 'Global *Translatio*: The "Invention" of Comparative Literature, Istanbul, 1933', *Critical Inquiry* 29 (2003); Jale Parla's essay ('The Object of Comparison') was published in a special issue of *Comparative Literature Studies* edited by Djelal Kadir (January 2004).

lyric poetry?' asks Prendergast; and Kristal: 'Why doesn't poetry
follow the laws of the novel?'[3]

It doesn't? I wonder. What about Petrarchism? Propelled by its
formalized lyrical conventions, Petrarchism spread to (at least)
Spain, Portugal, France, England, Wales, the Low Countries, the
German territories, Poland, Scandinavia, Dalmatia (and, according
to Roland Greene, the New World). As for its depth and duration,
I am sceptical about the old Italian claim that by the end of the
sixteenth century over two hundred *thousand* sonnets had been
written in Europe in imitation of Petrarch; still, the main disagreement seems to be, not on the enormity of the facts, but on the
enormity of their enormity—ranging from a century (Navarrete,
Fucilla), to two (Manero Sorolla, Kennedy), three (Hoffmeister,
Kristal himself), or five (Greene). Compared to the wave-like diffusion of this '*lingua franca* for love poets', as Hoffmeister calls it,
western novelistic 'realism' looks like a rather ephemeral vogue.[4]

---

3 'Conjectures', p. 58; 'Negotiating World Literature', pp. 120–1;
'"Considering Coldly . . ."', p. 62. Orsini makes a similar point for Indian
literature: 'Moretti's novel-based theses would seem to have little application to
the Subcontinent, where the major nineteenth and twentieth-century forms have
been poetry, drama and the short story, whose evolution may show quite different
patterns of change': 'Maps', p. 79.

4 See Antero Meozzi, *Il petrarchismo europeo (secolo xvi)* (Pisa 1934);
Leonard Forster, *The Icy Fire: Five Studies in European Petrarchism* (Cambridge
1969); Joseph Fucilla, *Estudios sobre el petrarquismo en España* (Madrid 1960);
Ignacio Navarrete, *Orphans of Petrarch* (California 1994); William Kennedy,
Authorizing Petrarch (Ithaca, NY 1994); Maria Pilar Manero Sorolla, *Introducción
al estudio del petrarquismo en España* (Barcelona 1987); Gerhart Hoffmeister,
Petrarkistische Lyrik (Stuttgart 1973); Roland Greene, *Post-Petrarchism: Origins
and Innovations of the Western Lyric Sequence* (Princeton 1991). Kristal's implicit
acknowledgement of the hegemony of Petrarchism over European and Latin
American poetry comes where he writes that 'the lyrical conventions of modern
Spanish poetry were developed in the 16th century by Boscán and Garcilaso de la
Vega . . . The first signs of a reaction against the strictest conventions of Spanish
prosody did not take place in Spain but in Spanish America in the 1830s':
'"Considering Coldly . . ."', p. 64.

Other things being equal, anyway, I would imagine literary movements to depend on three broad variables—a genre's potential market, its overall formalization and its use of language—and to range from the rapid wave-like diffusion of forms with a large market, rigid formulas and simplified style (say, adventure novels), to the relative stasis of those characterized by a small market, deliberate singularity and linguistic density (say, experimental poetry). Within this matrix, novels would be representative, not of the *entire* system, but of its most mobile strata, and by concentrating only on them we would probably overstate the mobility of world literature. If 'Conjectures' erred in that direction it was a mistake, easily corrected as we learn more about the international diffusion of drama, poetry and so on (here, Donald Sassoon's current work on cultural markets will be invaluable).[5] Truth be told, I would be very disappointed if all of literature turned out to 'follow the laws of the novel': that a single explanation may work *everywhere* is both very implausible and extraordinarily boring. But before indulging in speculations at a more abstract level, we must learn to share the significant facts of literary history across our specialized niches. Without collective work, world literature will always remain a mirage.

II

Is world-systems theory, with its strong emphasis on a rigid international division of labour, a good model for the study of world literature? On this, the strongest objection comes from Kristal: 'I am arguing, however, in favour of a view of world literature', he writes,

> in which the West does not have a monopoly over the creation of forms that count; in which themes and forms can move in several

5   See, for a preliminary account, his 'On Cultural Markets', *New Left Review* II/17 (September–October 2002).

directions—from the centre to the periphery, from the periphery to the centre, from one periphery to another, while some original forms of consequence may not move much at all.[6]

Yes, forms *can* move in several directions. But *do* they? This is the point, and a theory of literary history should reflect on the constraints on their movements, and the reasons behind them. What I know about European novels, for instance, suggests that hardly any forms 'of consequence' don't move at all; that movement from one periphery to another (without passing through the centre) is almost unheard of;[7] that movement from the periphery to the centre is less rare, but still quite unusual, while that from the centre to the periphery is by far the most frequent.[8] Do these facts imply that the West

---

6 '"Considering Coldly . . .'", pp. 73–4.

7 I mean here the movement between peripheral cultures which do not belong to the same 'region': from, say, Norway to Portugal (or vice versa), not from Norway to Iceland or Sweden, or from Colombia to Guatemala or Peru. Sub-systems made relatively homogeneous by language, religion or politics—of which Latin America is the most interesting and powerful instance—are a great field for comparative study, and may add interesting complications to the larger picture (like Darío's modernism, evoked by Kristal).

8 The reason why literary products flow from the centre to the periphery is spelt out by Even-Zohar in his work on polysystems, extensively quoted at the beginning of 'Conjectures': peripheral (or, as he calls them, 'weak') literatures 'often do not develop the same full range of literary activities . . . observable in adjacent larger literatures (which in consequence may create a feeling that they are indispensable)'; 'a weak . . . system is unable to function by confining itself to its home repertoire only', and the ensuing lack 'may be filled, wholly or partly, by translated literature'. Literary weakness, Even-Zohar goes on, 'does not necessarily result from political or economic weakness, although rather often it seems to be correlated with material conditions'; as a consequence, 'since peripheral literatures in the Western hemisphere tend more often than not to be identical with literatures of smaller nations, as unpalatable as this idea may seem to us, we have no choice but to admit that within a group of relatable national literatures, such as the literatures of Europe, hierarchical relations have been established since the very beginnings of these literatures. Within this (macro-)polysystem some literatures have taken peripheral positions, which is only to say that they were often modelled

has 'a monopoly over the creation of the forms that count'? Of course not.⁹ Cultures from the centre have more resources to pour into innovation (literary and otherwise), and are thus more likely to produce it: but a monopoly over creation is a theological attribute, not an historical judgment.¹⁰ The model proposed in 'Conjectures' does not reserve invention to a few cultures and deny it to the others: it specifies *the conditions under which it is more likely to occur*, and the forms it may take. Theories will never abolish inequality: they can only hope to explain it.

---

to a large extent upon an exterior literature.' Itamar Even-Zohar, 'Polysystem Studies', *Poetics Today*, Spring 1990, pp. 47, 81, 80, 48.

9   Nor does it have a monopoly over criticism that counts. Of the twenty critics on whose work the argument of 'Conjectures' rests, writes Arac, 'one is quoted in Spanish, one in Italian, and eighteen in English'; so, 'the impressive diversity of surveying some twenty national literatures diminishes into little more than one single means by which they may be known. English in culture, like the dollar in economics, serves as the medium through which knowledge may be translated from the local to the global': 'Anglo-Globalism?', p. 40. True, eighteen critics are quoted in English. But as far as I know only four or five are from the country of the dollar, while the others belong to a dozen different cultures. Is this less significant than the language they use? I doubt it. Sure, global English may end up impoverishing our thinking, as American films do. But for now, the rapid wide public exchanges it makes possible far exceed its potential dangers. Parla puts it well: 'To unmask the hegemony [of imperialism] is an intellectual task. It does no harm to know English as one sets out for the task.'

10   After all, my last two books end on the formal revolutions of Russian and Latin American narrative—a point also made (not 'conceded', as Kristal puts it, suggesting reluctance on my part) in an article on European literature ('an importer of those formal novelties that it is no longer capable of producing'), another one on Hollywood exports ('a counter-force at work within the world literary system') and in 'Conjectures' itself. See 'Modern European Literature: A Geographical Sketch', p. 42; 'Planet Hollywood', p. 105. 'Conjectures' pointed out that 'in those rare instances when the impossible programme succeeds, we have genuine formal revolutions' (p. 50, footnote 9), and that 'in a few lucky cases, the structural weakness may turn into a strength, as in Schwarz's interpretation of Machado' (p. 58, footnote 29).

III

Kristal also objects to what he calls the 'postulate of a general homology between the inequalities of the world economic and literary systems': in other words, 'the assumption that literary and economic relationships run parallel may work in some cases, but not in others'.[11] Even-Zohar's argument is a partial response to the objection; but there is another sense in which Kristal is right, and the simplifying euphoria of an article originally conceived as a thirty-minute talk is seriously misleading. By reducing the literary world-system to core and periphery, I erased from the picture the transitional area (the semi-periphery) where cultures move in and out of the core; as a consequence, I also understated the fact that in many (and perhaps most) instances, material and intellectual hegemony are indeed very close, but not quite identical.

Let me give some examples. In the eighteenth and nineteenth centuries, the long struggle for hegemony between Britain and France ended with Britain's victory on all fronts—except one: in the world of narrative, the verdict was reversed, and French novels were both more successful and formally more significant than British ones. Elsewhere I have tried to explain the reasons for the morphological supremacy of German tragedy from the mid eighteenth century on; or the key role of semi-peripheral realities in the production of modern epic forms. Petrarchism, which reached its international zenith when its wealthy area of origin had already catastrophically declined (like those stars which are still shining long after their death), is a particularly spooky instance of this state of affairs.

All these examples (and more) have two features in common. First, they arise from cultures which are close to, or inside the core of the system—but are not hegemonic in the economic sphere. France

---

11   '"Considering Coldly . . .",' pp. 69, 73.

may be the paradigm here, as if being an eternal second in the political and economic arena encouraged investment in culture (as in its feverish post-Napoleonic creativity, compared to the postprandial somnolence of the victorious Victorians). A—limited—discrepancy between material and literary hegemony does therefore exist: wider in the case of innovation per se (which does not require a powerful apparatus of production and distribution), and narrower, or absent, in the case of diffusion (which does).[12] Yet, and this is the second feature in common, all these examples *confirm the inequality of the world literary system*: an inequality which does not coincide with economic inequality, true, and allows some mobility—but a mobility *internal* to the unequal system, not alternative to it. At times, even the dialectic between semi-periphery and core may actually widen the overall gap (as in the instances mentioned in footnote 12, or when Hollywood quickly 'remakes' successful foreign films, effectively strengthening its own position). At any rate, this is clearly another field where progress will only be possible through the good coordination of specific local knowledge.

---

12 The fact that innovations may arise in the semi-periphery, but then be captured and diffused by the core of the core, emerges from several studies on the early history of the novel (by Armstrong, Resina, Trumpener and others: all written in total independence from world-systems theory), which have pointed out how often the culture industry of London and Paris discovers a foreign form, introduces a few improvements, and then retails it as its own throughout Europe (ending in the masterstroke of the 'English' novelist Walter Scott). As the picaresque declines in its native country, Gil Blas and Moll Flanders and Marianne and Tom Jones spread it all over Europe; epistolary novels, first written in Spain and Italy, become a continental craze thanks to Montesquieu and Richardson (and then Goethe); American 'captivity narratives' acquire international currency through *Clarissa* and the Gothic; the Italian 'melodramatic imagination' conquers the world through Parisian *feuilletons*; the German *Bildungsroman* is intercepted by Stendhal, Balzac, Dickens, Brontë, Flaubert, Eliot . . . This is of course not the only path of literary innovation, perhaps not even the main one; but the mechanism is certainly there—half swindle, half international division of labour—and has an interesting similarity to larger economic constraints.

IV

The central morphological point of 'Conjectures' was the contrast between the rise of the novel in the core as an 'autonomous development', and the rise in the periphery as a 'compromise' between a Western influence and local materials. As Parla and Arac point out, however, early English novels were written, in Fielding's words, 'after the manner of Cervantes' (or of someone else), thus making clear that a compromise between local and foreign forms occurred there as well.[13] And if this was the case, then there was no 'autonomous development' in western Europe, and the idea that forms have, so to speak, *a different history* at the core and at the periphery crumbles. The world-systems model may be useful at other levels, but has no explanatory power at the level of form.

Here things are easy: Parla and Arac are right—and I should have known better. After all, the thesis that literary form is *always* a compromise between opposite forces has been a leitmotiv of my intellectual formation, from Francesco Orlando's Freudian aesthetics to Gould's 'Panda principle', or Lukács's conception of realism. How on earth could I 'forget' all this? In all likelihood, because the core/periphery opposition made me look (or wish . . .) for a parallel morphological pattern, which I then couched in the wrong conceptual terms.[14]

So let me try again. 'Probably all systems known to us have emerged and developed with interference playing a prominent role', writes Even-Zohar: 'there is not one single literature which did not emerge through interference with a more established literature: and no

---

13 'Anglo-Globalism?', p. 38.
14 This seems a good illustration of the 'Kuhnian' point that theoretical expectations will shape facts according to your wishes—and an even better illustration of the 'Popperian' point that facts (usually gathered by those who disagree with you) will be finally stronger.

literature could manage without interference at one time or another during its history'.[15] No literature without interference . . . hence, also, no literature without compromises between the local and the foreign. But does this mean that all types of interference and compromise *are the same?* Of course not: the picaresque, captivity narratives, even the *Bildungsroman* could not exert the same pressure over French or British novelists that the historical novel or the *mystères* exerted over European and Latin American writers: and we should find a way to express this difference. To recognize when a compromise occurs as it were *under duress*, and is thus likely to produce more unstable and dissonant results—what Zhao calls the 'uneasiness' of the late Qing narrator.

The key point, here, is this: if there is a strong, systematic constraint exerted by some literatures over the others (and we all seem to agree that there is),[16] then we should be able to recognize its effects *within literary form itself*: because forms are indeed, in Schwarz's words, 'the abstract of specific social relationships'. In 'Conjectures', the diagram of forces was embodied in the sharp qualitative opposition of 'autonomous developments' and 'compromises'; but as that solution has been falsified, we must try something else. And, yes, 'measuring' the extent of foreign pressure on a text, or its structural

---

15 'Polysystem Studies', p. 59. A page later, in a footnote, Even-Zohar adds: 'This is true of almost all literatures of the Western hemisphere. As for the Eastern hemisphere, admittedly, Chinese is still a riddle as regards its emergence and early development.'

16 Except Orsini: 'Implicit in [Casanova's] view—explicit in Moretti's— is the traditional assumption of a "source" language, or culture—invariably carrying an aura of authenticity—and a "target" one, seen as in some way imitative. In place of this, Lydia Liu much more usefully proposed the concept of "guest" and "host" languages, to focus attention on the translingual practice through which the hosts may appropriate concepts and forms . . . Cultural influence becomes a study of appropriation, rather than of centres and peripheries': 'Maps', pp. 81–2. The culture industry as a 'guest' invited by a 'host' who 'appropriates' its forms . . . Are these concepts—or daydreams?

instability, or a narrator's uneasiness, will be complicated, at times even unfeasible. But a diagram of symbolic power is an ambitious goal, and it makes sense that it would be hard to achieve.

V

Two areas for future discussion emerge from all this. The first concerns the type of knowledge literary history should pursue. 'No science, no laws' is Arac's crisp description of Auerbach's project; and there are similar hints in other articles too. This is of course the old question of whether the proper objects of historical disciplines are individual cases or abstract models; and as I will argue at extravagant length for the latter in a series of forthcoming articles, here I will simply say that we have a lot to learn from the methods of the social and of the natural sciences. Will we then find ourselves, in Apter's words, 'in a city of bits, where micro and macro literary units are awash in a global system with no obvious sorting device'? I hope so . . . it would be a very interesting universe. So, let's start looking for good sorting devices. 'Formalism without close reading', Arac calls the project of 'Conjectures', and I can't think of a better definition. Hopefully, it will also be a formalism where the 'details' so dear to him and to Prendergast will be highlighted, not erased by models and 'schemas'.[17]

Finally, politics. Several articles mention the political pressure behind Auerbach's *Mimesis*, or Casanova's *République mondiale des lettres*. To them I would add Lukács's two versions of comparative literature: the one which crystallized around the First World War, when *The Theory of the Novel* and its (never completed) companion study on Dostoevsky mused on whether a world beyond capitalism could even still be imagined; and the one which took shape in the thirties, as a long meditation on the opposite political significance of

---

17   Arac, 'Anglo-Globalism?', pp. 41, 38; Apter, 'Global *Translatio*', p. 255.

German and French literature (with Russia again in the background). Lukács's spatio-temporal horizon was narrow (the nineteenth century, and three European literatures, plus Cervantes in *The Theory of the Novel*, and Scott in *The Historical Novel*); his answers were often opaque, scholastic, philistine—or worse. But his lesson lies in how the articulation of his comparative scenario (western Europe or Russia; Germany or France) is simultaneously an attempt to understand the great political dilemmas of his day. Or in other words: *the way we imagine comparative literature is a mirror of how we see the world*. 'Conjectures' tried to do so against the background of the unprecedented possibility that the entire world may be subject to a single centre of power—and a centre which has long exerted an equally unprecedented symbolic hegemony. In charting an aspect of the prehistory of our present, and sketching some possible outcomes, the article may well have overstated its case, or taken some wrong turns altogether. But the relationship between project and background stands, and I believe it will give significance and seriousness to our work in the future. Early March 2003, when these pages are being written, is in this respect a wonderfully paradoxical moment, when, after twenty years of unchallenged American hegemony, millions of people everywhere in the world have expressed their enormous distance from American politics. As human beings, this is cause to rejoice. As cultural historians, it is cause to reflect.

Evolution, World-Systems, Weltliteratur

Up to this point in time, the essays of Distant Reading *seem to be regulated by a sort of secret pendulum, which makes them oscillate back and forth between evolution ('Modern European Literature', 'Slaughterhouse'), and world-systems theory ('Conjectures', 'Planet Hollywood'). The thought that there may be something wrong with the pendulum itself—or, in plainer words, that the two theories may be incompatible—hardly ever occurred to me: they were both uncompromisingly materialistic; both historical; both supported by plenty of empirical evidence . . . What more could one ask for?*

An invitation to speak at Wallerstein's Fernand Braudel Center forced me to consider the matter more directly; and, retrospectively, 'Evolution, World-Systems, Weltliteratur' seems to do a good job at outlining the conceptual antithesis between the two theories, and a not-so-good job at correlating their differences with two long periods in the history of world literature itself.[1] But the fundamental problem posed by the adoption of natural science as a conceptual model for social history isn't really addressed in the article. By

---

1 The final section of the essay is one I would completely reformulate today, largely in the light of Alexander Beecroft's numerous empirical specifications in 'World Literature Without a Hyphen', *New Left Review* II/54 (November–December 2008).

'*fundamental problem*', *I don't mean the opposition between laws and individuals, explanation and interpretation, random and intentional, distant and close, and so on; in all these cases, I am squarely on the side of the natural sciences. But there is one question that I find truly insoluble: evolution* has no equivalent for the idea of social conflict. *Competition among organisms, or among similar species, yes; as well as arms races between predators and prey: but nothing like a conflict whose outcome may redefine the entire ecosystem. Nor is this a problem of evolution only; from what I understand complexity and network theory have exactly the same blind spot—which, clearly, no theory of culture and society can allow.*

My next long-term research project—on tragic collision and network theory—may help me gain some additional insight on this question. Meanwhile, as I was re-reading the article for this collection, I also realized that, beginning more or less around this time, both evolution and world-systems theory began to play a far less important role in my research. In part, it must have been the awareness of their possible weaknesses; but the decisive factor was certainly the growing importance of quantitative research that characterized my work at Stanford, and that eventually led to the creation of the Literary Lab in 2010. Not that quantitative data contradicted in any way the theses of evolution or of world-systems theory; but they produced such a large new body of evidence, for which I was so completely unprepared, that the need for a theoretical framework was for a few years forgotten in the heady mood of permanent exploration. As I write, the results of the explorations are finally beginning to settle, and the un-theoretical interlude is ending; in fact, a desire for a general theory of the new literary archive is slowly emerging in the world of digital humanities. It is on this new empirical terrain that the next encounter of evolutionary theory and historical materialism is likely to take place.

Although the term 'world literature' has been around for almost two centuries, we don't yet have a genuine theory of the object—however loosely defined—to which it refers. We have no set of concepts, no hypotheses to organize the immense quantity of data that constitutes world literature. We do not *know* what world literature is.

This paper will not fill the void. But it will sketch a comparison of two theories that have often struck me as excellent models for the task: evolutionary theory, and world-systems analysis. I will begin by outlining their potential contribution to literary history; then, I will discuss their compatibility; and finally, outline the new image of *Weltliteratur* that emerges from their encounter.[2]

I

It is easy to see why evolution is a good model for literary history: it is a theory that explains the extraordinary variety and complexity of existing forms on the basis of a historical process. In a refreshing contrast to literary study—where theories of form are usually blind to history, and historical work blind to form—for evolution form and history are really the two sides of the same coin; or perhaps, one should say, adopting a more evolutionary metaphor, they are the two dimensions of the same tree.

---

2   Embarrassingly enough, I have used evolution and world-systems analysis for over ten years—even in the same book!—without ever considering their compatibility. Evolution was crucial for the morphological argument of *Modern Epic* (London 1996), whose thematic aspect was in turn strongly shaped by world-systems analysis. A few years later, world-systems analysis played a major role in *Atlas of the European Novel* (London 1998), and in the articles 'Conjectures on World Literature' and 'More Conjectures', included in this volume; while evolution was the basis for 'The Slaughterhouse of Literature' (*Modern Language Quarterly*, 2000) and 'Graphs, Maps, Trees: Abstract Models for Literary History—III' (*New Left Review* II/28 [July–August 2004]; a few passages from this article are more or less repeated in the present text).

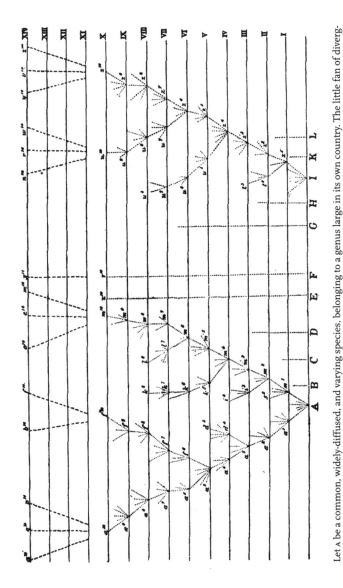

Let A be a common, widely-diffused, and varying species, belonging to a genus large in its own country. The little fan of diverging dotted lines of unequal lengths proceeding from A may represent its varying offspring. . . . Only those variations which are in some way profitable will be preserved or naturally selected. And here the importance of the principle of benefit being derived from divergence of character comes in; for this will generally lead to the most different or divergent variations (represented by the outer dotted lines) being preserved and accumulated by natural selection.

Figure 1: Divergence of character

Figure 1 is the only image in the entire *Origin of Species*; it appears in the fourth chapter, 'Natural Selection', in the section on 'Divergence of Character'. A tree, or a 'diagram', as Darwin calls it in the text, as if to emphasize that it is designed to visualize the interplay of two variables: history along the vertical axis, which charts the regular passage of time (every interval, 'one thousand generations')—and form along the horizontal axis, which follows for its part the morphological diversification that will eventually lead to 'well-marked varieties', or to entirely new species.

The horizontal axis follows formal diversification . . . But Darwin's words are stronger: he speaks of 'this rather perplexing subject', whereby forms don't just 'change', but do so by always *diverging* from each other (remember, we are in the section on 'Divergence of Character'). Whether as a result of geo-historical accidents, or under the action of a specific 'principle'—as far as I can tell, the question is still open—divergence pervades the history of life, defining its morphospace as an intrinsically expanding one. 'A tree can be viewed *as a simplified description of a matrix of distances,*' write Cavalli-Sforza, Menozzi and Piazza in the methodological prelude to their *History and Geography of Human Genes*; and Figure 2, where genetic groups and linguistic families branch away from each other in geography and morphology at once, makes clear what they mean: a tree is a way of sketching *how far* a given form has moved from another one, or from their common point of origin.

A theory that takes as its central problem the *multiplicity of forms* existing in the world; that explains them as the result of *divergence and branching*; and that bases divergence on a process of *spatial separation*: here is what evolutionary theory has to offer to literary history. Many different forms, in a discontinuous space: not a bad starting point, for the study of world literature.

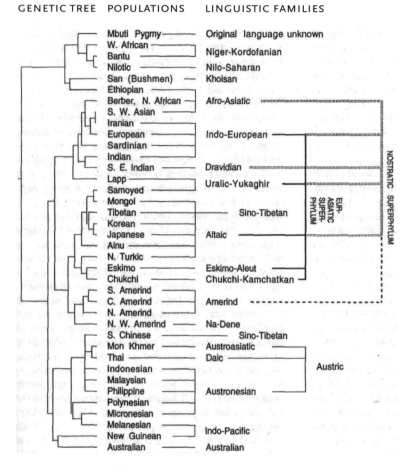

Figure 2: Linguistic trees

II

In world-systems analysis the coordinates change, as the onset of capitalism brusquely reduces the many independent spaces needed for the origin of species (or of languages) to just three positions: core, periphery, semi-periphery. The world becomes *one*, and *unequal*: one, because capitalism constrains production everywhere on the planet; and unequal, because its network of exchanges requires, and reinforces, a marked unevenness between the three areas.

Here, too, it's easy to understand the theory's appeal for literary study. On its basis, we can finally grasp the *unity* of world literature, as in Goethe's and Marx's *Weltliteratur*. And then, the theory illuminates the *internal articulations* of the literary system: like capitalism, *Weltliteratur* is itself one and unequal, and its various components—the world's many national and local literatures—are often thwarted in their development by their position within the system as a whole. Itamar Even-Zohar (whose 'polisystem theory' is quite similar to world-systems analysis) puts it very well when he observes that, within the international literary system, 'there is no symmetry': powerful literatures from the core constantly 'interfere' with the trajectory of peripheral ones (whereas the reverse almost never happens), thus constantly increasing the inequality of the system.

While studying the international market for eighteenth- and nineteenth-century novels, I reached very similar conclusions to Even-Zohar's. Here, the crucial mechanism by which the market operated was that of *diffusion*: books from the core were incessantly exported into the semi-periphery and the periphery, where they were read, admired, imitated, turned into models—thus drawing those literatures into the orbit of core ones, and indeed 'interfering' with their autonomous development. And then, this asymmetric diffusion imposed a stunning *sameness* on the literary system: wave after wave of epistolary fiction, or historical novels, or *mystères*, dominated the scene everywhere—often, like American action movies today, more thoroughly in the smaller markets of peripheral cultures than in their country of origin.

World literature as one and unequal: this was the contribution of the world-systems approach. The *international constraints* under which literature is written: the limits that the world market imposes on the imagination. 'Diffusion is the great conservative force in human history', wrote A. L. Kroeber—and he was absolutely right.

III

One can hardly imagine a more clear-cut antithesis. Evolution foregrounds the *diversification* of existing forms produced by speciation; world-systems analysis, the *sameness* (or at any rate, the limits on diversity) enforced by diffusion. I am simplifying of course, evolution includes mutation *and* selection (i.e. both the production and the elimination of diversity), just as world-systems analysis specifies *different* positions within the international division of labour. But still, think of those titles: *The Origin of* Species, plural, and *The Modern World*-System, singular: grammar is a good index of the opposite research projects. And the geographical substratum of the two theories duplicates the antithesis: Darwin's breakthrough famously occurred in an *archipelago*, because the origin of species (Ernst Mayr's 'allopatric speciation') needs a world made of separate spaces; but the long-distance trade of modern capitalism *bridges* the greatest of oceans, and subjects all societies to a single, continuous geography.

A theory of diversification; a theory of sameness. Clearly, the two are incompatible. Just as clearly, they both explain important aspects of world literature. They are both true: but they *cannot* both be true.[3] Or perhaps, better, they cannot be true—*unless literature itself functions in two completely incompatible ways.*

---

3 Obviously enough, I am here speaking of their truth *when applied to literature*; in their original fields (biology and economic history) the two theories are simply incomparable.

This sounds like an absurd idea; but it does have a historical and morphological rationale. The historical argument is simple: diversification and sameness are both present in literary history because they arise in different epochs, and from different social mechanisms. Diversification is the result of the (relative) isolation of human cultures from their origins until a few centuries ago; sameness appears much later, sometime around the eighteenth century, when the international literary market becomes strong enough to (begin to) subjugate those separate cultures. Here I am simplifying again, there have been earlier episodes of widespread diffusion (like the Petrarchist epidemics of late medieval Europe), just as there have been *later* episodes of diversification; but the point is that each of the two principles has an elective affinity with a different socio-historical configuration; and that, by and large, we have moved from the one to the other.

This, in broad strokes, is the historical argument. The morphological one is different. So far, I have implicitly accepted the evolutionary assumption that in literature, just as in nature, *diversity equals divergence*: that new forms only arise by branching out from pre-existing ones via some kind of mutation. Now, if this were the case, then diffusion (and with it the world-systems approach) would have very little to say on literary innovation: great at explaining how forms *move*, a theory of diffusion cannot account for how they *change*, for the simple reason that diffusion is not meant to multiply forms, but to *reduce* their number by maximizing the space occupied by just one of them. Diffusion is the great conservative—not creative—force of human history.

In literature, just as in nature, diversity equals divergence . . . But what if the *convergence* of distinct lineages could also produce new forms?

IV

This question will strike many readers as almost a rhetorical one. 'Darwinian evolution', writes Stephen Jay Gould, 'is a process of constant separation and distinction. Cultural change, on the other hand, receives a powerful boost from amalgamation and anastomosis of different traditions. A clever traveler may take one look at a foreign wheel, import the invention back home, and change his local culture fundamentally and forever.'[4] The clever traveller is a poor example (it's a case of diffusion, not of amalgamation), but the general point is clear, and well expressed by the historian of technology George Basalla: 'Different biological species usually do not interbreed', he writes: 'Artifactual types, on the other hand, are routinely combined to produce new and fruitful entities.'[5]

Routinely combined . . . That's it: for most scholars, convergence is the basic, if not the *only* mode of cultural history. I have criticized elsewhere this position, countering it with a sort of cyclical division of labour between divergence and convergence in the shaping of the literary morphospace.[6] Here, I will only add that the decisive historical watershed is again the establishment of an international market: divergence being the main path of literary change before its advent, and convergence afterwards. Thomas Pavel's morphological reflections in *La Pensée du Roman*—based on a very different conceptual framework from the present paper—offers excellent (because independent) corroboration for this thesis: divergence is for him the driving force in the first fifteen centuries of the novel's existence, and convergence from the eighteenth century onwards.

---

4   Stephen Jay Gould, *Full House: The Spread of Excellence from Plato to Darwin* (New York 1996), pp. 220–1.

5   George Basalla, *The Evolution of Technology* (Cambridge 1988), pp. 137–8.

6   See 'Graphs, Maps, Trees: Abstract Models for Literary History—III'.

From the eighteenth century onwards . . . Or in other words: convergence becomes active in literary life *at exactly the same time as diffusion.* And one wonders: is it merely a temporal coincidence, or is there a functional relationship between them?

V

Let me begin with a concrete example. Years ago, one of the greatest critics of our time, Antonio Candido, wrote a tryptich of essays (on Zola's *Assommoir* [1877], Verga's *Malavoglia* [1881], and Azevedo's *Cortiço* [1890]), in which he followed the diffusion of the naturalist novel from the core (France), through the semi-periphery (Italy) and into the periphery (Brazil) of the world literary system. And he discovered, among many other things, a sort of *internal asymmetry* in the diffusion of naturalism: whereas the structure of Zola's plot is largely retained by Verga and Azevedo, his *style* tends to be heavily transformed: in Verga, by his Sicilian-Tuscan orchestration of collective speech, and by the use of proverbs; in Azevedo, by the recourse to allegory, and the narrator's frequent ethical intrusions (especially in sexual matters).[7]

Now, Verga and Azevedo are far from being unique. In the late nineteenth century, as the diffusion of modern novels reaches peripheral cultures with increasing regularity, their greatest writers all subject western European models to a similar process of *stylistic overdetermination*: the analytico-impersonal style of nineteenth-century France is replaced by judgmental, loud, sarcastic, emotional voices, always somewhat at odds with the story they are narrating. In slightly different forms, we find the same arrangement in Multatuli's anti-imperialist classic, *Max Havelaar, or The Coffee Sales of the Netherlands Trading Company* (1860), and in Rizal's Filipino masterpiece *Noli me tangere* (1886–87); in Futabatei's *Drifting Clouds* (1887), the 'first modern

---

7   Antonio Candido, *O discurso e a cidade* (São Paulo 1993).

Japanese novel', and in Tagore's Rashomon-like political parable, *Home and the World* (1916).

Italy, Brazil, Indonesia, the Philippines, Japan, Bengal . . . The specifics obviously differ from case to case, but the formal logic is always the same: these novels are all 'amalgamations of different traditions'—and all of the same kind: they combine *a plot from the core*, and *a style from the periphery*.[8] The realist-naturalist plot of lost illusions and social defeat reaches the periphery of the literary system more or less intact; but in the course of the journey, it becomes somehow detached from the 'serious' tone that used to accompany it, and is joined to a new stylistic register.

But how is it possible for plot and style to become 'detached'?

VI

It is possible, because the novel is a *composite* form, made of the two distinct layers of 'story' and 'discourse'—or, in my slight simplification, of plot and style: plot presiding over the internal concatenation of the events, and style over their verbal presentation. Analytically, the distinction is clear; textually a little less so, because plot and style are usually so tightly interwoven that their separation is hard to imagine. And yet, *if diffusion intervenes, 'moving' novels across the literary system*, they do indeed separate: plot travels well, remaining fairly stable from context to context, whereas style disappears, or changes.

---

8 It can hardly be a coincidence that the greatest problematizer of narrative voice in western European literature—Joseph Conrad—had himself worked in the colonies, and owed his formal breakthrough (Marlow's laborious, defensive irony) to his wish to represent the periphery to a metropolitan audience. In his case, of course, the ingredients of the amalgamation are reversed: a plot from the periphery—and a style from the core.

Why this difference? Two reasons. First, plot is usually the main point of a novel, and hence it must be as solid as possible. To highlight how inextricable this narrative concatenation ought to be, Boris Tomashevsky coined in 1925 the metaphor of the 'bound motifs', which 'cannot be omitted . . . without disturbing the whole causal-chronological course of events'.[9] But if bound motifs 'cannot be omitted', neither can they really be *changed*: and so, concludes Tomashevsky, 'they are usually distinguished by their "vitality": that is, they appear unchanged in the works of the most various schools'—and just as unchanged, we may add, in the works of the most various countries.[10]

The second reason for the different destinies of plot and style is not structural, but linguistic. Diffusion usually means translation, and hence reformulation from one language into another. Now, plot is largely *independent* from language: it remains more or less the same, not only from language to language, but even from one sign system to another (from novel to illustration, film, ballet . . .) Style is however nothing *but* language, and its translation—*traduttore traditore*—is almost always an act of betrayal: the more complex a style

---

9   Boris Tomashevsky, 'Thematics' (1925), in Lee T. Lemon and Marion J. Reis, *Russian Formalist Criticism: Four Essays* (Nebraska 1965), p. 68.

10   Here, the analogy with biological mutation is arresting. 'In DNA and protein regions of vital importance for function, one finds perfect—or almost perfect—conservation', write Luigi Luca Cavalli-Sforza, Paolo Menozzi, and Alberto Piazza in *The History and Geography of Human Genes* (Princeton 1994), p. 15: 'This indicates strong selective control against changes that would be deleterious; it also shows that evolutionary improvement in this region is rare or absent. However, variation is quite frequent in chromosome regions that are not of vital importance.' Within narrative structure, bound motifs are the equivalent of those 'protein regions of vital importance for function', where one finds 'near perfect conservation'; whereas the 'chromosome regions that are not of vital importance', and where variation is therefore quite frequent, have their parallel in the 'free motifs' of Tomashevsky's model, which 'may be omitted without destroying the coherence of the narrative', and which are as a consequence quite variable ('each literary school has its characteristic stock [of free motifs]').

is, in fact, the greater the chance that its traits will be lost in the process.

So. As novelistic forms travel through the literary system, their plots are (largely) preserved, while their styles are (partly) lost— and are replaced by 'local' ones, as in Azevedo and the other novelists mentioned above. The result is a hybrid form that does indeed 'amalgamate different traditions', as Gould would have it. But for many of these texts, *dissonance* would be more precise than amalgamation: dissonance, disagreement, at times a lack of integration between what happens in the plot, and how the style evaluates the story, and presents it to the reader. *Form as a struggle*: this is what we have here: a struggle between the story that comes from the core, and the viewpoint that 'receives' it in the periphery. That the two are not seamlessly fused is not just an aesthetic given, then, but the crystallization of an underlying *political* tension. In this respect, the morphology of hybrid texts is an invaluable vantage point from which to observe the endless spiral of hegemony and resistance created by world literature.

VII

The term 'world literature' has been around for almost two centuries, but we still do not know what world literature is . . . Perhaps, because we keep collapsing under a single term *two distinct world literatures*: one that precedes the eighteenth century—and one that follows it. The 'first' *Weltliteratur* is a mosaic of separate, 'local' cultures; it is characterized by strong internal diversity; it produces new forms mostly by divergence; and is best explained by (some version of) evolutionary theory.[11] The 'second' *Weltliteratur*

---

11 Speaking of 'local' cultures does not exclude the existence of large regional systems (Indo-European, East Asian, Mediterranean, Meso-American, Scandinavian . . .), which may even overlap with each other, like the eight

(which I would prefer to call world literary system) is unified by the international literary market; it shows a growing, and at times stunning amount of sameness; its main mechanism of change is convergence; and it is best explained by (some version of) world-systems analysis.

What are we to make of these two world literatures? I think they offer us a great chance to rethink the place of history in literary studies. A generation ago, the literature of the past used to be the only 'great' literature; today, the only 'relevant' literature is that of the present. In a sense, everything has changed. In another, nothing has, because both positions are profoundly *normative* ones, much more concerned with value judgments than with actual knowledge. Instead, the lesson of the two world literatures is that the past and present of literature should be seen, not as 'better' or 'worse' epochs, but as *structurally so unlike each other* that they require completely different theoretical approaches. Learning to study *the past as past*, then, and *the present as present*: such is the intellectual challenge posed by *Weltliteratur* in the twenty-first century. But this is a very large topic, which deserves a study of its own.

---

thirteenth-century 'circuits' of Janet Abu-Lughod's *Before European Hegemony*. But these geographical units are not yet stably subordinated to a single center like the one that emerged in eighteenth-century France and Britain.

The End of the Beginning: A Reply to Christopher Prendergast

Along with 'Conjectures', my most criticized piece of writing has certainly been the book Graphs, Maps, Trees *(2005): in Italy, the new left daily which I have read for over forty years,* il manifesto, *evoked in its review—because people are crazy—the 'degenerate art' exhibition of Nazi Germany. In comparison, Christopher Prendergast's 'Evolution and Literary History' (*New Left Review *34 [July–August 2005]) is a model of intellectual sobriety. Here, I want to return to a couple of issues he raised, which acquired a growing importance in the years that followed.*

The first is the weakness of 'demonstrable causal relation' in some parts of my argument: a point Prendergast makes on page 50 of his article, and that I answer on pages 142–4. In retrospect, what is most striking is that Prendergast wanted a causal explanation. Usually, reactions to Graphs, Maps, Trees *take the opposite route, and end up gravitating around close and distant reading—are they complementary, compatible, opposite, do I really want people to stop reading books, etc. I have asked for it, so I won't complain, but it's not very interesting. The role of explanation in literature, however—this is* extremely *interesting. And Prendergast was right in criticizing a shaky explanation when he saw one.*

The second point concerns the role of the 'market' in my explanations; specifically, the fact that this notion ends up playing a greater role in 'Darwinian' pieces like 'Slaughterhouse', Trees, or 'Style, Inc.', than in explicitly 'Marxist' ones like 'Conjectures' or 'Planet Hollywood'. The reason for this seeming paradox is probably this: once literary history is conceived as an evolutionary process, it splits into two distinct (though interacting) series: on one side, the often random variations arising from formal experiments; on the other, the broad social processes that underlie cultural selection. Ideally, the analysis of these two series should form a unity; in practice, their two causal chains are so completely different that I have always ended up concentrating on one of the two, and evoking the other only in a simplified form. And this is what happened in the chapter criticized by Prendergast, where 'the market' is brought in largely as a place-holder for an analysis that is still to come.

The next essay in this collection presents the opposite type of one-sidedness: I spend several pages analyzing the features of novelistic markets in early modern China and Europe—and rely on a simplified summary of the morphological issues at stake. Maybe, one day, I will learn to do the two things together. But there is also something to be said for keeping them separate: 'tides are certainly connected to the phases of the moon', wrote Marc Bloch in The Historian's Craft, *'but in order to know it for sure one had first to independently determine the ones and the others'. The fact that* Distant Reading *is published alongside* The Bourgeois—*a book that couldn't be more unlike it in spirit and execution—makes me think that I prefer studying tides and moon independently of each other. Whether or not a synthesis will follow, remains to be seen.*

Christopher Prendergast's critique of *Graphs, Maps, Trees* in 'Evolution and Literary History' raises objections of an empirical, theoretical and political nature.[1] The main disagreement is this: for Prendergast, nature and culture function in such incomparable ways that evolutionary theory, which was devised to account for the one, cannot possibly work for the other. This conceptual misalignment makes evolutionary 'explanations' of literature incapable of mastering any actual historical evidence, and forces them to rely on circular reasoning and various forms of *petitio principii* instead. In this analytical void, the market acquires an exaggerated importance, that makes it appear as 'a cognate of Nature'; and the final result is that *Graphs, Maps, Trees*' 'no-nonsense realism . . . deteriorates fast into the language of the winner-takes-all attitude' that is typical of social Darwinism.[2]

Predictably, I dissent from this diagnosis, and will explain why in the pages that follow. But in the course of writing this reply I have also become increasingly (and uneasily) aware of how few concrete results have emerged so far from the models discussed in *Graphs, Maps, Trees*, and from others of a similar cast. As they are all rather recent, this fact does not invalidate them: they have gaps, yes, but for me they are still better than the existing alternatives. Still, a good method should prove itself by producing interesting findings, and the title of this article expresses my impatience with the purely methodological reply which, unfortunately, is what I am able to offer at present. 'La metodologia è la scienza dei nullatenenti', wrote Lucio Colletti in *Marxism and Hegel*: methodology is the science of those who have nothing (but *nullatenente* is harsher, loaded with sarcasm). A bitter truth, about which I will say more at the end.

---

1   Christopher Prendergast, 'Evolution and Literary History', *New Left Review* II/34 (July–August 2005); *Graphs, Maps, Trees: Abstract Models for Literary History*, London/New York 2005 (henceforth, ELH and GMT).
2   ELH, p. 61.

CLUES

Prendergast's opening comments concern the 'trees' of detective fiction discussed in the last chapter of *Graphs, Maps, Trees*. For him, those images embody 'an implicit syllogism: Doyle was to prove the most popular of the thriller writers; Doyle comes to use clues in a uniquely special way; therefore the way he uses clues explains his enduring popularity'.[3] Had I foregrounded clues because Doyle 'used them in a uniquely special way', he would be absolutely right: when the choice of the evidence predetermines the results of the investigation, the reasoning is circular indeed. But that was not why I focused on clues in *Graphs, Maps, Trees* (nor in the earlier article on which it was based): rather, I did so because all theories of detective fiction place clues at the very centre of the genre's structure, thus singling them out as its crucial morphological variable.[4] Between Conan Doyle and clues, in other words, there was no inevitable a priori agreement—if anything, it is striking how erratically and inconsistently they are used, throughout the Sherlock Holmes cycle.[5] But although Doyle's solution was far from perfect, it was still *better than those of his rivals*, and this fact seemed to offer a good explanation for their different destinies. Readers liked clues, and so they chose Conan Doyle's stories over those of his rivals.

Readers liked clues . . . But Prendergast doesn't like that 'like'. Having rightly noticed that 'what readers like serves as the equivalent—or analogue—of "environment" in evolutionary thinking', he then dismisses 'this characterization of reading practices and preferences [as] a curiously lightweight scaffolding to build a theoretical model'.[6] But why lightweight? What more powerful agent of selection can there be

---

3   Ibid., p. 49; GMT, pp. 70–8, Figs 29 & 30.
4   'The Slaughterhouse of Literature', *Modern Language Quarterly*, March 2000, reproduced above, pp. 71–2; henceforth: SL.
5   Ibid., pp. 74–5; GMT, p. 74.
6   ELH, p. 50.

than the choices of contemporary readers? Sure, there are publishing, and distribution, and their various appendices (reviewing, advertising, etc.); but even in the film industry, where their role is clearly much greater than in the book market of a century ago, genuine hits don't acquire their typical momentum when these external pressures are at their strongest (that is to say, right away), but only weeks later, when they have largely been replaced by a chain of informal exchanges— 'I really liked that film'—among common movie-goers.[7]

Which brings me to that disgraceful 'like'. It was, obviously, shorthand for something more complicated, on which I have so often insisted, from *Signs Taken for Wonders* on, that I have become reluctant to repeat it (especially as it's not an original idea: Freud, Lévi-Strauss, Althusser, Orlando, Jameson, Eagleton and several others have all offered their version of it). In a nutshell, the idea is that literary genres are problem-solving devices, which address a contradiction of their environment, offering an imaginary resolution by means of their formal organization. The pleasure provided by that formal organization is therefore more than just pleasure—it is the vehicle through which a larger symbolic statement is shaped and assimilated. When readers of detective fiction 'like' clues, in other words, it is because the structure provided by clues makes them feel that the world is fully understandable, and rationalization can be reconciled with adventure, and individuality is a great but dangerous thing . . . [8]

---

7 'Film audiences make hits or flops . . . by discovering what they like . . . This information is transmitted to other consumers and demand develops dynamically over time . . . A hit is generated by an information cascade . . . A flop is an information bandwagon too; in this case the cascade kills the film': Arthur De Vany and W. David Walls, 'Bose-Einstein Dynamics and Adaptive Contracting in the Motion Picture Industry', *Economic Journal*, November 1996, p. 1493. Now in Arthur De Vany, *Hollywood Economics*, London/New York 2004, p. 28; for the statistical data on the temporal trajectories of box office hits, see pp. 48–64.

8 On this, see SL, and 'Clues', in my *Signs Taken for Wonders*, London/New York 2005.

Until proved wrong, then, I will stand by the idea that literary history is shaped by the fact that readers select a literary work, keeping it alive across generations, because they like some of its prominent traits. But where is the 'demonstrable causal relation'[9]— where is the evidence that readers liked clues?

'DEMONSTRABLE CAUSAL RELATION'

That readers selected Doyle because of his use of clues, writes Prendergast, 'cannot simply be *affirmed*. It may well be that Doyle's success can be accounted for in this way, but, subject to further investigation, it may well also be that it was due to quite different factors (for example, a fascination with the figure of Sherlock Holmes, the gentleman from Baker Street).'[10]

It may well also be. But since Prendergast does not explain why a gentleman (which Holmes, incidentally, is not) would be so fascinating in a mystery story—whereas we *do* know what makes clues valuable in that type of narrative—I see no reason to abandon a solid hypothesis for one that, right now, is a mere possibility. And then, unlike gentlemen, clues are a *formal* trait of detective fiction, and since form is the repeatable element of literature, they are more likely to play a role in the replication and long-term survival of a literary genre.[11] Still: is this a 'demonstrable causal relation'? No;

---

9   ELH, p. 50.
10 Ibid., p. 51.
11 In recent years, I have found several other instances of this interdependence of genre and device: analytical descriptions, and historical novels; narrative fillers, free indirect discourse, and, respectively, the tempo and style of 'realistic' conventions; the stream of consciousness, and the modernist koine. In all these cases, the new device allowed Goethe and Scott, Austen and Flaubert, Doyle and Joyce to capture a salient aspect of a historical transformation, and 'fix' it for generations to come: from the prosaic reordering of bourgeois existence in the case of fillers, to the spread of conservative thought in Restoration Europe (description); from the socialization of the modern individual (free

or at least, not yet. Right now, it's just a hypothesis, whereas a genuine demonstration would provide evidence, not only that readers 'liked' clues, but that they managed to 'see' them in the first place. In the 1890s, remember, not even writers were sure of how clues really worked;[12] how then could *readers* recognize them distinctly enough to select them? 'How is the reader influenced by formal properties without being fully conscious of the influence?' asks Steven Johnson in a comment on the book; '*Graphs, Maps, Trees* is silent on the question.' And the question is important:

> If a mind picks up a form, and can recognize it without being fully aware of it, what is really going on in that act of formal perception? It would be interesting to have a model for how form infiltrates the mind that's engaging with it, without actually making the mind fully aware of what's going on.[13]

It would be *very* interesting. But on this point, alas, *Graphs, Maps, Trees* was indeed silent: instead of providing an explanatory 'mechanism', it placed a 'black box' right in the middle of the argument,[14] thus justifying Prendergast's scepticism. In retrospect, I think that my reasoning must have proceeded like this: given the centrality of clues in detective fiction, and Doyle's success with its early readers,

---

indirect style), to the impact of rationalization over adventure (clues), and the multiplication of metropolitan stimuli (stream of consciousness). On fillers, analytical description, and free indirect style, see 'Serious Century', my *The Novel*, Princeton 2006, vol. I, pp. 364–400; on the stream of consciousness, see *Modern Epic*, London/New York 1996, pp. 123–81.

12   SL, pp. 71–5, 79–83; GMT, pp. 72–5.

13   The first passage is in Steven Johnson, 'Distant Reading Minds', available at thevalve.org; the second occurred in a private exchange.

14   The terms 'mechanism' and 'black box' come from Elster's *Explaining Technical Change*: 'To explain is to provide a mechanism, to open up the black box and show the nuts and bolts, the cogs and wheels of the internal machinery . . . A mechanism provides a continuous and contiguous chain of causal or intentional links; a black box is a gap in the chain.' Jon Elster, *Explaining Technical Change*, Cambridge 1983, p. 24.

there *must* be a way in which his use of clues was perceived by those readers. 'There must be': that's the black box. As a small consolation, now at least we have an idea of what may be 'in' the box: the mental mechanisms—perception, processing, pleasure, cognition—through which a form interacts with the environment (and whose clarification may well come, as Johnson suggests, from cognitive science). And if delimiting what needs to be explained is not much, it's not nothing either: to use Chomsky's famous distinction, it takes what used to be 'mysteries', and turns them into 'problems'.[15] And, with a little patience, all problems get solved.

WINNERS' HISTORY?

'In Chekhov's complete works, it is the volume containing his short stories that shows the most wear and tear', wrote Viktor Shklovsky in *Theory of Prose*; and then, with typical effervescence: 'it is high time for Chekhov not only to be republished but re-examined as well. Everyone who does so will surely admit that his most popular stories are also the most formally perfect.'[16] The most popular as the most formally perfect . . . Questionable, of course. But the hyperbole is a good prologue to another of Prendergast's objections: if evolution explains Doyle's survival with the superiority of his formal design—the most popular as the most formally perfect— then all it does is to 'reiterate the verdict' passed by the market: 'If certain texts are lost to us, that is because they are natural born losers.' But this 'equation of market and nature under the aegis of

---

15 'I would like to distinguish roughly between two kinds of issues that arise in the study of language and mind: those that appear to be within the reach of approaches and concepts that are moderately well understood—what I will call "problems"; and others that remain as obscure to us today as when they were originally formulated—what I will call "mysteries"': Noam Chomsky, *Reflections on Language*, New York 1998 (1975), p. 137.

16 Viktor Shklovsky, *Theory of Prose*, Elmwood Park, IL 1990 (1929), pp. 57, 61.

evolutionary biology', he goes on, 'is exactly the move of social Darwinism': no more, and no less, than 'a naturalized representation of winners' history'.[17]

Strong words. But mistaken. What happened is this: I set out to explain the logic behind literary survival and oblivion; I studied a specific historical episode; and then I described what I found: namely, that the texts that survived were formally and symbolically more suited to their environment than their competitors. Since I don't believe that the market produces the best of all possible literatures[18]—after all, half of the *Atlas of the European Novel* examines its stifling effects in nineteenth-century Europe, and 'Planet Hollywood' (see Chapter 4) does the same for film—I would have been *delighted* to find complex, meaningful detective stories unfairly sacrificed to Holmes's success. But—I have not found them. Nor has Prendergast. Nor has anyone else. And in the total absence of contrary evidence, why on earth should I drop a perfectly plausible explanation? Because it sounds politically *wrong*? I doubt this is what a libertarian spirit like Prendergast wants—but I see no other outcome for this type of argument.

And then, cultural markets are peculiar creatures. In the entertainment industry, writes Sherwin Rosen in 'The Economics of Superstars', there is 'a strong tendency for both market size and reward to be skewed toward the most talented people' because

---

17   ELII, pp. 61–2.

18   I doubt Prendergast has any idea what apologies for cultural markets really sound like. Here is an excerpt from Tyler Cowen's *In Praise of Commercial Culture* (Cambridge, MA 1998, pp. 22, 35): 'A quick walk through any compact disc or book superstore belies the view that today's musical and literary tastes are becoming increasingly homogeneous ... Today's video stores are treasure chests of modern cultural achievement, following along the lines of the ancient Ptolemaic library in Alexandria.'

a performer or an author must put out more or less the same effort whether 10 or 1,000 people show up in the audience or buy the book. More generally, the costs of production (writing, performing, etc.) do not rise in proportion to the size of a seller's market, [and] the implied scale economy of joint consumption allows relatively few sellers to service the entire market.[19]

A few sellers for the entire market; just like Holmes for the mystery niche. But it's important to disentangle the two discrete processes that converge onto this single outcome: the process that centres on readers, and on their selection of Doyle's formal solution over those of his rivals; and the other one, in which the market amplifies that initial selection over and over again. Readers and markets, in other words, are both causal agents, but in different ways: in the sense that readers *select*, and then markets *magnify*. Did Doyle deserve to sell ten times more than Huan Mee and McDonnell Bodkin? Yes. A hundred times? Doubtful. A thousand—a hundred thousand times? Of course not: this order of magnitude no longer has anything to do with actual morphological differences, but only with the perverse market logic—to those who have, more shall be given—that goes by the name of increasing returns.

Do morphological trees embody 'a naturalized representation of winners' history', then? No; if anything, they show *how close* Doyle and his rivals were, before the market's feedback loop seized on their differences—real, but limited—and hyperbolically exaggerated them. We should learn to recover 'the plurality of potential outcomes' of literary history, writes Prendergast, and I agree. But that's exactly what evolutionary trees do: you look at them, and what leaps to the eye is the proximity between the road that was

---

19   Sherwin Rosen, 'The Economics of Superstars', *American Economic Review*, December 1981, pp. 845–7. For this winner-takes-all logic of information markets see also De Vany's *Hollywood Economics*.

actually taken—and the many, many more that were not.[20] I don't know what better 'imaginative grip on counterfactual thinking' one could ever find.[21]

FROM GEOGRAPHY TO MORPHOLOGY

Prendergast's next target is the tree of free indirect style, where he objects in particular to the geographical explanation advanced in the book. 'The fact of geographical displacement', he writes, is not 'a sufficient reason' for 'the ever-new sprouting of the branches of the tree . . . we could just as well posit the changes [the evolutionary model] allegedly explains as random events, as stuff that happens to happen'.[22]

Well, stuff does happen to happen. But what the tree shows is that—as free indirect style travels across the world literary system—very *different* stuff happens from place to place, because different pressures are exerted upon its configuration. And since this style is so uniquely located 'halfway between social doxa and

---

20   In Giulio Barsanti's brilliant reconstruction of the three most widespread metaphors of nature in early modern Europe—the ladder, the map and the tree—the main difference lies precisely in the way they visualize the relationship between actual and potential outcomes. The ladder was the favourite metaphor of those who 'thought that god (or nature) had generated its products according to *one choice* only, therefore following *a single* path'; the map was adopted by those who 'thought that god (or nature) had made *no choice at all*, and had therefore proceeded equally in *every* direction'; and the tree was the favourite image of those who 'thought that god (or nature) had neither chosen a single path, nor proceeded in every direction, but had followed a middle road, operating *a few specific choices* . . . The tree is the only one of these images entirely constructed *a posteriori.*' (Giulio Barsanti, *La scala, la mappa, l'albero: Immagini e classificazioni della natura fra Sei e Ottocento*, Florence 1992, pp. 77–8; all italics are in the original.)

21   ELH, p. 61.

22   Ibid., pp. 54–5; GMT, pp. 81–91, and Fig. 33.

individual voice',[23] a correlation rapidly emerges between formal metamorphoses (first or second person; conflict, or acquiescence; comedy, or utter seriousness), and, not just 'the fact of geographical displacement', but the geopolitical variations in the type of social consensus (more unstable in Russia than in the West; oral in southern Europe; buried in the unconscious in the modernist metropolis, etc. etc.).

Different doxas that 'nudge' free indirect style in this or that morphological direction: here is the explanation that Prendergast does not find in *Graphs, Maps, Trees*.[24] And this correlation between space and style is also the reason I refer to Ernst Mayr's theory of 'allopatric speciation': exactly as the theory predicts, all major transformations occur when the device enters a new cultural habitat. But—no. 'Does it really make sense', asks Prendergast,

> to construe [the travels of free indirect style] in terms of the concept of 'allopatric speciation'? If this means the emergence, in the literary sphere, of a 'new species', then the evidence is distinctly underwhelming . . . the travelling device or genre is far more likely to appear as so many variations within a species than as a series of

---

23   GMT, p. 82.

24   The interactions between the social environment and free indirect style are described in detail in 'Serious Century' (for Austen and Flaubert), *Atlas of the European Novel* (Dostoevsky), and *Modern Epic* (Joyce). A section of the *Atlas* also anticipates Prendergast's question about Russia and Dostoevsky: 'what is it specifically about Russia that made possible this adaptive transformation of free indirect style? Why would the Russian context—environment—prove favourable to a mutation of the device?' (ELH, p. 55.) What was specific to Russia, and favourable to a mutation, was the geo-political uniqueness of 'a country that was both inside and outside Europe', and that could therefore 'call into question modern Western culture, and subject it (with Dostoevsky) to genuine "experiments"'. (*Atlas of the European Novel*, London / New York 1998, pp. 29–32, and Fig. 11.) Russia's geo-cultural ambivalence towards western Europe is of course hardly an original idea; I merely charted some of its formal consequences.

fundamental species-changes . . . Even Moretti's own formulation hesitates: 'allopatric speciation' as a 'new species', but then hastily qualified by the parenthetical 'or at any rate a new formal arrangement'. The terms in brackets do not equate with those outside them.[25]

Yes: the two sets of terms do not equate, and I describe 'so many variations within a species' rather than a new species. So? Prendergast here confuses the validity of a theory with the results of a specific investigation. Mayr's concept posits that a change in the environment encourages the spread of morphological novelties, of which speciation is *the most significant*, but hardly the only one. I found that a change in the environment encouraged the spread of morphological novelties, although less dramatic than speciation would have been. Shouldn't we be working on this relationship between style and space, instead of pursuing terminological perfectionism?

BRANCHING

Having objected to this and that aspect of 'Trees', Prendergast concludes by calling into question the very premise of the chapter as a whole: the idea that evolutionary trees—with their typical pattern of diverging branches—offer a good model for the study of cultural history. 'From the mix of historical records and presently observable conditions', he writes, 'it is clear that, in the matter of culture, convergence is "primordial"': and if this is the case—if, in other words, culture usually changes by amalgamating disparate lineages—then describing it as the result of a branching pattern is not just wrong, but *completely* so.[26]

---

25   ELH, p. 58.
26   Ibid., p. 57.

I have my doubts about the lessons of history: after all, the human artifact that has been most thoroughly studied—language—is unquestionably the result of branching. Still, many natural scientists share Prendergast's position, and would agree with Stephen Jay Gould that, unlike 'Darwinian evolution . . . cultural change receives a powerful boost from amalgamation . . . of different traditions'.[27] Reflecting on the evolution of musical instruments, Niles Eldredge has reached a similar conclusion: with cultural products, he writes, 'theft of idea renders straightforward classification impossible, as the shape of the evolutionary "tree" becomes almost hopelessly complex, its branches thoroughly entangled'.[28]

Its branches thoroughly entangled—as in Kroeber's tree of culture, reproduced in *Graphs, Maps, Trees* (Figure 32). But if 'a single taxonomy' is not plausible, Eldredge continues, 'a multi-level classification nonetheless remains feasible . . . What we need is a classificatory scheme with multiple levels and criteria.' 'When we study phylogenies in culture and language', adds another recent essay, 'our analyses will necessarily produce numerous trees. We should expect many trees for any population, each tracing the history of particular traits or sets of traits.'[29]

---

27   See GMT, pp. 78ff.

28   Niles Eldredge, 'Biological and Material Cultural Evolution: Are There Any True Parallels?' in François Tonneau and Nicholas S. Thompson, eds, *Perspectives in Ethology*, vol. 13, *Evolution, Culture and Behavior*, New York 2000, p. 120.

29   Ibid., p. 126; Carl Lipo, Michael O'Brien, Mark Collard and Stephen Shennan, 'Cultural Phylogenies and Explanation: Why Historical Methods Matter', in Lipo et al., eds, *Mapping Our Ancestors: Phylogenetic Approaches in Anthropology and Prehistory*, New Brunswick/London 2006, p. 15. Similar theses have been advanced by Robert Boyd and Peter J. Richerson in *The Origin and Evolution of Cultures* (Oxford 2005, p. 54), and by other recent studies. Moreover, evidence that branching patterns are quite frequent in cultural history (even above the level of the 'single trait') is rapidly growing: 'statistics do not support the hypothesis that blending is more important than branching in macroscale cultural evolution', write Mark Collard, Stephen Shennan and Jamshid Tehrani:

Trees that trace the history of particular traits: like clues, or free indirect style. But even assuming that some cultural artifacts do indeed change in a branching pattern—why is this so? Since the cultural 'interbreeding' of amalgamation is always possible, and it works so much more flexibly and rapidly than branching, why does the latter occur at all? Why doesn't cultural change *always* occur by amalgamation?

Among anthropologists, the usual reply is that—in order to amalgamate cultural traits—populations must mix: which is not always possible. (A recent study of Turkmen textiles, for instance, explains the persistence of certain formal patterns by the endogamy of the groups involved.)[30] But in the modern world, where ideas travel rapidly and easily everywhere, this answer would be patently absurd. So the question remains: why doesn't amalgamation monopolize the process of cultural change?

The answer seems to be: because literary forms are complex arrangements, for which the macroscopic mutation of amalgamation, tempting as it may be, is actually a serious threat: symbolic structures have their own inner logic, which cannot be altered at will overnight. Take the diffusion of the modern novel between the late eighteenth and the early twentieth centuries: a tumultuous

---

'On average, the cultural datasets appear to be no more reticulate than the biological datasets.' ('Branching versus Blending in Macroscale Cultural Evolution: A Comparative Study'; in Lipo et al., *Mapping Our Ancestors*, p. 57.) In the same collection, Lee Lyman and Michael O'Brien discuss several series of objects—pots, paddles, helmets, swords—put together independently of the evolutionary paradigm, where branching is a more frequent mechanism of change than blending. ('Seriation and Cladistics: The Difference Between Anagenetic and Cladogenetic Evolution', in Lipo et al., *Mapping Our Ancestors*, pp. 71ff.)

30 Jamshid Tehrani and Mark Collard, 'Investigating Cultural Evolution through Biological Phylogenetic Analyses of Turkmen Textiles', *Journal of Anthropological Archaeology* 21: 4 (2002), p. 456.

blending of disparate traditions if ever there was one—and yet, for that very same reason, a process beset by 'uneasiness', 'disunity', 'problems', 'fallacies', 'incompatibilities', 'cracks', 'impossible programmes', and more.[31] Because this is the trouble with amalgamation: its potential is always great; its reality, often the reverse. And the slower, less brilliant mechanism of branching emerges as a safer way to change and survive.

EXPLANATION, INTERPRETATION

At the end of *Graphs, Maps, Trees*, casting a retrospective glance at the models discussed in its three chapters, I observed that they all shared a certain preference 'for the explanation of general structures over the interpretation of individual texts'. Implacable, Prendergast counters the claim: not only does interpretation play—'and *has* to play—a major part' in literary history, but 'how large a role it performs in the argument [of *Graphs, Maps, Trees*] is something the argument itself does not fully acknowledge'.[32]

In one respect, my observation was certainly wrong, as it collapsed two issues that should remain conceptually distinct: the difference between (causal) explanation and (teleological) interpretation, and that between the 'nomothetic' attempt to discover general laws and the 'idiographic' desire to account for the specificity of individual cases.[33] So, let me try again, this time in the terms formulated by

---

31   On these morphological impasses, see 'Conjectures on World Literature', above, pp. 54–9 Its macro-historical findings are now being confirmed, at a microscopic level, by an (unfinished) study that analyses the incipits of all novels published in Britain in five sample years of the early nineteenth century (1800–01, 1814–15, 1830). So far, the most interesting result is how many of these beginnings try to blend together elements from disparate generic conventions—and how often do these wild attempts at amalgamation result in messiness, unreadability and ultimately oblivion.

32   GMT, p. 91; ELH, p. 45.

33   To be sure, there is an elective affinity between causal explanation and

Paul Ricœur in *Freud and Philosophy*. Simplifying somewhat: for Ricœur, interpretation is what establishes a relationship between two meanings: it is a process that shows how 'A' actually means 'B'. The 'real' meaning of Old Testament narrative is an ethical norm; of an absurd oneiric image, a certain forbidden desire. No matter how apparently unrelated the two meanings are, interpretation is the activity, more or less systematic, which transforms the one into the other, and understands it as such.

Whereas interpretation relates meaning to meaning, for explanation meaning is only half of the story. In Ricœur's paradigmatic example (Freud's *Traumdeutung*), to explain a text implies a movement *outside* the semantic sphere, whereby the dream's double meaning—'the relation of the hidden to the shown' defined by interpretation—is itself re-defined as the effect of a 'deformation, or disfiguration, which can only be stated *as a compromise of forces*'.[34] Forces that (de-)form meanings: I will return to this in a moment. Right now, let's focus on the epistemological relationship outlined by Ricœur. 'In the *Interpretation of Dreams*', he writes, 'the systematic explanation is placed at the end of a process . . . that is accessible only in and through the work of interpretation. The explanation, therefore, *is explicitly subordinated to interpretation*.' Explanation subordinated to interpretation; but then, two pages later:

> interpretation *cannot be developed without calling into play concepts of an entirely different order, energy concepts*. It is impossible to achieve the first task of interpretation—viz, to discover the thoughts, ideas or wishes that are 'fulfilled' in a disguised way—without

---

nomothetic models (although Weber's view of historical explanation proves that it is far from inevitable), just as there is an affinity—for which the history of hermeneutics offers abundant evidence—between teleological interpretation and the idiographic impulse.

34 Paul Ricœur, *Freud and Philosophy*, New Haven 1977 (1965), p. 92.

considering the 'mechanisms' that constitute the dreamwork and bring about the 'transposition' or 'distortion' of the dream-thoughts into the manifest content.[35]

Explanation that presupposes interpretation, that in its turn presupposes explanation. So, Prendergast is right: interpretation '*has* to play' a large role in the study of literature. My point in *Graphs, Maps, Trees*, however, had less to do with general principles than with concrete praxis. 'There are many tasks that confront criticism', wrote Jonathan Culler some time ago, 'many things we need to advance our understanding of literature, but one thing we do not need is more interpretations of literary works.'[36] We do not need more interpretations, I take Culler to mean, not because they have nothing to say, but because, by and large, *they have already said what they had to*. A lot of good work has been done on the relation between meaning and meaning; far too little on meanings and forces. Some of it is excellent, of course, and in some cases—like Lukács's *Historical Novel*, or Watt's *Rise of the Novel*—it has even survived the dismissal of (most of) its factual basis. But when all is told, the state of literary studies cannot but recall a page from Chomsky's *Reflections on Language*:

> Roughly, when we deal with cognitive structures . . . we face problems, but not mysteries. When we ask how humans make use of these cognitive structures, how and why they make choices and behave as they do . . . when we turn to such matters as causation of behaviour, it seems to me that no progress has been made, that we are as much in the dark as to how to proceed as in the past.[37]

As much in the dark . . . Compared to Lukács and Watt, we know a lot more about eighteenth-century narrative, or early historical

---

35   Ibid., pp. 88, 90; my emphases.
36   Jonathan Culler, *The Pursuit of Signs*, Ithaca, NY 1981, p. 6.
37   Chomsky, *Reflections on Language*, p. 138.

novels; but in 'such matters as causation of behaviour', we know a lot less. In this situation, 'defending' interpretation from explanation misses the point: where the real challenge lies, and the hope for genuine breakthroughs, is in the realm of causality and large-scale explanations. What we really need are more books like *The Rise of the Novel*.

KNOWLEDGE, CRITIQUE, SELF-CRITIQUE

Let me conclude by addressing a different type of objection from the ones discussed so far. In 2003, after hearing an early version of *Graphs, Maps, Trees* as a series of lectures, Roberto Schwarz observed that, yes, those patterns emerging from the literary system were interesting, and a 'Darwinian' history was certainly appropriate to the current state of the world. But . . . was this kind of literary history still trying to be (also) a form of social critique—or had it entirely abandoned that project?

Friendly and radical at once, Schwarz's words catapulted me back to the short-lived but (in Italy) intense discussion on 'the crisis of Marxism' of the late 1970s. For me, the issue was shaped by Colletti's idea that the trouble with historical materialism was that it wasn't really that materialistic after all: its conception of history was too imbued with teleology, its categories too dialectical to undergo the test of falsifiability. In the wake of these reflections, the pursuit of a sound materialistic method, and of testable knowledge, occupied more and more of my attention, until finally—slowly, imperceptibly—it ended up overshadowing the more substantive aspects of my historical work. Methodology had replaced critique. And Schwarz's words came as a sudden jolt: have I lost my way?

Before attempting an answer, a brief aside on Schwarz's own position on the matter, as it emerges from his work on Machado de Assis. Machado's stroke of genius, he writes in a recent piece, consisted in a shift in narrative viewpoint that, although at first sight quite perplexing, allowed him to expose the worst secrets of the Brazilian ruling class:

> Instead of a narrator siding with the weak, whose pleas led nowhere, he contrived one who not only sides with social injustice and its beneficiaries, but brazenly relishes being of their party. This turning of the coat might seem odious, but it is more duplicitous than at first appears. For what, with high artistry, it achieved was a complete, intimate exposure of the very viewpoint it ostensibly adopted.[38]

To expose the adopted viewpoint; or perhaps—as the ending of *A Master on the Periphery of Capitalism* puts it, miniaturizing an entire *ars critica* in its very last word—to '*imitate*'.[39] What the italics mean, here, is that, at the same time that Machado is truthfully reproducing the nature of the Brazilian elite ('imitating', in the usual sense of the term), he is also accentuating ('*imitating*', italicized, as in a Brechtian estrangement) those traits that lay it open to a merciless critique. The form of his novels thus functions like a 'structural reduction' (Antonio Candido), or an 'abstract' (Schwarz) of existing social relations: a synthesis that makes it possible to intuitively grasp the social whole, and hence also to judge it.[40]

---

38 'A Brazilian Breakthrough', *New Left Review* II/36 (November–December 2005), p. 102.

39 'Contrary to what the present vogue for antirealism might make one think, historical mimesis, duly imbued with critical sense, did not lead to provincialism, nationalism, or backwardness. And if one part of our intelligentsia imagined that the most advanced and universal of Brazilian writers passed by, at a considerable distance, from the systematic injustice thanks to which their country was inserted into the contemporary world, it must be thanks to a blindness that is also historical, a more or less distant relative of that impudence that Machado *imitated*.' Roberto Schwarz, *A Master on the Periphery of Capitalism*, Durham, NC 2001 (1990), p. 164.

40 A similar combination of truthfulness, stylization and critique emerges

Form as the abstract of social relations. The second chapter of *Graphs, Maps, Trees*, where maps brought to light 'the direct, almost tangible relationship between social conflict and literary form', operated on a similar wavelength.[41] But most of the book took a different course, where the interaction between force and form gave way to the more abstract methodological question of the 'proper' object of literary history. A page by Krzysztof Pomian, which at the time I didn't know, explains it better than I ever could. 'Whether it be demographic evolution', he writes in *L'Ordre du temps*,

> attitudes towards death, sexuality, the body, literacy, power relations, cities . . . the objects studied by contemporary historians have always been constructed. They are also invisible objects, in the sense that no one has ever seen them, and no one *could* ever have seen them . . . thanks to seriation, and the use of long stretches of time, historians conjure up objects that have no equivalent within lived experience.[42]

Objects that have no equivalent within lived experience: this is what *Graphs, Maps, Trees* is made of. The graph on the rise of the novel in five distinct countries, and the generational cycles of British literature; the circular patterns of village stories, and the trees of clues and free indirect discourse: what these images represent, *personne ne les a jamais vus*. But if no one can see these objects, why bother with

---

from other Marxist interpretations of high bourgeois art: Benjamin on Baudelaire, for instance, and Oehler on Heine and Flaubert; Adorno on Schoenberg, or T. J. Clark on Manet. In all these cases, Lukács's periodization of decadence is exactly reversed: the contraction of bourgeois horizons in the wake of the June massacres stimulates a *sharpening* of the realistic impulse, fuelled by a profound (self-) contempt for bourgeois existence, and invisibly sheltered by the new autonomy of the aesthetic field (which also allows for 'unrealistic' distortions whenever they are needed).

41   GMT, p. 64.

42   Krzysztof Pomian, *L'Ordre du temps*, Paris 1984, p. 31.

them? For me, the answer is this: they signal a clear break with the literary tradition as we know it. In the 'invisible objects' of *Graphs, Maps, Trees*, not only does literature 'look' very different from the one we are used to, but it also no longer 'speaks' to the historian: it remains perfectly still—inert, even—until the right question is asked. And the epistemological alterity thus instituted between subject and object contains the seed and the potential for critique.

For critique? Yes and no. Yes, to the extent that an estranged tradition leaves us free to advance new, irreverent hypotheses. But no, or not quite, because it remains to be seen whether this is the type of critique that Schwarz had in mind. To find out, one must bid farewell to the ethereal elegance of methodological abstractions, and return to the messy realities of social history. Which is precisely what I plan to do.

The Novel: History and Theory

In 2007, Nancy Armstrong invited me to speak at a conference on the novel, at Brown University. A few years earlier, while editing the 5,000 pages of Il romanzo, I had become extremely impatient with the stranglehold of European 'realism' over the theory and the history of the novel, and this explains the brisk opening of the piece, with its threefold call for renewal along the lines of prose, adventures, and Chinese novels. Five years later, a first personal balance-sheet is perhaps in order.

Prose has proved to be a very fecund object of study, both in The Bourgeois, where it has become a sort of hidden protagonist of the book, and in several collective projects of the Literary Lab. On adventures, on the other hand, I have made no progress at all: I still find them important and interesting, but I don't know how to think about them. (And it's not just me: we tried as hard as we could to find someone for Il romanzo, but nothing.) Perhaps there is something intrinsically difficult in analyzing an impetuous narrative flow; or it may be the cultural significance of adventures that has become hard to fathom. Be that as it may, on this point we are still, more or less, where Nerlich's Ideology of Adventure had left the matter thirty-five years ago.

But the pièce de resistance of the essay was clearly the pages on the Chinese novel, which I saw as a unique opportunity for removing all *aspects of 'inevitability' from the history of the European novel; not in the name of abstract anti-teleological principles, but on the basis of the very concrete fact that this major tradition had developed in a completely different way. The theme returns in 'Network Theory, Plot Analysis', with the discussion of Dickens's and Cao Xueqin's narrative networks: a modest attempt at the* comparative morphology *that comparative literature has seldom managed to be. And in truth, I can think of no other historical case whose systematic introduction into the Western field of vision will be as significant—and as challenging—as classical Chinese literature. And comparative literature has everything to gain from a radical change of its past, which has remained exceedingly stable for over a century.*

Decidedly future-oriented, for its part, is the follow-up study that materialized from the pages on Leserevolution *and 'extensive reading', which inspired Natalie Phillips (at the time, a graduate student at Stanford) and me to design an experiment which uses fMRI—functional magnetic resonance imagery—to test the existence of a neuro-physiological basis for Engelsing's typology of 'intensive' and 'extensive' reading. Needless to say, fMRI will never tell us whether a shift from the one to the other occurred (or not) during the eighteenth century; but it can prove whether concentrated and relaxed reading turn out to be correlated to a differential activation of brain areas. As I am writing this page, Phillips has solved most of the technical obstacles we have encountered along the way, and— though being strapped inside a narrow metal tube bombarded by a hammering noise is hardly the best way to read novels—she has also begun to see some extremely interesting results. For literary research it would be, for once, a very* real *step forward.*

There are many ways of talking about the theory of the novel, and mine will consist in posing three questions: Why are novels in prose? Why are they so often stories of adventures? And, Why was there a European, but not a Chinese rise of the novel in the course of the eighteenth century? Disparate as they may sound, the questions have a common source in the guiding idea of the collection *The Novel*: 'to make the literary field longer, larger, and deeper': historically longer, geographically larger, and morphologically deeper than those few classics of nineteenth-century western European 'realism' that have dominated the recent theory of the novel (and my own work).[1] What the questions have in common, then, is that they all point to processes that loom large in the history of the novel, but not in its theory. Here, I will reflect on this discrepancy, and suggest a few possible alternatives.

I

Prose. Nowadays, so ubiquitous in novels that we tend to forget that it wasn't inevitable: ancient novels were certainly in prose, but the *Satyricon* for instance has many long passages in verse; the *Tale of Genji* has even more (and crucially so, as hundreds of *tanka* poems stylize sadness and longing throughout the story); French medieval romances had a prodigious early peak in verse with Chrétien de Troyes; half of the old *Arcadia* is eclogues; Chinese classic novels use poetry in a variety of ways ... Why did prose eventually prevail so thoroughly, then, and what did this mean for the form of the novel?

---

1   This article was originally presented at the conference 'Theories of the Novel', organized by *Novel*, at Brown University, in the autumn of 2007. Except for a couple of passages, expanded in the light of the discussion that followed, I have left the text more or less as it was, only adding a few footnotes. I am very grateful to Nancy Armstrong, who persuaded me to write the paper in the first place; and to D. A. Miller and William Warner, with whom I have discussed it at length. The sentence from *The Novel* comes from the brief preface ('On *The Novel*') that can be found in both volumes of the Princeton edition (see footnote 2), on p. x.

Let me begin from the opposite side, of verse. Verse, *versus*: there is a pattern that turns around and comes back: there is a symmetry, and symmetry always suggests permanence, that's why monuments are symmetrical. But prose is not symmetrical, and this immediately creates a sense of im-permanence and irreversibility: prose, *provorsa*: forward-looking (or front-facing, as in the Roman *Dea Provorsa*, goddess of easy childbirth): the text has an orientation, it leans forwards, its meaning 'depends on what lies ahead (the end of a sentence; the next event in the plot)', as Michal Ginsburg and Lorri Nandrea have put it.[2] 'The knight was defending himself *so bravely that his assailers could not prevail*'; 'Let's withdraw a little, *so that they will not recognize me*'; 'I don't know that knight, but he is *so brave that I would gladly give him my love*.' I found these passages in a half page of the prose *Lancelot*, easily, because consecutive and final constructions—where meaning depends so much on what lies ahead that a sentence literally falls into the following one—these forward-looking arrangements are everywhere in prose, and allow it its typical acceleration of narrative rhythm. And it's not that verse ignores the consecutive nexus while prose is nothing *but* that, of course; these are just their 'lines of least resistance', to use Jakobson's metaphor; it is not a matter of essence, but of relative frequency— but style is *always* a matter of relative frequency, and consecutiveness is a good starting point for a stylistics of prose.

But there is a second possible starting point, which leads, not towards narrativity, but towards *complexity*. It's a point often made by studies of *dérimage*, the thirteenth-century prosification of courtly romances which was one of the great moments of decision,

---

2 Michal Ginsburg and Lorri Nandrea, 'The Prose of the World', in Franco Moretti, ed., *The Novel*, vol. II, Princeton 2006, p. 245. On this topic, I have also learned a lot from Kristin Hanson and Paul Kiparsky, 'The Nature of Verse and its Consequences for the Mixed Form', in Joseph Harris and Karl Reichl, eds, *Prosimetrum: Cross-Cultural Perspectives on Narrative in Prose and Verse*, Cambridge 1997.

so to speak, between verse and prose, and where one thing that kept happening, in the transfer from one into the other, was that the number of subordinate clauses—increased.[3] Which makes sense. A line of verse can to a certain extent stand alone, and so it encourages independent clauses; prose is continuous, it's more of a construction, I don't think it's an accident that the myth of 'inspiration' is so seldom evoked for prose: inspiration is too instantaneous to make sense there, too much like a gift; and prose is not a gift; it's work: 'productivity of the spirit', Lukács called it in the *Theory of the Novel*, and it's the right expression: hypotaxis is not only laborious—it requires foresight, memory, adequation of means to ends—but truly productive: the outcome is more than the sum of its parts, because subordination establishes a hierarchy among clauses, meaning becomes articulated, aspects emerge that didn't exist before . . . That's how complexity comes into being.

The acceleration of narrativity; the construction of complexity. Both real: and totally at odds with each other. What did prose mean for the novel . . . ? It allowed it to play on two completely different tables—popular and cultivated—making it a uniquely adaptable and successful form. But, also, an extremely *polarized* form. The theory of the novel should have greater morphological depth, I said earlier, but depth is an understatement: what we have here are stylistic extremes that in the course of 2,000 years not only drift further and further away from each other, but turn *against* each other: the style of complexity, with its hypothetical, concessive, and conditional clauses, making forward-looking narrative seem hopelessly simple-minded and plebeian; and popular forms, for their part, mutilating complexity wherever they find it—word, sentence, paragraph, dialogue, everywhere.

---

3   See, for instance, Wlad Godzich and Jeffrey Kittay, *The Emergence of Prose: An Essay in Prosaics*, Minneapolis 1987, pp. 34ff.

A form divided between narrativity and complexity: with narrativity dominating its history, and complexity its theory. And, yes, I understand why someone would rather study sentence structure in *The Ambassadors* than in its contemporary *Dashing Diamond Dick*. The problem is not the value judgment, it's that when a value judgment becomes the basis for concepts, then it doesn't just determine what is valued or not, but what is *thinkable* or not, and in this case, what becomes unthinkable is, first, the vast majority of the novelistic field, and, second, its very shape: because polarization disappears if you only look at one of the extremes, whereas it shouldn't, because it's the sign of how the novel participates in social inequality, and duplicates it into cultural inequality. A theory of the novel should account for this. But to do so, we need a new starting point. 'Veblen explains culture in terms of kitsch, not vice-versa', writes Adorno in *Prisms*, disapprovingly:[4] but it's such a tempting idea. Taking the style of dime novels as the basic object of study, and explaining James's as an unlikely by-product: that's how a theory of prose should proceed—because that's how *history* has proceeded. Not the other way around.

Looking at prose style from below . . . With digital databases, this is now easy to imagine: a few years, and we'll be able to search just about all novels that have ever been published, and look for patterns among billions of sentences. Personally, I am fascinated by this encounter of the formal and the quantitative. Let me give you an example: all literary scholars analyze stylistic structures—free indirect style, the stream of consciousness, melodramatic excess, whatever. But it's striking how little we actually know about the genesis of these forms. Once they're there, we know what to do; but how did they get there in the first place? How does the 'confused thought' (Michel Vovelle) of *mentalité*, which is the substratum for

4   Theodor Adorno, 'Veblen's Attack on Culture', in *Prisms*, Cambridge, MA 1990, p. 79.

almost all that happens in a culture—how does messiness crystallize into the elegance of free indirect style? Concretely: what are the steps? No one really knows. By sifting through thousands of variations and permutations and approximations, a quantitative stylistics of the digital archive may find some answers. It will be difficult, no doubt, because one cannot study a large archive in the same way one studies a text: texts are designed to 'speak' to us, and so, provided we know how to listen, they always end up telling us something; but archives are not messages that were meant to address us, and so they say absolutely nothing until one asks the right question. And the trouble is, we literary scholars are not good at that: we are trained to listen, not to ask questions, and asking questions is the *opposite* of listening: it turns criticism on its head, and transforms it into an experiment of sorts: 'questions put to nature' is how experiments are often described, and what I'm imagining here are questions—put to culture. Difficult; but too interesting not to give it a try.

II

All this lies in the future. My second point lies in the past. Novels are long; or rather, they span a very wide range of lengths—from the 20,000 words of *Daphnis and Chloe* to the 40,000 of Chrétien, 100,000 of Austen, 400,000 of *Don Quixote*, and over 800,000 of *The Story of the Stone*—and one day it will be interesting to analyze the consequences of this spectrum, but for now let's just accept the simple notion that they are long. The question is, How did they get to be that way? And there are of course several answers, but if I had to choose a single mechanism I would say: adventures.[5] Adventures

---

5 If I had to choose a single mechanism . . . And if I could choose two: adventures—and love. One mechanism to expand the story, and one to hold it together: a conjunction that is particularly clear in the ancient novels, where love is the one source of permanence in a world where everything else is scattered by fortune to the four winds, and acts therefore as a figure *for the social bond in*

expand novels by opening them to the world: a call for help comes—
the knight goes. Usually, without asking questions; which is typical
of adventure, the unknown is not a threat here, it's an opportunity,
or more precisely: there is no longer any distinction between threats
and opportunities. 'Who leaves the dangerous path for the safe',
says Galessin, one of the knights of the Round Table, 'is not a
knight, is a merchant': true, capital doesn't like danger for its own
sake, but a knight does: he has to: he can't accumulate glory, he
must renew it all the time, so he needs this perpetual motion machine
of adventure . . .

. . . perpetual, especially if a border is in sight: across the bridge,
into the forest, up the mountain, through the gate, at sea.
Adventures make novels long because they make them wide; they
are the great explorers of the fictional world: battlefields, oceans,
castles, sewers, prairies, islands, slums, jungles, galax-
ies . . . Practically all great popular chronotopes have arisen when
the adventure plot has moved into a new geography, and acti-
vated its narrative potential. Just as prose multiplies styles, then,
adventure multiplies stories: and forward-looking prose is perfect
for adventure, syntax and plot moving in unison, I'm not sure
there is a main branch in the family of forms we call the novel, but
if there is one, it's this: we would still recognize the history of the

---

general: the freely chosen union from which, in antithesis to the adventures
despotically imposed by Tuche, a larger organism can somehow be glimpsed.
But this balance between love and adventure breaks down in chivalric romances,
as errant knights start to actively *look* for adventures (the Quest), and new figures
for the social contract emerge (the Court, the Round Table, the Grail). In this
new situation, love becomes functionally subordinated to adventure—and the
theme of adultery, which immediately arises, is at once the symptom of its abiding
strength, and of its newly problematic position. This redistribution of narrative
tasks, from which love has never fully recovered, is the reason why I decided to
focus exclusively on adventures; besides, love has long been recognized by the
theory of the novel (especially in the English tradition), and I wanted to shift our
attention towards the historically broader phenomenon.

novel without modernism, or even without realism;[6] without adventures in prose, no.

Here, too, the novelistic field is profoundly polarized between adventures and the everyday; and here, too, the theory of the novel has shown very little interest (aside from Bakhtin, and now Pavel) for the popular side of the field. But I won't repeat that aspect of the argument, and will turn instead to the odd *narrowness* that—in spite of all its plasticity—seems typical of adventure. A social narrowness, fundamentally. The whole idea had been 'a creation of the petty nobility of penniless knights', for whom '"*aventure*" was a way to survive—and possibly, to marry an heiress', writes Erich Köhler, who was the great sociologist of this convention.[7] But if knights needed adventures, for other social classes the notion remained opaque. 'I am, as you see, a knight seeking what I cannot find', says Calogrenant to a peasant at the beginning of *Yvain*. 'And what do you want to find?' 'Adventure, to test my courage and my strength. Now I pray and beseech you to advise me, if you know, of any adventure or wonder.' 'I know nothing of adventure, nor have I ever heard about it.'[8] What a reply; only a few years earlier, in the *chanson de geste*, the nature of knightly action was clear to everybody; not any more. The chivalric ethos has become 'absolute . . . both in its ideal realization and in the absence of any earthly and practical purpose', writes Auerbach in *Mimesis*: 'no political function . . . no practical reality at all'. And yet, he goes on, this unreal ethos 'attained

---

6 Hopefully, modernism (that is to say: the host of centrifugal experiments—Stein, Kafka, Joyce, Pilniak, De Chirico, Platonov . . . — attempted in the years around the First World War) will play a larger role than realism in any future theory of the novel, as a cluster of incompatible extremes should reveal something unique about what a form can—and cannot—do. So far, however, this has not been the case.

7 Erich Köhler, 'Il sistema sociologico del romanzo francese medievale', *Medioevo Romanzo* 3 (1976), pp. 321–44.

8 Lines 356–67.

acceptance and validity in the real world' of Western culture for centuries to come.[9] How could it be?

For Köhler, the reason was that adventure became 'stylized and moralized' in the much wider ideal—launched by the Crusades, and sublimated by the Grail—of 'the Christian redemption of the warrior'.[10] Which sounds right, but in its turn opens another problem: How could these starkly feudal coordinates of adventure, not only survive into the bourgeois age, but inspire all of its most popular genres?

III

Before I attempt an answer, some thoughts on the third question, the Chinese–European comparison. Until well into the nineteenth century, almost the end in fact, east Asian and west European novels developed independently of each other; which is great, it's like an experiment history has run for us, the same form in two . . . laboratories, it's perfect for comparative morphology, because it allows us to look at formal features not as givens, as we inevitably tend to do, but as *choices*: and choices that eventually add up to alternative structures. Beginning, for instance, with how often the protagonists of Chinese novels are not individuals, but *groups*: the household in the *Jin Ping Mei* and *The Story of the Stone* (or *Dream of the Red Chamber*), the outlaws in *The Water Margin*, the literati in *The Scholars*. Titles are already a clue—what would European titles do without proper names—but here, not even one; and these are not just random novels, they are four of the six 'great masterpieces' of the Chinese canon, their titles (and their heroes) matter.

---

9   Erich Auerbach, *Mimesis*, Princeton 2003, pp. 134, 136. On this, see also Erich Köhler, 'Quelques observations d'ordre historico-sociologique sur les rapports entre la chanson de geste et le roman courtois', in *Chanson de geste und höfischer Roman*, Heidelberg 1963, *passim*.

10   Köhler, 'Il sistema sociologico', p. 326.

So, groups. Large; and with even larger character-systems around them: Chinese critics have identified over 600 characters in *The Scholars*, 800 in *The Water Margin* and the *Jin Ping Mei*, 975 in *The Story of the Stone*. And since size is seldom *just* size—a story with a thousand characters is not like a story with fifty characters, only twenty times bigger: it's a different story—all this ends up generating a structure which is very unlike the one we are used to in Europe. With so many variables, one would expect it to be more unpredictable, but the opposite is actually more often the case: a great attempt at *reducing* unpredictability, and re-balancing the narrative system. Let me give you an example from *The Story of the Stone*: after six or seven hundred pages, the two young undeclared lovers, Bao-yu and Dai-yu, have one of their many fights; Dai-yu leaves, and Bao-yu, left alone, falls into a sort of trance; his maid Aroma arrives, but he doesn't notice her, and in his dream-like state proceeds to express for the first time his love for Dai-yu; then he 'awakes', sees Aroma, is bewildered, runs away, and one can imagine all sorts of sequels here: Aroma has been sleeping with Bao-yu for some time, and could feel wounded; or she could side with Dai-yu, and tell her what Bao-yu has just said; or she could betray her to the other young woman who is in love with Bao-yu . . . Many ways of making the episode generate narrative (after all, we've been waiting for this declaration of love for hundreds of pages); and instead, what Aroma immediately thinks is 'how she could arrange matters so as to prevent any scandal developing from those words'. *Preventing* developments: that's the key. Minimizing narrativity. *The Story of the Stone* is often described as a Chinese *Buddenbrooks*, and they are certainly both stories of the decline of a great family, but *Buddenbrooks* covers a half century in five hundred pages, and *Stone* a dozen years in two *thousand* pages: and it's not just a matter of rhythm, here (although that is obviously also the case), but of the hierarchy between synchrony and diachrony: *Stone* has a 'horizontal' dominant, where what really matters is not what lies 'ahead' of a given event, as in 'forward-looking' European prose, but what lies 'to the side' of it: all the vibrations that ripple across this immense narrative system—and all the *counter*-vibrations that try to keep it stable. Earlier, I pointed out how the breakdown of symmetry allowed European prose to intensify irreversibility; irreversibility is present also in Chinese novels, of course, but instead of intensifying it they often try to *contain* it, and so symmetry regains its centrality: chapters are announced by couplets that neatly divide them into two halves; many important passages are couched in the wonderfully named 'parallel prose' ('Every evening devoted to the pursuit of pleasure; Every morning an occasion for deluded dalliance'); in the novel's overall architecture there are blocks of ten, twenty, even fifty chapters that mirror each other across hundreds of pages . . . It's really an alternative tradition.

Alternative, but *comparable*: up to the eighteenth century, the Chinese novel was arguably greater in both quantity and quality than any in Europe, with the possible exception of France. 'The Chinese have novels by the thousand, and already had them when our ancestors were living in the forests', said Goethe to Eckermann in 1827, on the day he coined the concept of *Weltliteratur* (while reading a Chinese novel). But the figures are wrong: by 1827 novels by the thousand existed in France, or Britain, or indeed in Germany—but not in China.

Why?

IV

When we discuss the destinies of eighteenth-century core areas, writes Kenneth Pomeranz in *The Great Divergence*,

> we should make our comparisons . . . truly reciprocal . . . that is, look for absences, accidents and obstacles that diverted England from a path that might have made it more like the Yangzi Delta or

Gujarat, along with the more usual exercise of looking for block-ages that kept non-European areas from reproducing implicitly normalized European paths . . . view both sides of the comparison as 'deviations' when seen through the expectations of the other, rather than leaving one as always the norm.[11]

The European rise of the novel as a deviation from the Chinese path: as soon as you start thinking in these terms, it immediately leaps to the eye how much more *seriously* the novel was taken in China than in Europe. Despite all the attacks by the Confucian literati, by the early seventeenth century Chinese culture already had a novelistic canon; Europe wasn't even thinking about it. For the epic or tragedy it had one, or the lyric; not for the novel. And the canon is just the tip of the iceberg: there was in China an immense investment of intellectual energies in the editing, revision, continuation, and especially *commentary* of novels. These were already very long books, *The Romance of the Three Kingdoms*, 600,000 words, the inter-lineal commentary made it almost a million—but it added so much 'to the enjoyment . . . of the novel', writes David Rolston, 'that editions without commentary . . . went out of circulation'.[12]

'The novel has less need of . . . commentary than other genres', writes Watt in *The Rise of the Novel*,[13] and for Europe he's right. But Chinese novels needed them, because they were seen as—art. Since at least the *Jin Ping Mei*, around 1600, 'Chinese *xiaoshuo* went through an . . . extended aesthetic turn', writes Ming Dong Gu: 'a self-conscious emulation and competition with the dominant literary

---

11 Kenneth Pomeranz, *The Great Divergence: China, Europe, and the Making of the Modern World Economy*, Princeton 2000, pp. 7–8.
12 David L. Rolston, *Traditional Chinese Fiction and Fiction Commentary: Reading and Writing Between the Lines*, Stanford 1997, p. 4.
13 Ian Watt, *The Rise of the Novel*, Berkeley 1957, p. 30.

genres . . . a poeticization'.[14] We should look for absences that
diverted the European novel from the Chinese path . . . and here is
one: the aesthetic turn of the European novel occurred in the late
nineteenth century, with a delay of almost three hundred years.[15]

Why?

V

For Pomeranz, one reason for the great divergence was that in
eighteenth-century Europe 'the wheels of fashion were spinning
faster',[16] stimulating consumption, and through it the economy as a
whole; while in China, after the consolidation of the Qing dynasty,
consumption 'as a motor of change' came to a halt for over a century,
not triggering that 'consumer revolution' McKendrick, Brewer and
Plumb have written about. Revolution is a big word, and many
have questioned the extent of consumption before the mid

---

14   Ming Dong Gu, *Chinese Theories of Fiction: A Non-Western Narrative
System*, New York 2006, p. 71.
15   The divergence of the two models is well illustrated by the role played
by *Don Quixote* and the *Jin Ping Mei*—two novels that were written in the same
years, and are often compared to each other (more by sinologists than by
hispanists, it must be said)—in their respective traditions: for at least two
centuries, if not longer, the *Jin Ping Mei*'s influence on the theory and practice of
the novel in China was incomparably greater than that of *Don Quixote* in Europe.
A similar parting of the ways occurs in the late eighteenth century, when the peak
of the Chinese aesthetic turn (*The Story of the Stone*) could have found its match
in an incredibly gifted generation of German poet-novelists (Goethe, Hölderlin,
Novalis, Schlegel, Von Arnim, Brentano)—if only they hadn't been roundly
ignored by European readers (except for Goethe, of course; but even Goethe
kept the 'poetic' first version of *Meister* in a drawer, as if sensing that it wasn't the
right book for the times). Incidentally, that the *Jin Ping Mei* could be hailed as the
masterpiece that would change the Chinese novel is another striking instance of
the difference between the two traditions: that European culture could produce—
and appreciate!—an erotic corpus as explicit as the Chinese one is quite
unimaginable.
16   Pomeranz, *The Great Divergence*, p. 161.

nineteenth century; still, no one really doubts that 'superfluous things', to use a Chinese expression, multiplied during the eighteenth century, from interior decoration to mirrors, clocks, porcelain, silverware, jewellery—and concerts, journeys and books. 'In any consideration of leisure', writes Plumb, 'it would be quite wrong not to put cultural pursuits in the foreground.'[17] So: what did 'the birth of a consumer society' mean for the European novel?

First of all, a giant quantitative leap. From the first to the last decade of the century, new titles increased seven times in France (even though, in the 1790s, the French had more to do than write novels); fourteen in Britain; and about thirty in the German territories. Also, by the end of the eighteenth century print runs had become a little larger, especially for reprints; many novels that are not included in the standard bibliographies were published in magazines (some of which had a very wide audience); the strengthening of family ties encouraged reading aloud at home (providing the training ground for Dr Bowdler's vocation); finally, and most significantly, the diffusion of lending libraries made novels circulate much more efficiently than before, eventually leading to the imposition of the three-decker on writers and publishers alike, so as to lend each novel to three readers at once. Hard though it is to quantify these various factors, if all of them combined increased the circulation of novels between two and three times (a conservative estimate), then the presence of novels in western Europe would have gone up between thirty and sixty times in the course of the eighteenth century. For McKendrick, the fact that consumption of tea rose fifteenfold in a hundred years is a great success story of the consumer revolution. Novels increased more than tea.

---

17   J. H. Plumb, 'The Commercialization of Leisure in Eighteenth-Century England', in Neil McKendrick, John Brewer, J. H. Plumb, *The Birth of a Consumer Society: The Commercialization of Eighteenth-Century England*, Bloomington 1982, pp. 265–6.

Why? The answer used to be, Because readers did. But the current consensus—which is slippery, like all that has to do with literacy, but has been stable for a few decades now—is that between 1700 and 1800, readers doubled; a little less than that in France, a little more in England, but that's the horizon. They doubled; they didn't increase fifty times. But, they were reading *differently*. 'Extensive' reading, Rolf Engelsing has called it: reading a lot more than in the past, avidly, at times passionately, but probably more often than not also superficially, quickly, even a little erratically; quite different from the 'intensive' reading and re-reading of the same few books— usually devotional ones—that had been the norm until then.[18] And Engelsing's thesis has often been criticized, but with novels multiplying so much more quickly than readers, and readers behaving like the famous John Latimer, of Warwick, who from mid January to mid February 1771 borrowed a volume a day from Clay's circulating library,[19] it is hard to imagine how the whole process could have worked without a major increase in—let's call it distraction.

Let's call it that, because, even though Engelsing never mentions Benjamin, extensive reading looks very much like an early version of that 'perception in a state of distraction' described at the end of 'The Work of Art in the Age of its Technological Reproducibility'. Distraction in that essay is *Zerstreuung*—absent-mindedness, and entertainment: the perfect mix for novel-reading—and for Benjamin it is the attitude that becomes necessary at those 'historical turning points' when the 'tasks' facing 'the human apparatus of perception' are so overwhelming that they can't be 'mastered' by way of concentrated attention:[20] and distraction emerges as the

---

18   Rolf Engelsing, *Der Bürger als Leser: Lesergeschichte in Deutschland 1500–1800*, Stuttgart 1974, esp. pp. 182ff.

19   Jan Fergus, *Provincial Readers in Eighteenth-Century England*, Oxford 2006, p. 113.

20   Walter Benjamin, 'The Work of Art in the Age of Its Technological Reproducibility', 1935, in *Selected Writings III: 1935–1938*, Cambridge, MA

best way to cope with the new situation—to keep up with those 'faster-spinning wheels of fashion' that have so dramatically widened the market for novels.[21]

What did the birth of a consumer society mean for the European novel? More novels, and less attention. Dime novels, not James, setting the tone of the new way of reading. Jan Fergus, who knows more about lending libraries' records than anyone else, calls it

---

2002, p. 119. The passage returns virtually unchanged in the third version of the essay, in 1939.

21   As I hope is clear, my focus on consumption, fashion and distraction is not meant to erase capitalism from literary history, but to specify which of its aspects play a more direct causal role in the novel's take-off. Unquestionably, capitalist expansion as such created some key general pre-conditions: a larger, more literate population; more disposable income; and more free time (for some). But since new novelistic titles increased four times faster than printed matter in general during the eighteenth century (even including the flood of pamphlets at the end of the century: see James Raven, *The Business of Books: Booksellers and the English Book Trade 1450–1850*, New Haven, CT 2007, p. 8), we must also explain this different rate of growth: and that peculiar exaggeration of consumer mentality embodied by distraction and fashion (and which seems to play a lesser role for drama, poetry, and most other types of cultural production) seems to be the best explanation we have found so far. That consumption could play such a large role in the history of the novel depends, in its turn, on the fact that the suspicion towards reading for pleasure was beginning to fade, in line with Constant's idea of the Liberty of the Moderns as 'the enjoyment of security in private pleasures' (Benjamin Constant, *Political Writings*, Cambridge 2007, p. 317). Pleasure, by the way, is another blindspot of the theory of the novel: though we 'know', more or less, that the novel was from the very beginning a form of 'light reading' (Thomas Hägg, 'Orality, Literacy, and the "Readership" of the Early Greek Novel', in R. Eriksen, ed., *Contexts of Pre-Novel Narrative*, Berlin/New York 1994, p. 51), we still work as if reading for pleasure were basically the same as reading 'for serious reasons—religious, economic, or social' (J. Paul Hunter, *Before Novels: The Cultural Contexts of Eighteenth Century English Fiction*, New York/London 1990, p. 84: one of the few to pose the problem in an interesting way). This is yet another issue on which specific historical studies are well ahead of theoretical reflection: the dramatic enlargement of the ancient novelistic field, for instance, would have been impossible without a shift towards popular, light, and even vulgar forms of writing.

'desultory' reading: borrowing the second volume of *Gulliver's Travels* but not the first, or the fourth, out of five, of *The Fool of Quality*. And Fergus then hails this as 'readers' agency, their power of choice'[22]—but, frankly, the choice here seems to be, giving up all consistency, in order to be always somehow in touch with what the market has to offer. Leaving the TV on all day long, and watching it every now and then—that's not agency.

VI

Why was there no rise of the Chinese novel in the eighteenth century—and no European aesthetic turn? The answers mirror each other: taking the novel seriously as an aesthetic object slowed down consumption—while a quickened market for novels discouraged aesthetic concentration. 'When reading the first chapter, the good reader has already cast his eyes towards the last', says a commentary to the *Jin Ping Mei* (which is two thousand pages long); 'when reading the last chapter, he is already recalling the first.'[23] This is what intensive reading is like: the only true reading is *re*-reading, or even 'a *series* of re-readings', as some commentators seem to assume. 'If you don't put your pen into action, it cannot really be considered reading', as Mao once put it. *Study*; not one-volume-per-day consumption. In Europe, only modernism made people study novels. Had they read with pen and commentary in the eighteenth century, there would have been no rise of the European novel.

VII

Typically, the great theories of the novel have been theories of modernity, and my insistence on the market is a particularly brutal version thereof. But with a complication, suggested by another

---

22   Fergus, *Provincial Readers*, pp. 108–16, 117.
23   Rolston, *Traditional Chinese Fiction*, p. 126.

research project I'm engaged in at present, on the figure of the bourgeois, in the course of which I have been often surprised by how *limited* the diffusion of bourgeois values seems to have actually been. Capitalism has spread everywhere, no doubt about that, but the values which—according to Marx, Weber, Simmel, Sombart, Freud, Schumpeter, Hirschmann . . . —are supposed to be most congruous with it have not, and this has made me look at the novel with different eyes: no longer as the 'natural' form of bourgeois modernity, but rather as that through which the *pre*-modern imaginary continues to pervade the capitalist world. Whence, adventure. The anti-type of the spirit of modern capitalism, for *The Protestant Ethic*; a slap in the face of realism, as Auerbach saw so clearly in *Mimesis*. What is adventure doing in the modern world? Margaret Cohen, from whom I have learned a lot on this, sees it as a trope of expansion: capitalism on the offensive, planetary, crossing the oceans. I think she is right, and would only add that the reason adventure works so well within this context is that it's so good at imagining *war*. Enamoured of physical strength, which it moralizes as the rescue of the weak from all sorts of abuses, adventure is the perfect blend of might and right to accompany capitalist expansions. That's why Köhler's Christian warrior has not only survived in our culture—in novels; films; videogames—not only survived, but dwarfed any comparable bourgeois figure. Schumpeter put it crudely and clearly: 'The bourgeois class . . . needs a master.'[24]

It needs a master—to help it rule. In finding distortion after distortion of core bourgeois values, my first reaction was always to wonder at the loss of class identity that this entailed; which is true, but, from another perspective, completely irrelevant, because hegemony doesn't need purity—it needs plasticity, camouflage, collusion between the old and the new. Under this different

---

24　Joseph A. Schumpeter, *Capitalism, Socialism and Democracy*, New York 1975 (1942), p. 138.

constellation, the novel returns to be central to our understanding of modernity: not despite, but *because* of its pre-modern traits, which are not archaic residues, but functional articulations of ideological needs. To decipher the geological strata of consensus in the capitalist world—here is a worthy challenge, for the history and the theory of the novel.

Style, Inc.: Reflections on 7,000 Titles (British Novels, 1740–1850)

How does a literary historian end up writing on 7,000 titles?[1] In the presentation of 'The Slaughterhouse of Literature' I used the metaphor of the snowball, and that's really how it felt, during these twenty years; at the beginning, I had no idea I would end up doing quantitative research; all I was interested in was evolution, the great theory of how forms change in time; while I was studying evolution, however, Ernst Mayr's theory of speciation made me aware of the role of geography in the generation of new forms; so I turned to cartography, to make literary maps; but maps need homogeneous data, so I started to extract small series from novels (beginnings and endings in Austen, Balzac's young men in Paris), and, later, to make diagrams of library holdings and translation flows. Evolution, geography, maps, series, diagrams . . . One step led to the next; one step asked for the next. And one day I realized that the study of morphological evolution had itself morphed into the analysis of quantitative data.

---

1   This article has been greatly improved by exchanges with Sam Bowles, David Brewer, Bob Folkenflik, Matthew Jockers, David Krakauer, and Michael Silverstein: to all of them, my thanks. A further, more abstract study (co-authored with Matthew Jockers and David Krakauer) should soon extend and refine the argument that follows.

But there was a problem. The more 'literary' series (Austen, Balzac, etc.) revealed interesting formal patterns, but had a weak quantitative foundation; the data from book history were more solid, but much further removed from formal analysis. I could find form—or I could find data; but, it seemed, not both of them together. Then, with 'Style, Inc.', the two sides finally clicked, in a full-blown instance of that 'formalism without close reading' that I mentioned in the presentation of 'Slaughterhouse'—or of the 'quantitative formalism' of the first pamphlet of the Literary Lab. But since quantification can only occur if its basic units are reasonably well-defined—and since the units of language are much *better defined than those of plot—at this point it was* form *that split into two, making the formalism of 'Style, Inc.' focus entirely on the analysis of language, with virtually no reference to plot. It's another case, it seems, of the analytical one-sidedness I mentioned in the presentation to 'The End of the Beginning'—which returns one more time in the last piece of this collection, which errs unreservedly in the opposite direction: an analysis of* Hamlet's *plot, conducted as if Shakespeare's characters didn't utter a single word in the entire play. Clearly, I like to put on 'blinders', as Weber wrote in his lecture on 'Science as a Profession'. It must be the* longue durée *of my Marxist formation (the work of Della Volpe and Colletti), whose ferociously anti-dialectical stance urges me to devote all my energies to analysis, and none to synthesis. And, as I said, I like it.*

One last thing that became clear, while working at 'Style, Inc.', was the enormous difference between the archive of the Great Unread, and the world of the canon. You enter the archive, and the usual coordinates disappear; all you can see are swarms of hybrids and oddities, for which the categories of literary taxonomy offer very little help. It's fascinating, to feel so lost in a universe one didn't even know existed; but it's hard to extract a rational picture from this Walpurgisnacht *of discordant voices. And then, to make matters worse, there is the opposite problem, too: working with large quantities, the* average *becomes an inevitable presence—and the average means loss of distinction, slowness, boredom . . . Too much polyphony, and too much monotony: it's the Scylla and Charybdis of digital humanities. The day we establish an intelligible relationship between these two, a new literary landscape will come into being.*

The British novel, from 1740 to 1850. Peripheral, often despised at the beginning of the period, by its end the novel has moved very close to the core of the national culture. So, this is an important century, for this literary form. But, truth be told, the historical framework of this study has been largely dictated by an extrinsic reason: unlike earlier and later periods, from 1740 to 1850 we have very good bibliographies. Which is to say, good lists of titles; in a few years, we will have a digital archive with the full texts of (almost) all novels ever published; but for now, titles are still the best way to go beyond the 1 per cent of novels that make up the canon, and catch a glimpse of the literary field as a whole. And then, titles are not just a good research tool: they are important in themselves—Walter Scott's first word as a novelist, literally, was 'title' ('The title of this work has not been chosen without the grave and solid deliberation . . . ')— and they are important because, as Claude Duchet has put it, they are 'a coded message—in a market situation'.[2] A code, in the market: half sign, half ad, the title is where the novel as language meets the novel as commodity, and their encounter can be extremely illuminating. In what follows, I focus on three moments of this history: first, I describe a major metamorphosis of eighteenth-century titles, and try to explain its causes; next, I suggest how a new type of title that emerged around 1800 may

---

2   Claude Duchet, '"La fille abandonnée" et "La bête humaine"; éléments de titrologie romanesque', *Littérature* 12 (1973), p. 50.

have changed what readers expected of novels; and finally, I make a little attempt at quantitative stylistics, examining some strategies by which titles point to specific genres. Three sections; three pieces in the large puzzle of the literary field.

I

The major metamorphosis of eighteenth-century titles is simple: in the space of two generations, they become much, much shorter. In Figure 1, where their length is measured in the number of words, the median oscillates between ten and twenty words for the first twenty-five years; it drops quickly to ten, around 1770; then to six, by 1790; and it remains there (with minor ups and downs) until the mid nineteenth century.[3] From fifteen or twenty words, to six. And titles don't just become shorter, in the course of these 110 years, they also become much more similar to each other: in Figure 2, the steep drop of the standard deviation (which measures the degree of variation within a system) indicates precisely how rapidly the

---

3   The chart in Figure 1 follows both mean and median length in order to offer a more complete picture of how titles vary: the mean (or average) provides information about the often extravagant length of some titles—while the median draws attention to the 'central' length of each given year (that is to say, that which has an equal number of results above and below it). The difference between the two forms of measurement becomes particularly clear in years such as 1780 (with the 346-word long *History of Miss Harriot Fairfax*), or 1784 (with the 273 words of *The Maid of the Farm; Or memoirs of Susannah James*): in these two instances, the mean balloons to 37.9 and 19.7 respectively, while the median (8.5 and 7) is hardly affected.

Unless otherwise indicated, the sources of all the figures are the following: 1740–49, Jerry C. Beasley, *Novels of the 1740s*, Georgia, 1982; 1750–69, James Raven, ed., *British Fiction 1750–1770: A Chronological Checklist of Prose Fiction Printed in Britain and Ireland*, Delaware, 1987; 1770–1829, Peter Garside, James Raven, and Rainer Schöwerling, eds, *The English Novel 1770–1829: A Bibliographical Survey of Prose Fiction Published in the British Isles*, vols. I and II, Oxford 2000; 1830–36, online database 'The British Novel 1830–36', directed by Peter Garside at Cardiff University; 1837–50, Andrew Block, ed., *The English Novel 1740–1850*, London 1968.

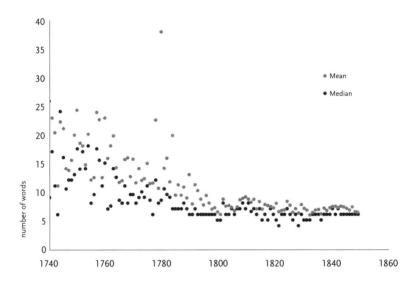

Figure 1: Length of Titles

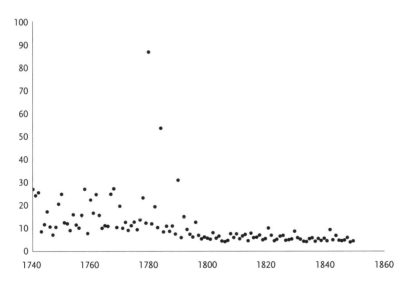

Figure 2: British novels 1740-1850, standard deviation from the mean

range of options is shrinking. To understand what this means, look at the distribution of mid-eighteenth-century titles in Figure 3: many of them are already quite short, with between one and ten words, but there is still a lot of variety, with plenty of titles which use fifteen words, twenty, twenty-five, thirty, forty, or more. A hundred years later (Figure 4) this 'tail' is gone, and long titles have virtually vanished.[4] It's not just that all titles are becoming shorter, in other words; it's also that a certain type of title disappears altogether. How long is 'long' is of course an open question, but if we set the limit at fifteen or twenty words—which is quite long, for a title—then long titles were between 40 and 60 per cent of the total in the mid eighteenth century (Figure 5, overleaf); by 1800 their number had already dropped to 5 to 10 per cent; eventually, they just disappeared. Why?[5]

---

4   The thirty novels in the *New York Times* best-seller list in November 2006 used between one and six words; the forty in November 2008, between one and seven. In both cases, the mean was around 2.7 words—slightly higher than Austen's 2.0.

5   Counting the number of words in a title . . . But what exactly *is* a title? Among the novels for the year 1802, Peter Garside's masterful bibliography lists *Delaval. A Novel. In three Volumes.* But are expressions that point so explicitly to *extra*-textual realities like 'in three Volumes' (or 'dedicated to Her Royal Highness The Dutchess of York', 'from the French of M. Victor Hugo', and so on) really part of the title? In my opinion, no; and so, useful as such information is in other respects, I have removed it from the database, leaving the title in question as *Delaval. A Novel.* But what about 'A Novel' ('A Romance', 'A Tale', 'In a Series of Letters')? Here, the reference is not so much extra-, as *meta*-textual: all these markers designate a *class*, rather than a specific book: invaluable for the analysis of novelistic sub-genres, they have little or nothing to say about individual cases. As a consequence, I have preserved them the first few times they appear in a title (when they are presumably indicating something new and specific about the given book), and deleted them thereafter; making an exception for those bizarre cases where the wider class is evoked only in order to estrange it: 'A Rhapsodical Romance', 'A Dramatic Novel', 'A Neapolitan Tale'—and also, sure enough, 'A Novel Without a Hero'. This said, since my choices may strike some readers as not merely subjective but perverse, Figure 6 charts the length of titles as they appear in the bibliographical sources, without any intervention on my part. As a comparison with Figure 1 shows, the general trend does not

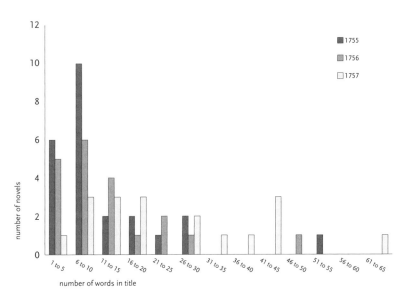

Figure 3: Mid-18th century titles

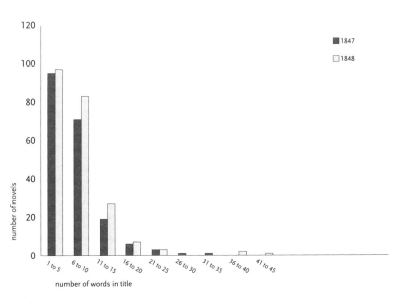

Figure 4: Mid-19th century titles

And, before coming to that, what were they like, those long titles—what did they *do*, with all those words? Usually, they provided a summary of the novel: *A letter from H—g—g, Esq; One of the Gentlemen of the Bedchamber to the Young Chevalier, And the Only Person of his Retinue that attended him from Avignon, in his late Journey through Germany, and elsewhere; Containing Many remarkable and Affecting Occurrences which happened to the P— during the course of his mysterious Progress. To a Particular Friend.* Today, this sounds odd; but actually, a summary at the beginning of a novel makes sense: a novel is a narrative, and the title—the title-*page*, here one sees why books needed a whole page for their title—the title-as-summary was a *shorter* narrative: it presented the main events of the story, the characters, the setting, the ending. It made sense.

But the cultural ecosystem was changing in a way that was incompatible with it: in the course of the eighteenth century, the publication of novels in Britain grew dramatically (Figure 7, overleaf), from a few books a year in the early decades, to twenty-five or so in mid-century, seventy to eighty around 1800, and about a hundred a year in early Victorian times. And as more novels circulated, two things happened. In the third, and even more so in the fourth quarter of the eighteenth century, the *Monthly* and other magazines started to publish reviews of many new novels, making title-page summaries somewhat superfluous: as the literary system grew, in other words, some of its functions became more specialized, 'freeing' titles from having to provide a detailed description. And then, as the number of new novels kept increasing, each of them had inevitably a much smaller 'window' of visibility on the market, and it became vital for a title to catch quickly and effectively the eye of the public. Summaries were not good at that. They were good at describing a

change much: the decline in length is slightly less dramatic (the median being significantly higher for the first forty years, and then stabilizing around seven or eight words rather than six), but equally evident.

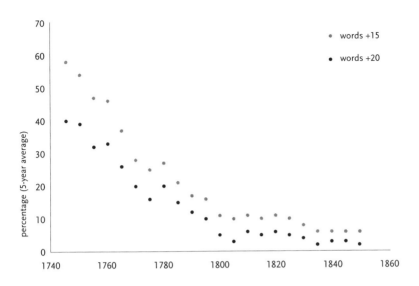

Figure 5: Novels with very long titles

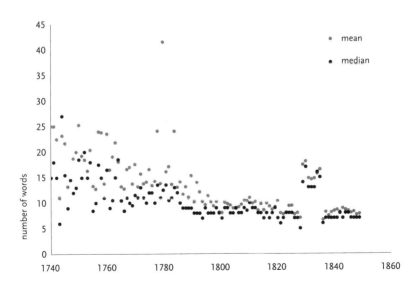

Figure 6: Length of titles (unedited)

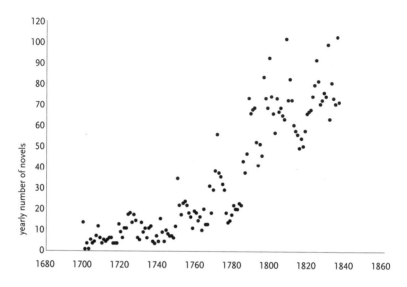

Figure 7: Publication of British novels, 1700-1836

Additional source: 1700–39, William H. McBurney, ed., *A Check List of English Prose Fiction, 1700–1739*, Harvard 1960. The chart stops in 1836 because it seems very likely that Block's bibliography (*The English Novel 1740–1850*) significantly overstates the number of novels published after that date.

book in isolation: but when it came to standing out in a crowded marketplace, short titles were better—much easier to remember, to begin with (but not only). That's why long titles disappeared: because between the size of the market, and the length of titles, a strong negative correlation emerged: as the one expanded, the other contracted. Nothing much had changed, in the length of titles, for a century and a half, as long as the production of novels had remained stable around five or ten per year; then, as soon as publishing took off in earnest, titles immediately shrank (Figure 8). By 1790, their 'quantitative' transformation was virtually complete.[6]

---

6   The other type of title that disappeared in the late eighteenth century was the 'title-compilation', like the 1772 *The Egg, Or the Memoirs of Gregory Giddy,*

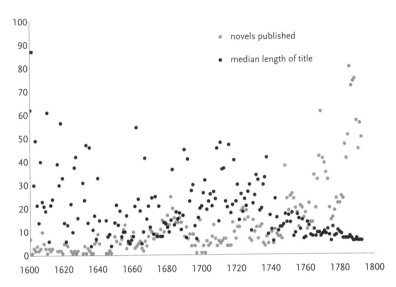

Figure 8: Size of the literary market, length of novelistic titles

Additional source: 1600–1700, Charles C. Mish, ed., *English Prose Fiction, 1600–1700: A Chronological Checklist*, Charlottesville, VA 1967.

As long as only a few novels per year are published, the median length of titles keeps oscillating between 10 and 40–50 words; after the first 'rise' of the 1720s and '30s, however, it drops below 20, and below 10 during the late-eighteenth century take-off first noticed by Clifford Siskin. Earlier on, more ephemeral publishing spurts (1655–60; the 1680s) had also coincided with a marked drop in the length of titles.

Esq: With the Lucubrations of Messrs. Francis Flimsy, Frederick Florid, and Ben Bombast. To which are Added Private Opinions of Patty Pout, Lucy Lucious, and Priscilla Positive. Also the Memoirs of a Right Honourable Puppy. Or Bon Ton Display'd: Together with Anecdotes of a Right Honourable Scoundrel. Conceived by a Celebrated Hen, and Laid Before the Public by a Famous Cock-feeder. Just as summaries drew the reader's attention to the multiplicity of episodes along the diachronic axis, compilations foregrounded a 'horizontal' proliferation of perspectives, characters, and locations—a naive, picaresque-like poetics of 'variety' (to use a keyword of the age), at the very moment when novelistic structure was becoming tighter and more homogeneous. Out of step with the times, summaries and compilations became even more unimaginable in the nineteenth century.

The market expands, and titles contract. Figure 8 showed the temporal correlation of the two processes; a closer look at the market adds a specific causal relationship. Because 'market', in the late eighteenth century—when readers almost never bought novels—really means: circulating libraries. Commercial enterprises, which disseminated the novel throughout Britain (and France, and Germany: one of Brecht's early plays, *In the Jungle of Cities*, opens in one of these libraries), and whose catalogues have frequently survived until today. Catalogues: lists of titles. But not quite the same titles we find in Raven and Garside. In Sander's library, in 1780s Derby, *Capacity and Extent of the Human Understanding; Exemplified in the Extraordinary Case of Automathes: A Young Nobleman; who was Accidentally left in his Infancy, upon a desolate Island, and continued Nineteen Years in that solitary State, separate from all Human Society. A Narrative abounding with many surprising Occurrences, both Useful and Entertaining to the Reader*, becomes: *History of Automathes, A Young Nobleman*. At Phorson's, in Berwick, in 1790, *Unfortunate Sensibility; or, the Life of Mrs L*****. Written by Herself. In a Series of Sentimental Letters. Dedicated to Mr. Yorick, in the Elysian Fields* becomes *Unfortunate Sensibility*. At Sael's, in the Strand, in 1793, *Emmeline, the Orphan of the Castle* becomes *Emmeline*. And so on.

A coded message, in a market situation. And the key institution of the market takes the code, and *compresses* it: typically, to a proper name. Libraries couldn't waste space on a catalogue page; they didn't want any confusion between this novel and that; the spine of the book had only room for a few words anyway; and then, readers were getting used to novels, and needed less 'guidance' from titles.[7]

---

7   If everything was really pushing towards shorter titles—observed Sam Bowles during a discussion of this paper—shouldn't these be 'rewarded' by the cultural ecosystem, and be on average more successful than other types? Yes, they should; and since James Raven had already identified which of the 1,400 novels published between 1770 and 1799 had been reprinted at least five times by 1829 (see his 'Historical Introduction: the Novel Comes of Age', in *The English*

So, the average length decreased, long titles disappeared, and, at the opposite end of the spectrum, titles with only one, two, or three words multiplied rapidly (Figure 9, overleaf): they were 5 per cent in the 1740s and '50s, but by 1800 they were already around 20 to 30 per cent, and had completely traded places with the long titles which had been their predecessors (Figure 10). It's the same thing that happened in advertising a hundred years later, when the detailed descriptions of the nineteenth century were replaced by the evocative oblique brevity of today's ads; *literally* the same thing: title-pages with long summaries of novels were often used as flyers, and

---

Novel 1770–1829: A Bibliographical Survey of Prose Fiction Published in the British Isles, vol. I, Oxford 2000, p. 40), I compared the lengths of these sixty-five titles to the median for their years—fully expecting them to be significantly shorter. That, however, turned out not to be the case: thirty-two of the titles were indeed shorter than the median, but twenty-nine were longer (at times, *much* longer), and four were exactly the same length.

What these results seem to suggest is that—although a crowded market does exert a strong *negative* pressure against long titles—it remains relatively neutral once a certain length has been reached: it prohibits at one end of the spectrum, but it does not prescribe at the opposite one. Comparative work in other European traditions should provide additional evidence on this matter; meanwhile, and more anecdotally, a look at some canonical British novelists is as inconclusive as the wider bibliographical investigation. If Edgeworth and Austen use much shorter titles than their contemporaries, and Fielding, Smollett, and Burney remain slightly below the median, Richardson and Radcliffe behave in an average way, while Scott and Galt and Dickens often enjoy playing with extremely long titles (which, by their time, are a quaintly obsolete choice): *Tales of My Landlord, Collected and Arranged by Jedediah Cleishbotham, Schoolmaster and Parish-Clerk of Gandercleugh*; *The Annals of the Parish; or, The Chronicle of Dalmailing; During the Ministry of the Rev. Micah Balwhidder. Written by himself*; *Dealings with the Firm of Dombey and Son, Wholesale, Retail and for Exportation.*

Now, if neither 'successful' nor 'canonical' novelists took the lead in shortening titles, then, inevitably, *someone else* must have done so: writers who—as we will see in the next section—were neither particularly popular, nor especially good. Perhaps, once the literary system had started moving in a certain direction, some developments were so inevitable that they didn't require any special talent. Or perhaps—as suggested in footnote 11, below—in this case the key variable was not literary, but political.

pasted around to advertise a book. But short titles, as we
will see, were not just better titles—they were better *ads*,
too.

Titles allow us to see a larger literary field, I said at the beginning
of this study; and the first thing we see in this larger field, at this
moment in history, is *the force of the market*: how its growth creates
a major constraint on the presentation of novels. This of course
doesn't mean that all titles gave the same answer to the pressure of
the market; but it does mean that they all had to face the same
question: How could one shorten a message—without losing
information? There was a lot of information in summaries: what
happened to it? Was it—gone? reformulated? replaced by something else? I will return to this in a moment; now let me close this
first section by acknowledging a limit of this investigation: I began
by showing the average length of titles, but I then shifted to very
long and very short titles—and I did so, because these trends are
much more dramatic than the slow decline of the average, and
thus also much easier to talk about. Which is not exactly *wrong*
(after all, those trends are real!), but, even aside from a question
of completeness—of the 7,000 titles in the study, around 900 are
'long', 1,600 'short', and 4,500 somewhere in between—the focus
on extremes misses a decisive aspect of quantitative work: what
really counts, here, are not a few major and rapid changes, but
many small and slow ones.

But the trouble is, we literary historians don't really know how to
think about what is frequent and small and slow; that's what makes
it so hard to study the literary field as a whole: we must learn to
find meaning in small changes and slow processes—and it's difficult. Especially so, in the case of titles: which are by definition the
most public part of a book, hence the most subject to censorship:
what we find in titles reflects the 'legitimate irradiation' of existing
ideas, wrote Jean-Louis Flandrin, and it's true, titles are so

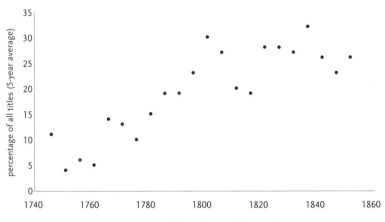

Figure 9: novels with very short titles

'On the twenty-seventh evening, *Nanine*, by M. de Voltaire, was performed. *Nanine?* asked so-called critics when this piece first appeared in 1749: what sort of a title is that? what idea does that give us? Nothing more and nothing less than a title should. A title must be no bill of fare. The less it betrays of the contents, the better it is. It is better for both poet and spectator. The ancients rarely gave to their comedies any other than insignificant titles.' Lessing, *Hamburg Dramaturgy*

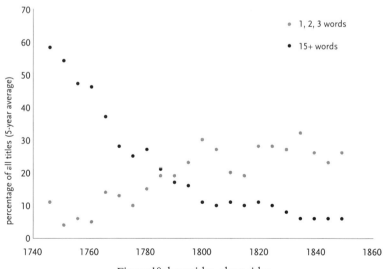

Figure 10: long titles, short titles

'respectable'; and again, how do you make respectable messages interesting . . . ?[8]

II

Very short titles: one, two, or three words. Where the question that interests me is, How can a couple of words stand in for hundreds of pages? What does it mean, that they should do so? For summaries, it's clear: they are scaled-down versions of the whole story. Two words? So, I started looking at these short titles, and found three main clusters within the group: proper names (*Octavia*; *George Barnwell*), which make up around one-third of the total; the article-noun (*The Steam-Boat*; *The Smuggler*) and article-adjective-noun combinations (*The Tuscan Vase*; *The Invisible Gentleman*) just below 30 per cent; and conceptual abstractions (*Fatality*; *Enthusiasm not Religion*) around 10 per cent. 'A large change in size inevitably carries with it a change of form', wrote J. B. S. Haldane, and here one sees how right he was: a title

---

8   Jean-Louis Flandrin, 'Sentiments et civilisation. Sondage au niveau des titres d'ouvrages', *Annales*, September–October 1965, p. 939. Later I hope to study the 'average title' of these 110 years, taking as a starting point the formula in 'or' (*Pamela, or Virtue Rewarded*; *Vensenshon; or, Love's Mazes*; *Manfrone; or, The One-Handed Monk*). There are over 2,000 such titles in the database, most of which use between three and fifteen words, thus occupying exactly the middle of the field. To get a sense of the morbid diffusion of 'or' in eighteenth-century titles, let me just say that it is the fourth-most-frequent word of the database, following 'the', 'of', and 'a' (and preceding 'and'!); by contrast, in Gaskell's *North and South*, 'or' is the forty-fourth-most-frequent word; in *Our Mutual Friend*, the fifty-fifth.

A side from quantitative reasons, the formula in 'or' is important because it codified the form of the 'double' title, where the second (on the right of the 'or') is an explication of the first: Waverley, *that is to say*, events of sixty years ago; Pamela, a story in which virtue is rewarded. Here, we are clearly beyond the title as summary, though not quite yet in the world of *Belinda* or *Persuasion*: as if the 'or' were a sort of afterthought—a hiccup: maybe one word is not really enough for a title, let's add something else, just to be sure. A compromise formation that coexisted first with summaries, then with short titles, the formula in 'or' thus mediated between explanatory and intuitive strategies; but as readers became more comfortable with allusion, it lost its *raison d'être*. By 1900, it had become a thing of the past.

with twenty words and one with two are not the same creature, one larger and one smaller; they are different animals altogether. Different *styles*. There is a 'less is more' elegance to short titles—*Persuasion*; *Emma*; *Mansfield Park*—that was unthinkable in summaries; there, the aim was to squeeze as many things as possible into the front page— more is more, as it were—and if the title turned out to be a mess, so be it: *Robinson Crusoe*'s mentioned an episode that doesn't even appear in the novel (*An Account how he was at last as strangely deliver'd by PYRATES*: pyrates? what pyrates?)—it didn't really matter. But a short title is a delicate structure, sensitive to every small change. Consider the article-noun, and article-adjective-noun combinations: similar forms, similar semantic horizon—*The Monk*, 1796; *The New Monk*, 1798—and so at first I assumed that the adjective wouldn't change much: the monk and the new monk: big deal; the adjective would specify the noun, as adjectives do, but no more than that.

And instead, it turns out that the adjective does not specify the semantic field; it transforms it. In the article-noun combination, half of the titles describing a social type evoke an exotic-transgressive field—*The Fakeer*, *The Vampyre*, *The Fire-eater*, *The Pirate*, *The Sabbath-Breaker*, *The Spectre*, *The Rebel*, *The Epicurean*, *The Mussulman*, *The Libertine*, *The Parricide* . . . —and only a small minority evokes the idea of the 'familiar' (wife, brother, father, daughter, etc.). But when an adjective is added to the title, the ratio is exactly reversed (Figure 11, overleaf): fakeers and libertines drop from 50 to 20 per cent, while wives and daughters rise from 16 to 40 per cent: *The Unfashionable Wife*, *The Discarded Daughter*, *The Infidel Father*, *The Rival Brothers*, *The Posthumous Daughter*, *The False Friend*, *The Maniac Father* . . . Without adjectives, we are in a world of adventures; with adjectives, in a destabilized domesticity. The adjective is the only change, but it changes everything. And of course, once you think about it, it makes sense: if all that is in the title is a noun, then that noun must guarantee an interesting story all by itself, and vampires and parricides are a very good choice; but if an adjective is present, then even the most familiar figures can be

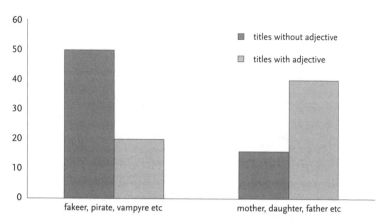

Figure 11: Semantic fields in very short titles: the role of adjectives

estranged into infidel fathers and posthumous daughters. The adjective relocates narrative from substance to accident, as it were. And again, it makes sense: the adjective introduces *predication* within the title, and predication is the germ of storytelling. 'The wife' is a stable quantity; the *unfashionable* wife is a question mark: why is she unfashionable? what does her husband think? her daughters? This is why short titles are so interesting: they are on the border: between two and three words lies the invisible barrier that separates storytelling from—something else, which we'll see in a minute.

Common nouns are frequent, in short titles, but proper names are even more frequent, especially at the turn of the century (Figure 12), when one title in twelve (1786–90), then one in ten (1791–95), then almost one in seven (1796–1800), consists of a proper name, and nothing else: *Emily*; *Henry*; *Georgina*. The growth of the market forced titles to become shorter, and, as we saw in circulating libraries' catalogues, proper names were a great way to do so: one word, and a novel was immediately singled out from the rest.[9] Singled out, by pointing to

---

9   Needless to say, different names—Evelina, Mary and Moll; Edward, Tom and Dick—evoked very different semantic associations: a great topic for further study.

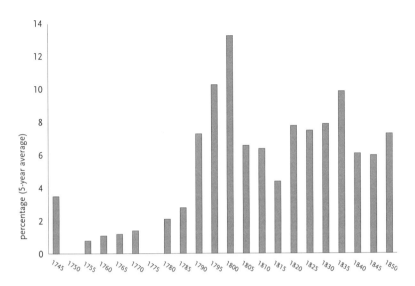

Figure 12: Short titles consisting only of a proper name

'If the Name [...] is a sign, it is a voluminous sign, a sign always pregnant and crammed full of meanings that no use can reduce or flatten [...] It is immune from any kind of selective restriction, and the syntagm in which it is located is a matter of indifference to it. In a certain sense, the name is thus a semantic monstrosity.' Barthes, 'Proust and Names'.

its protagonist; a choice which was not inevitable—of the 'six master-pieces' of the Chinese canon, for instance, none was ever shortened to a proper name, because none had a name in the title to begin with—but which has been typical of European narrative since Greek and medieval times (probably, because in our tradition the central charac-ter has always played a greater role). And of course, in the late eighteenth century, protagonist mostly means *female* protagonist (Figures 13 and 14, overleaf): a woman's name, and often just a *first* name (Figures 15 and 16): *Lucy, Caroline, Belinda, Emma* . . . Heroines who lack a last name: a very simple, very crude hint, typical of the British marriage plot (which reaches its apex in these decades): they lack a husband. But the wider field charted in Figures 13 through 16

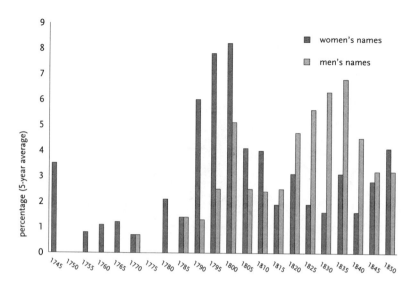

Figure 13: Short titles consisting only of a proper name

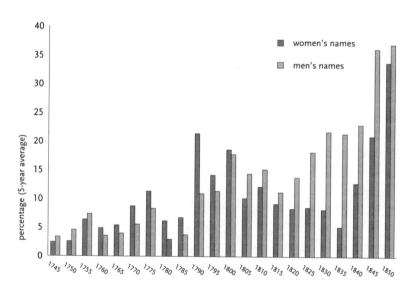

Figure 14: All titles including a proper name

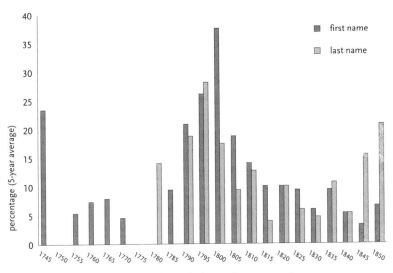

Figure 15: Short titles including only a woman's name

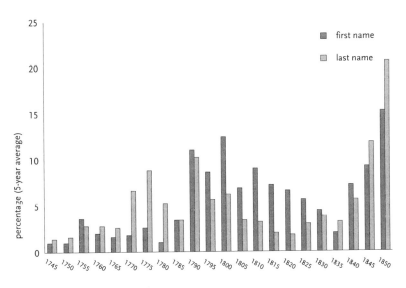

Figure 16: All titles including a woman's proper name

also shows how quickly the gender asymmetry was reversed in the 1820s and '30s, and how frequent the heroine's *last* name could actually be.[10] In both cases, the main changes were almost certainly caused by shifts in the system of genres: the historical novel's rise to prominence after 1815, for instance, with its mostly male heroes;[11] or the marriage plot becoming embedded within genres like the *Bildungsroman* and the industrial novel, where the heroine acquired a public life, which was promptly mirrored in titles like *Jane Eyre* or *Mary Barton*. Again, see how much can be done with how little, in short titles: one word, and the image of the heroine rotates 180 degrees: from private, to public. Short titles were a constraint imposed by the market, yes, but the constraint could also be a fantastic opportunity for the literary imagination: the art of allusion, of condensation: the title as trope, ultimately. Odd twist: the market promoting—style.

The market expanded, titles contracted; by 1790, as we have seen, the issue of length had been settled, and didn't really change for at least sixty years. But something else *did* change, between 1790 and 1850, and the last type of title I will discuss in this section—abstractions—will help us to understand what. Abstractions were usually a single word (*Generosity*, *Indiscretion*, *Independence*, *Delusion*), or a conceptual pair (*Liberality and Prejudice*, *Jesuitism and Methodism*),

---

10   That female protagonists are more often indicated by their full name than by their first name is one of the surprises of this study. In the century under investigation, the old aristocratic (and often French) form of the proper name—*Rosa de Montmorien*, *Eloise de Montblanc*—found a newer, 'bourgeois' (and British) incarnation in *Alice Lemington*, or *Margaret Graham*; the golden age of the marriage plot, and of titles mentioning first names only, falls in between these two alternative typologies.

11   If one looks at the entire period in question, men's names outnumber women's by about 10 percent, probably because many novelistic subgenres—most travel narratives, nautical tales, later 'Irish' novels, war stories, Newgate novels—were quite unlikely to have female protagonists. That the 'Emma' type of title should immediately come to mind when thinking of proper names in titles, is a sign of its exceptional power of allusion, and of the centrality of the marriage plot in the modern English novel.

and although they were never very frequent, in the first quarter of the century, and especially in the 1820s, they were not insignificant, thanks largely to the tireless Barbara Hofland, who in the five years from 1823 to 1827 published, one after the other, *Integrity*, *Decision*, *Patience*, *Moderation*, *Reflection*, and *Self-Denial*. And as you read these titles you realize that abstractions here really means—ethics. Nineteenth-century ethics; previously, abstractions had often emphasized moral violations (*Disobedience*, *Indiscretion*, *Fatality*, *Retribution*, *False Gratitude*, *The Relapse*, *Conscious Duplicity* . . .), but after 1800 it is the *construction* of the ethical that is highlighted (Figure 17): *Self-Control*, *Conduct*, *Discipline*, *Correction*, *Decision*, *Reformation*. Morality not as purity, but as *work*: one takes one's own self and transforms it, in a process that is both spiritual and pragmatic. Hofland's *Moderation*, wrote the *Monthly Review* in 1825, is 'fabricated . . . to . . . strongly enforce a precept in morals of great practical utility'—and that moral precept fabricated for practical utility is really the dawn of Victorianism.

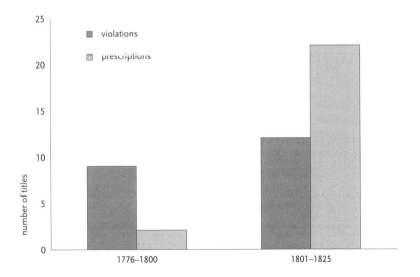

Figure 17: Ethical content of abstractions in short titles

When titles were summaries, they of course used verbs (*The misfor-tunes in which this young woman has been cruelly involved* etc. etc.); but once summaries disappear, so do verbs (aside from the occa-sional *Says She to Her Neighbour, What?*), and titles like *Patience* or *Moderation* are the logical endpoint of the process: titles that sound more and more like nominal sentences. A grammatical form that 'places the utterance beyond all temporal or modal localization, and beyond the subjectivity of the speaker', wrote Benveniste in his classic analysis of this type of sentence: beyond subjectivity, beyond temporal localization . . . the telos of nominal sentences is *the abolition of contingency*: 'they don't describe a situation', Benveniste again, 'they posit an absolute'.[12] *Self-Control*; *Patience*; *Integrity*: they don't describe a situation, not even in the minimal way of maniac fathers and unfashionable wives; they don't allude to what happens in the novel, or to where and when it takes place; they posit an absolute, and that absolute is of course *the meaning of the novel*. This was the great historical achievement of abstrac-tions: they made titles meaning-ful: nothing *but* meaning, as if the essence of the novel had been distilled and purified of all narrative contingency. And readers, faced with this type of title, have to change their expectations: the first thing they are told about the novel asks them to imagine, not so much a story, but *the point* of the story: the point of the story as a single, unifying concept. And this is important. That titles became short is interesting, yes, but in the end, So what? That by becoming short they adopted a signi-fying strategy that made readers look for a unity in the narrative structure—this is a perceptual shift which has persisted for 200 years. And mediocre conservative writers did more to make it happen than anyone else.[13]

---

12   'The Nominal Sentence', in *Problems in General Linguistics*, 1966, Miami 1971, pp. 138, 142.

13   Why them? Perhaps, because there was much in common between the conservative reaction to the French Revolution (for which basic social values had to be preserved from historical transformation), and the type of titles I am

I have discussed abstractions next to proper names, because they both make for very short titles; but, clearly, their relationship to plot is completely different: proper names are a *part* of the story, whereas abstractions are an *interpretation* of it. It would be tempting to say that names have a metonymic relationship to the novel, and abstractions a metaphoric one; but if characters' names (and the— rarer—place names like *Minerva Castle* or *Mansfield Park*) are indeed metonymies of the plot, abstractions are not quite metaphors,[14] and in fact it is curious how *few* metaphors are there, in these 7,000 titles.[15] By the end of the century they are everywhere (*The Belly of Paris*, *The Doll*, *Ghosts*, *The Octopus*, *Heart of Darkness*, *The Beast in the Jungle*), so they must have taken root sometime in the third quarter of the nineteenth century, and the glimpses one gets suggest a lot of hesitation on the part of writers: Gaskell shift- ing at the last minute from *Margaret Hale* to *North and South* (proper name to metaphor); Dickens doing the opposite, from *Nobody's Fault* to *Little Dorrit*. Announcing a story with a metaphor must have seemed strange—and it is strange: if abstractions are removed from the plot, then metaphors are twice removed: interpretations that *require an interpretation*, as it were. But it is precisely this 'diffi- culty' of metaphors that holds the secret of the title as ad.

---

discussing here (for which fundamental ethical absolutes had to be freed from narrative relativization).

14   Nor are they allegories or personifications: Hofland's *Moderation* is not meant to come alive and be part of a story like its homonym in the 1669 *History of Moderation; or, The Life, Death and Resurrection of Moderation: together with her Nativity, Country, Pedigree, Kindred, Character, Friends, and also her Enemies*.

15   It's only at the very end of the period that they begin to appear: *Loss and Gain* (1848), *Rough and Smooth* (1849), *Shadows and Sunshine, Flies in Amber* and *The Swan's Egg* (1850). In general, if the years between 1790 and 1830 see the establishment of metonymies and abstractions, no further novelties seem to emerge between 1830 and 1850: instead of looking for new forms of brevity, writers seem to devote their best energies to the second title, as if that were the key to the problem: *Helen Halsey. A Tale of the Borders. A Romance of Deep Interest*; *The Slave Captain; A Legend of Liverpool; Goals and Guerdons: Or, The chronicles of a life. By a very old lady*; *Rebecca and Rowena. A Romance Upon Romance*.

Eighteenth-century summaries told readers a lot of things about the novel, yes; but they never really engaged their intelligence. And instead, by puzzling and challenging readers, metaphors induced them to take *an active interest in the novel* from the very first word. If you are trying to sell a product, that's exactly what you want.

Summaries, adjectives, proper names, nominal sentences, metonymies, metaphors . . . In a minute I will turn to articles (and am thinking of sections on conjunctions and participles). This is a quantitative study: but its units are linguistic and rhetorical. And the reason is simple: for me, formal analysis is the great accomplishment of literary study, and is therefore also what any new approach—quantitative, digital, evolutionary, whatever—must prove itself against: prove that it can do formal analysis, better than we already do. Or at least: equally well, in a different key. Otherwise, what is the point?

III

As the market expands, titles contract; as they do that, they learn to compress meaning; and as they do *that*, they develop special 'signals' to place books in the right market niche. 'Had I, for example, announced in my frontispiece, "Waverley, a Tale of other Days", must not every novel-reader have anticipated a castle scarce less than that of Udolpho . . . a "Sentimental Tale" would . . . have been a sufficient presage of a heroine with a profusion of auburn hair . . . "a Tale of the Times" [of] a dashing sketch of the fashionable world' . . . *Tale of other Days, Sentimental Tale, Tale of the Times*: that these words would make readers think of specific genres is of course true—and trivial: it's obvious. The code may be in the market, but it remains transparent. And instead, the interesting cases are the opaque ones: where the signal works, and we somehow know what kind of a novel we have in our hands, but we don't know why we know it, because it is all conveyed by traits that escape our attention; 'subliminal', as we used to say.

Let me illustrate this point with two genres—the so-called anti-jacobin and 'new woman' novels—that are separated by a hundred years:[16] two explicitly ideological genres, which rely heavily on contemporary politics, and whose titles have thus a lot in common—except for one detail. Among anti-jacobin titles, 36 per cent begin with the definite article (*The Banished Man, The Medallion, The Parisian, The Democrat*) and 3 per cent with the indefinite; a result which is perfectly aligned with the rest of the field, since at the time the overall frequencies are 38 and 2 per cent.[17] New woman titles, no; the definite article is obviously still present, in 24 per cent of the cases, but the use of the indefinite leaps from 2, or 3, to *30* per cent of the cases (Figure 18, overleaf). Now, this is odd, not only because it is completely out of scale with anything else I have found, but because in many other ways the conventions of the two genres are quite similar. *The* democrat; *A* blue-stocking: two well-known figures of the contemporary political scene; why is the article different? *The* infidel father; *A* hard woman; the same grammar, the same dissonance between adjective and noun; why is the article different? What do the articles *do*, that they need to be different? An essay by Harald Weinrich offers an answer; for Weinrich, the starting point to understand linguistic categories is always the text, and, since all texts are linear, 'there are always two main directions in which the attention of the reader may be directed': backwards, or forwards: backwards, towards what we already know from the text, and forwards, towards what we don't.[18] And the simplest way to alert

---

16   See the bibliographies included in M. O. Grenby, *The Anti-Jacobin Novel*, Cambridge 2001, and Ann Ardis, *New Women, New Novels*, New Brunswick 1990.

17   In the *New York Times* best-seller list of November 2008, 38 per cent of the titles began with the definite article, and 6 per cent with the indefinite: not that different from two centuries earlier.

18   Harald Weinrich, 'The Textual Function of the French Article', in Seymour Chatman, ed., *Literary Style: A Symposium*, Oxford 1971, p. 226.

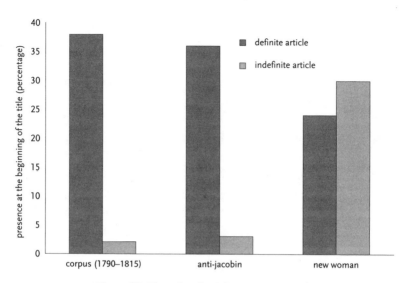

Figure 18: The role of articles as genre signals

the reader's attention is—articles: the definite article announcing a noun as something that we already know (thus directing our attention backwards); and the indefinite suggesting the opposite: Take heed, here comes something that you haven't encountered yet. The first time the wolf appears in *Little Red Riding Hood* it is 'a' wolf; afterwards, 'the' wolf, forever. So: *A Girton Girl, A Hard Woman, A Mummer's Wife, A Domestic Experiment, A Daughter of Today, A Semi-detached Marriage*: what the article 'says' is that we are encountering all these figures *for the first time*; we think we know what daughters and wives are, but we actually don't, and must understand them afresh. The article announces the novel as a challenge to received knowledge. And instead, 'the' democrat, 'the' parisian, 'the' infidel father . . . we know these people! Anti-jacobin titles don't want to change received ideas, they want to *use* them: the French Revolution has multiplied your enemies—beware.

Here is a modest example of what quantitative stylistics could do: take those units of language that are so frequent we hardly notice them

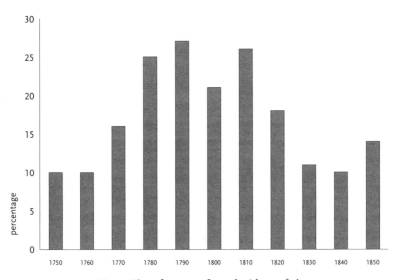

Figure 19: A fortunate formula: 'the x of y'

and show how powerfully they contribute to the construction of meaning.[19] Which is also the point of my last example: a formula that, at first sight, looks as flat and uninspiring as could be: *The Duchess of York*, *The Novice of Corpus Domini*, *The Heir of Montgomery Castle*: let's call it 'the x of y'. As Figure 19 shows, the formula has always been quite frequent in titles, never dropping below 10 per cent of the total; but around 1800 its frequency increases, and if we look more closely at those decades, we find that the surge does not occur evenly everywhere, but is almost entirely concentrated in a single genre, which is the gothic. There, 'the x of y' appears three times more often than in the rest of the corpus (Figure 20), which is too big a difference to be the product of chance, especially since something very similar also occurs within the gothic itself: we all know that the word 'castle' was the shibboleth of the genre's imagination, from *The Castle of*

---

19   The model here remains John Burrows's analysis of Austen's characters' styles in *Computation into Criticism*; that he did it twenty years ago, without the help of today's technology, puts us all to shame.

Otranto onwards; well, in gothic titles 'the x of y' occurs *three times more often* than 'castle'.

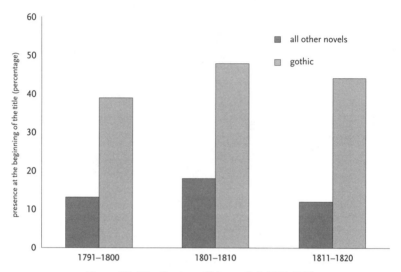

Figure 20: Distribution of 'the x of y', 1791-1820

But why? Castles in gothic titles, it makes sense. The x of y? Here semantics helps; if we look at the 'x' in the formula, we find that 'romance' appears in 7 per cent of the cases (*The Romance of the Pyrenees*), a cluster of genre indicators like mysteries, horrors, secrets, adventures in 13 per cent (*The Horrors of Oakendale Abbey*), personal nouns in 34 per cent (*Emmeline, or the Orphan of the Castle*), and space nouns in 41 per cent of the total (Figure 21): from *The Castle of Otranto* in 1764 to *The Mines of Wielitzka* and *The Rock of Glotzden* a half century later. So, in three-quarters of the cases 'the x of y' specifies an 'x' which is either a person or a space. And when we move from the subject of the formula to its predicate—from the x to the y—what we find is so striking that I don't even need a graph to point it out: *The Romance of the Pyrenees, The Horrors of Oakendale Abbey, The Orphan of the Castle, The Castle of Otranto, The Mines of Wielitzka, The Rock of Glotzden* . . . in 82 per

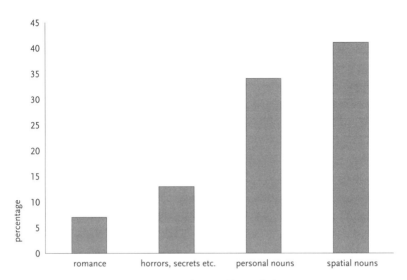

Figure 21: The x in 'the x of y'

cent of the cases, the 'y' is a space: a person defined by a space, or, most frequent of all, a space defined by another space. *The Castle of Otranto*: a spatial noun specified by a place name.

There are many intriguing traits to gothic titles—this is the genre that discovers that readers like villains, for instance, and shamelessly parades them in titles—but space is really the cornerstone of the convention: place names are much more frequent than human proper names; spatial nouns like castle, abbey, forest, cave, etc., show up in 50 per cent of the cases; and there are even other kinds of geographical signals, like *A Sicilian Romance* or *The Danish Massacre*. Nothing is as typical of gothic titles as this fixation with space; and of course this is true not just of titles, but of gothic *novels*: where space is dark, labyrinthine, cold; it imprisons, it terrifies, it kills . . . 'The x of y' takes this power of space, and activates it at two scales at once: human, and geographical. *The Castle of Otranto*: there is a building; there is a town; they are both gothic. Escape from the castle, you're still in southern Italy. There is no way out.

'Literature is the fragment of fragments', wrote Goethe in *Wilhelm Meister's Years of Wandering*, the great sad novel of his old age: 'the least part of all that ever happened and was spoken was written down, and of what was written only the least part has survived . . .'. 'Of this history we possess the last volume alone', wrote Darwin in *The Origin of Species*: 'of this volume, only here and there a short chapter has been preserved, and of each page, only here and there a few lines'. There are differences, of course, between the history of nature and that of culture: the 'fossils' of literary evolution are often not lost, but carefully preserved in some great library, like most of those 7,000 novels whose titles I have discussed here; but for the purposes of our knowledge, it's as if they too had crumbled into dust, because we have never really tried to read the entire volume of the literary past. Studying titles is a small step in that direction.

Network Theory, Plot Analysis

'Style, Inc.' had sketched out some hypotheses for quantitative stylistics; 'Network Theory, Plot Analysis' was an attempt to do the same for plot, thus providing an essential—and still missing—piece to the computational analysis of literature. Once I started working in earnest, however, I soon realized that the tools for a large-scale gathering of data were not (yet) available to me, and the essay retreated from quantification into a qualitative analysis of plot: space and time, network regions, central characters, periphery, and so on. And then a second shift followed: though in a couple of cases—the pages on clustering, and on guanxi in Chinese novels—the essay did engage the categories of network theory, its main claims were independent from its conceptual architecture. Did I really need network theory to discuss Horatio and the State, or 'symmetry' in Dickens?

No, I didn't need the theory; but I needed the networks. Though Horatio is an old fixation of mine, I had never fully understood his role in Hamlet until I looked at the play's network structure. The keyword, here, is 'looked'; what I took from network theory was its basic form of visualization: the idea that the temporal flow of a dramatic plot can be turned into a set of two-dimensional signs—vertices (or nodes) and edges—that can be grasped at a single glance. 'We construct, and construct, and yet, intuition remains a good thing', Klee once wrote, *and that's exactly how I proceeded here, (mis-)using network theory to bring some order into literary evidence, but leaving my analysis free to follow any course that happened to suggest itself.*

Intuition is a good thing, but concepts are better, and, as I write this page, a much larger study of drama and network theory is in progress at the Literary Lab: a collective project, on hundreds of plays from a variety cultures and historical periods. But this is a different story, which ought to be told in a different book.

In the last few years, literary studies have experienced what we could call the rise of quantitative evidence. This had happened before of course, without producing lasting effects, but this time it is probably going to be different, because this time we have digital databases and automated data retrieval. As a recent article in *Science* on 'Culturomics' made clear, the width of the corpus and the speed of the search have increased beyond all expectations: today, we can replicate in a few minutes investigations that took a giant like Leo Spitzer months and years of work.[1] When it comes to phenomena of language and style, we can do things that previous generations could only dream of.

When it comes to language and style. But if you work on novels or plays, style is only part of the picture. What about plot—how can that be quantified? This paper is the beginning of an answer, and the beginning of the beginning is network theory. This is a theory that studies connections within large groups of objects: the objects can be just about anything—banks, neurons, film actors, research papers,

---

1 Jean-Baptiste Michel, Erez Lieberman Aiden et al., 'Quantitative Analysis of Culture Using Millions of Digitized Books', *Science*, December 2010.

friends . . . —and are usually called nodes or vertices; their connections are usually called edges; and the analysis of how vertices are linked by edges has revealed many unexpected features of large systems, the most famous one being the so-called 'small-world' property, or 'six degrees of separation': the uncanny rapidity with which one can reach any vertex in the network from any other vertex. The theory proper requires a level of mathematical intelligence which I unfortunately lack; and it typically uses vast quantities of data which will also be missing from my paper. But this is only the first in a series of studies we're doing at the Stanford Literary Lab; and then, even at this early stage, a few things emerge.

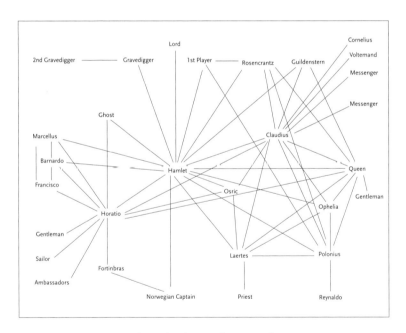

Figure 1: The Hamlet network

CHARACTER-NETWORK

A network is made of vertices and edges; a plot, of characters and actions: characters will be the vertices of the network, interactions the edges, and this is what the *Hamlet* network looks like: Figure 1.[2] There are some questionable decisions here, mostly about *The Murder of Gonzago*, but, basically, two characters are linked if some words have passed between them: an interaction is a speech act. This is not the only way to do things, the authors of a previous paper on Shakespeare had linked characters if they had speaking parts during the same scene, even if they did not address each other: so, for instance, for them the Queen and Osric are linked (because they both have speaking parts, and are on stage together in the last scene of the play), whereas here they are not, because they don't speak to each other.[3] My network uses explicit connections, theirs adds implicit ones, and is obviously denser, because it has all of my edges plus some; both are plausible, and both have at least two flaws. First, the edges are not 'weighted': when Claudius tells Horatio in the graveyard scene, 'I pray thee, good Horatio, wait upon him', these eight words have in this figure exactly the same value as the four *thousand* words exchanged between Hamlet and Horatio. This can't be right. And then, the edges have no 'direction': when Horatio

---

2   As will become clear from the text, the visual evidence relevant to this article can easily be increased to fifty or more images; the full series can be found on the website of Stanford's Literary Lab (litlab.stanford.edu).

3   'The network structure calculations were obtained by treating each speaking character as a vertex, and deeming two characters to be linked if there was at least one time slice of the play in which both were present (that is, if two characters spoke to each other or were in each other's presence, then they have a link)': James Stiller, Daniel Nettle, Robin I. M. Dunbar, 'The Small World of Shakespeare's Plays', *Human Nature* 14: 4 (2003), p. 399. Another application of network theory to narrative (R. Alberich, J. Miro-Julia and F. Rosselló, 'Marvel Universe Looks Almost Like a Real Social Network', 11 February 2002, available at arXiv.org) uses a similar premise, by stating that 'two characters are linked when they jointly appear in a significant way in the same comic book'; since, however, we are never told what exactly constitutes a 'significant' interaction, as opposed to an insignificant one, the basis for quantification remains fundamentally opaque.

addresses the Ghost in the opening scene, his words place an edge between them, but of course that the Ghost would not reply and would speak only to Hamlet is important, and should be made visible.[4] But I just couldn't find a non-clumsy way to visualize weight and direction; and turning to already-existing software didn't help, as its results are often completely unreadable. So, the networks in this study were all made by hand, with the very simple aim of maximizing visibility by minimizing overlap. This is not a long-term solution, of course, but these are small networks, in which intuition can still play a role; they're like the childhood of network theory for literature; a brief happiness, before the stern adulthood of statistics.

Anyway. Four hours of action, that become this. Time turned into space: a character-*system* arising out of many character-*spaces*, to use Alex Woloch's concepts in *The One vs the Many*. Hamlet's space, Figure 2: in bold, all the direct links between him and other characters; Hamlet and Claudius, Figure 3: see how much of the network they capture, between the two of them. Ophelia and Gertrude, Figure 4: the much smaller space of the two women in the play. And so on. But before analyzing spaces in detail, why use networks to think about plot to begin with? What do we gain, by turning time into space? First of all, this: when we watch a play, we are always in the present: what is on stage, is; and then it disappears. Here, nothing ever disappears. What is done, cannot be undone. Once the Ghost shows up at Elsinore things change forever, whether he is onstage or not, because he is never not there in the network. The past becomes past, yes, but it never disappears from our perception of the plot.

---

4   The reason weight and direction are particularly important in literary networks is that, whereas the systems studied by network theory have easily thousands or millions of vertices, whose relevance can be directly expressed in the number of connections, plots have usually no more than a few dozen characters; as a consequence, the mere existence of a connection is seldom sufficient to establish a hierarchy, and must be integrated with other measurements.

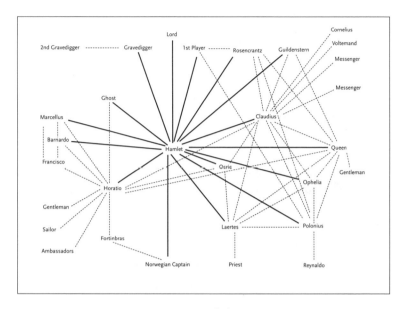

Figure 2: Hamlet's space

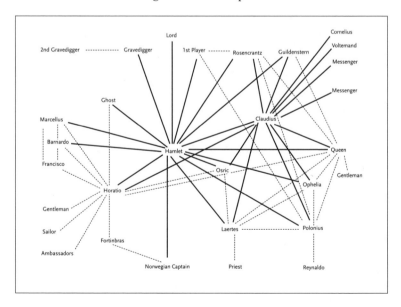

Figure 3: Hamlet and Claudius

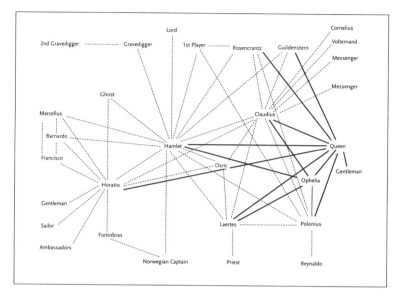

Figure 4: Gertrude and Ophelia

Making the past just as visible as the present: that is one major change introduced by the use of networks. Then, they make visible specific 'regions' within the plot as a whole: sub-systems, which share some significant property. Take the characters who are connected to both Claudius and Hamlet in Figure 5: except for Osric and Horatio, whose link to Claudius is however extremely tenuous, they are all killed. Killed by whom, is not always easy to say: Polonius is killed by Hamlet, for instance—but Hamlet has no idea that it is Polonius he is stabbing behind the arras; Gertrude is killed by Claudius—but with poison prepared for Hamlet, not for her; Hamlet is killed by Laertes, with Claudius's help, while Laertes, like Rosencrantz and Guildenstern before him, is killed by Hamlet but with Claudius's weapons. Individual agency is muddled; what is truly deadly, is the characters' position in the network, chained to the warring poles of king and prince. Outside of that bold region, no one dies in *Hamlet*. The tragedy is all there.

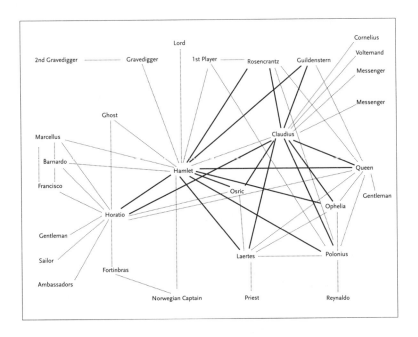

Figure 5: Hamlet: the region of death

MODELS, EXPERIMENTS

Third consequence of this approach: once you make a network of a play, you stop working on the play proper, and work on a *model* instead. You reduce the text to characters and interactions, abstract them from everything else, and this process of reduction and abstraction makes the model obviously much less than the original object—just think of this: I am discussing *Hamlet*, and saying nothing about Shakespeare's words—but also, in another sense, much *more* than it, because a model allows you to see the underlying structures of a complex object. It's like an X-ray: suddenly, you see the region of death of Figure 5, which is otherwise hidden by the very richness of the play. Or take the protagonist. When discussing this figure, literary theory usually turns to concepts of 'consciousness' and

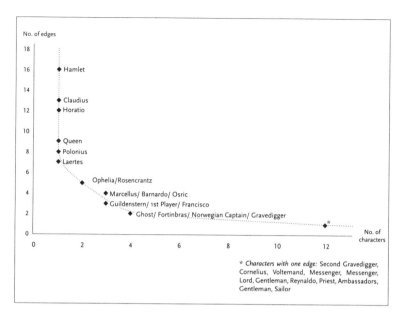

Figure 6: Centrality in Hamlet

'interiority'—even Woloch's structural study takes this path. When a group of researchers applied network theory to the Marvel comics series, however, their view of the protagonist made no reference to interiority; the protagonist was simply 'the character that minimized the sum of the distances to all other vertices';[5] in other words, the *centre* of the network. In their case, it was a character called Captain America; in ours, it is Hamlet. One degree of separation from sixteen of the characters; two degrees from the others; average distance from all vertices in the network, 1.45. And if we visualize these results in the form of a scatter-plot (Figure 6), we find the skewed distribution that is characteristic of all networks: very few characters with many edges on the left, and very many characters with just one or two edges on the right. The result is the same if we add all the characters from

---

5   Alberich et al., 'Marvel Universe'.

Macbeth, Lear and *Othello*. What we have here is the opposite of a Gaussian curve: there is no central tendency in the distribution, no 'average'; that is to say, there is no 'typical' vertex in the network, *and no typical character in the plays*. So, speaking of Shakespeare's characters 'in general' is wrong, at least in the tragedies, because these characters-in-general don't exist: all there is, is this curve leading from one extreme to the other without any clear solution of continuity. And the same applies to the binaries with which we usually think about character: protagonist versus minor characters, or 'round' versus 'flat': nothing in the distribution supports these dichotomies; what it asks for, rather, is a radical reconceptualization of characters and of their hierarchy.

What is done is never undone; the plot as a system of regions; the hierarchy of centrality that exists among characters; finally—and it is the most important thing of all, but also the most difficult—one can *intervene* on a model; make experiments. Take the protagonist again. For literary critics, this figure is important because it is a very meaningful part of the text; there is always a lot to be said about it; we would never think of discussing *Hamlet*—without Hamlet. But this is exactly what network theory tempts us to do: take the *Hamlet*-network, and *remove* Hamlet, to see what happens: Figure 7. And what happens is that the network almost splits in half: between the court on the right, and the region that includes the Ghost and Fortinbras on the left all that remains are the three edges linking Horatio to Claudius, Gertrude and Osric: a few dozen words. If we used the first Quarto, the breakdown would be even more dramatic.

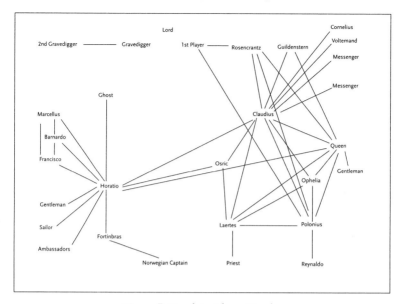

Figure 7: Hamlet without Hamlet

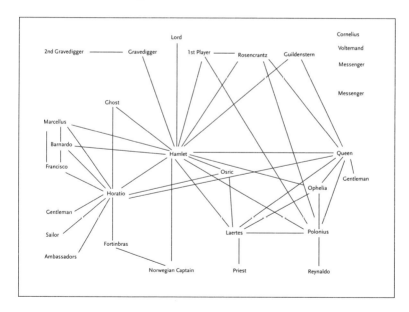

Figure 8: Hamlet without Claudius

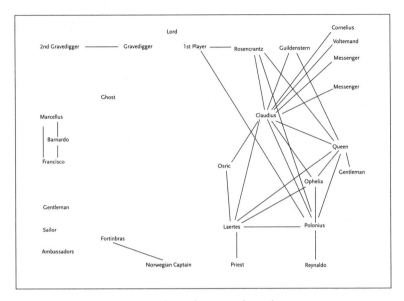

Figure 9: Hamlet without Hamlet and Horatio

Why is the protagonist significant here? Not for what is 'in' it; not for its essence, but for its function in the stability of the network. And stability has clearly much to do with centrality, but is not identical to it. Take the second-most-central character of the play: Claudius. In quantitative terms, Claudius is almost as central as Hamlet (average distance of 1.62, versus 1.45); but in structural terms not so, when we remove him from the network (Figure 8), what happens is that a handful of peripheral characters are affected, but the network as a whole not much. Even if we remove, first Hamlet, and then Claudius, his subtraction does not do much. But if we remove, first Hamlet, and then *Horatio* (Figure 9), then the fragmentation is so radical that the Ghost and Fortinbras—which is to say, the beginning and the ending of the play—are completely severed from each other and from the rest of the plot. *Hamlet* no longer exists. And yet, Horatio is slightly less central than Claudius in quantitative terms (1.69 versus 1.62). Why is he so much more important in structural terms?

CENTRALITY, CONFLICT, CLUSTERING

Let me take a brief step back, and add something on Hamlet's centrality first. Shakespeare's major tragedies are reflections on the nature of sovereignty, in which an initial figure of legitimacy is ousted by a usurper, who is in his turn defeated by a second figure of legitimacy. But there are differences. In *Macbeth* and *Lear* legitimate rulers have very solid connections to the rest of the network: Duncan and Malcolm (in grey and bold, in Figure 10), have a powerful antagonist in Macbeth (dots), but the two fields are basically balanced; and this is even truer for *Lear*, with its scattering of sovereign power (Figure 11). In *Hamlet*, no: between old Hamlet and Fortinbras on one side and Claudius on the other there is a total disproportion; the usual balance of power is not there,[6] and Hamlet finds himself caught between the space of the Court and that of the anti-Court: the soldiers who still remember the old king, the ghost, the Norwegian pretender, the carnivalesque of the Gravedigger. It's a duality that emerges in all the great Court scenes, from that which sets up the pattern in Act I (Figure 12), to the arrival of the players, the play within the play (Figure 13), and the two final scenes of the tragedy (Figure 14). Always two hubs in the network: Claudius inside the Court, and Hamlet (half-)outside it.

Claudius inside the Court . . . This is the densest part of the network: the hexagon formed by Hamlet, Claudius, Gertrude, Polonius, Ophelia and Laertes, where everybody is connected to everybody else, and clustering reaches 100 per cent. Clustering is a technical concept of network theory, which Mark Newman explains thus: 'If vertex A is connected to vertex B and vertex B to vertex C, then there is a heightened probability that vertex A will also be connected to vertex C. In the language of social networks, the

---

6   *Why* the balance is not there—why choose a ghost and a Norwegian as figures of legitimacy—is a different question, on which network theory has probably nothing to say. *That* it is not there, is one of those things that it makes visible.

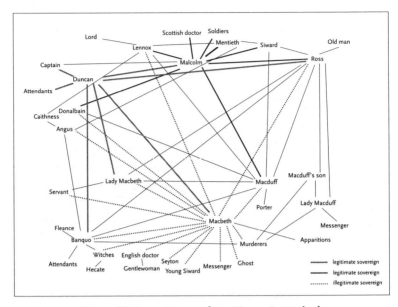

Figure 10: Sovereignty and Legitimacy in Macbeth

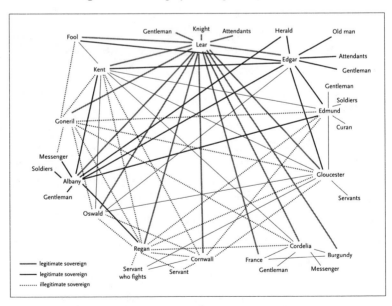

Figure 11: Sovereignty and Legitimacy in King Lear

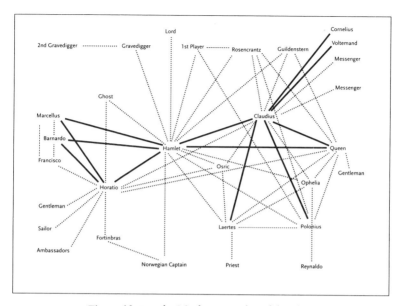

Figure 12: Hamlet i.2: the two poles of the play

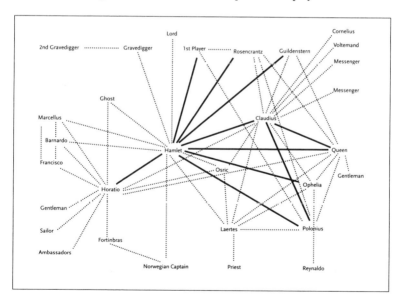

Figure 13: Hamlet iii.2

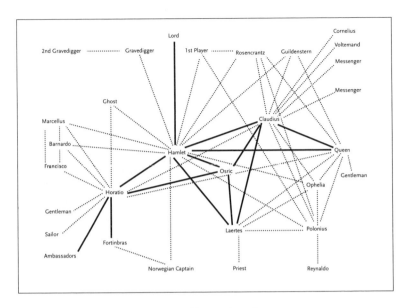

Figure 14: Hamlet v.2

friend of your friend is likely also to be your friend.'[7] This is what clustering means: A and C connect, the triangle closes, and when that happens the resilience of that part of the network increases. *And this is why removing Claudius has such little effect on the network*: he belongs to a region which is already very interconnected, and that remains just as solid with or without him.[8]

---

7   Mark Newman, 'The Structure and Function of Complex Networks', SIAM *Review* 45: 2 (2003), p. 183, available at arXiv.org.

8   Hamlet also belongs to the hexagon, of course; but although he shares those five edges with Claudius (plus that to Horatio, and to those other Court creatures, Rosencrantz, Guildenstern and Osric), their remaining edges are quite different: in Claudius's case, they link him to minor characters who are emanations of the Court, and hence add nothing to his role in the structure; in Hamlet's case, they lead into other regions of the play, increasing his structural significance. Moreover, whereas Hamlet's exchanges with the five Court characters amount only to 28 per cent of the words he speaks in the play, in Claudius's case—though he barely speaks to Ophelia, and not much to Polonius, either—the figure rises to 48 per cent (or 60 per cent, if we

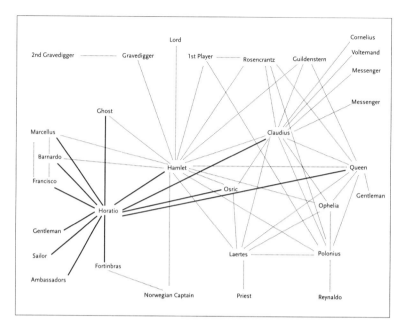

Figure 15: Horatio's space

Horatio is the opposite: he inhabits a part of the network where clustering is so low (Figure 15) that, without him, it disintegrates. In this, he is a good gateway to the region that is the exact antithesis of the 100 per cent clustering of the Court: the periphery of *Hamlet*, where we find the *least* connected of its characters—those with just one link to the network; at times, just one sentence. Very little. But as a group, these peripheral characters do something unique: they point to the world *beyond Elsinore*: the gentleman, sailor and ambassadors who speak to Horatio, and one of the messengers to Claudius, are links to the 'English' subplot; Cornelius and Voltemand, to 'Norway'; Reynaldo, to Laertes's 'France'; the Priest and

---

include his speeches to the Court as a whole): in other words, most of Claudius's verbal energy is spent within this very small circle. This is one case where 'weighting' the edges would significantly modify the initial X-ray of *Hamlet*.

Gravedigger, to the world of the dead. These centrifugal threads—
'tendrils', as they are sometimes called—contribute to the uncanny
feeling that Elsinore is just the tip of the tragic iceberg: geography
as the hidden dimension of fate, like genealogy in Greek tragedy.
Genealogy, vertical, rooted in myth; geography, horizontal, in
something like the nascent European state system.

HORATIO

I may be exaggerating here, projecting onto the periphery of this
diagram Napoleon's words at Erfurt on politics as the fate of the
moderns. But Horatio's space—ambassadors, messengers, senti-
nels, talk of foreign wars, and of course the transfer of sovereignty
at the end—all this announces what will soon be called, not Court,
but State. The Court, the space of 100 per cent clustering, where
one is always seeing and being seen, as in Elias's *Court Society*, is
really two families: Ophelia, Laertes and Polonius; Claudius,
Gertrude and Hamlet. Horatio's world is more abstract: he
exchanges just a couple of sentences with Claudius and Gertrude,
and none at all with Polonius, Ophelia and Laertes. Here, incidentally, you see the difference between my network and that of the
other Shakespeare study: for the latter Horatio *is* linked to Polonius,
Laertes and Ophelia, because they are on stage together, which
seems to me to miss the point of his character: his being a 'weak tie',
unlike those hyperconnected families-at-Court. Weak, that is to
say: less intense, but with a wider radius; and more impersonal,
almost bureaucratic, like the ties described by Graham Sack in his
study of *Bleak House*.[9]

---

9 Alexander Graham Sack, '*Bleak House* and Weak Social Networks',
unpublished thesis, Columbia University, 2006. The concept of 'weak tie' was
first formulated by Mark Granovetter in 'The Strength of Weak Ties', *American
Journal of Sociology* 78: 6 (May 1973).

I may be making too much of this; or, Horatio may really be a fantastic half-intuition on Shakespeare's part; and I say 'half', because there is something enigmatically undeveloped about him. Think of Posa, in Schiller. *Don Carlos* is to a large extent a remake of *Hamlet*, and Posa is certainly a remake of Horatio: another lonely friend of another sad prince in another oedipal play. But Posa has a reason for being so central: he is that new figure, so important for modern drama: the ideologue. There is something he wants to *do*. Horatio? Kent is near Lear out of loyalty; Macduff, near Malcolm to avenge his family. Horatio?

Horatio has a function in the play, but not a motivation. No aim, no emotions—no *language*, really, worthy of *Hamlet*. I can think of no other character that is so central to a Shakespeare play, and so flat in its style. Flat, just like the style of the State (or at least, of its bureaucracy). Flat, like the typical utterances we encounter at the periphery of *Hamlet*: orders and news: 'And we here dispatch / You, good Cornelius, and you, Voltemand' (I.2.33–4); 'Sea-faring men, sir. They say they have letters for you' (IV.6.2–3). Orders and news must avoid ambiguity, and so, around them, the play's 'figurality rate' (to use a concept of Francesco Orlando's) drops; language becomes simple. Conversely, as we move towards the centre of the network figurality rises, all the way to Hamlet's puns in response to Claudius, and to the soliloquies that occupy, so to speak, the centre of the centre. You see the possibility here: different uses of language emerging in different network regions. Style, integrated within plot as a *function* of plot. It would be a breakthrough, and not just for literary analysis—which has never been able to create a unified theory of plot and style—but for the analysis of culture more broadly. Because plot and style could provide a small-scale model to study two general properties of human societies: plot, to understand how the simple exchange between two individuals evolves into complex patterns made of thousands of interactions; and style, to study how human beings make sense of their actions. A model for the relationship between what we do, and how we think about it: this is what a plot–style continuum could provide. But we are definitely not there yet.

SYMMETRY

Networks are made of vertices and edges; plot networks, of characters and verbal exchanges. In plays this works well, because words are deeds, deeds are almost always words, and so, basically, a network of speech acts is a network of actions. In novels, no, because much of what characters do and say is not uttered, but narrated, and direct discourse covers only a part of the plot—at times, a very small part. This makes the transformation of plots into networks a lot less accurate, but the idea is too tempting to just let it go, and so I will show a few networks of verbal exchanges from *The Story of the Stone* and *Our Mutual Friend* just the same. A couple of years ago I conjectured that the number of characters could be a major source of morphological differences between Chinese and Western novels, and networks seem to be a good way to test the idea.

Unlike with *Hamlet*, however, I won't present networks for the entire text, but only chapter-networks; I could perhaps manage *Our Mutual Friend* (even though, by Western standards, it has a lot of characters), but certainly not the hundreds and hundreds of characters of *The Story of the Stone*, in which each chapter has between five and twenty-eight different speaking characters, with a median of fourteen. *Our Mutual Friend* is less crowded: between three and fourteen speaking characters per chapter, with a median of six. And here is one of them: Chapter 1 of Book II of the novel (Figure 16), which introduces Jenny Wren and Headstone; Chapter 2, a variation on this (Figure 17), with Lizzie's other suitor, Wrayburn, and Jenny's father; Chapter 4, with the revenge of the Lammles over Podsnap via his daughter (Figure 18). And so on.

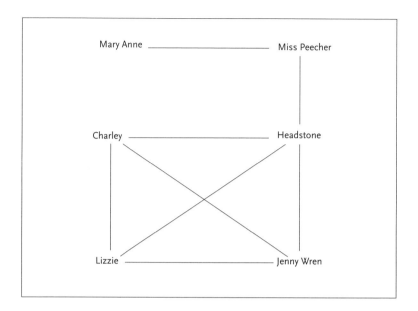

Figure 16: Our Mutual Friend, ii.1

Now, in Western novelistic poetics, aside from a few neo-classical moments, symmetry has never been an important category. But you look at these networks (and others) from *Our Mutual Friend* and it is stunning how regular they are. Probably, there are two reasons for this. The first is that Dickens's building blocks are usually binary pairs: husband and wife, parent and child, brother and sister, suitor and beloved, friend and friend, employer and employee, rival and rival . . . And, second, these binaries can project their dualism onto the chapter as a whole because there is very little 'noise' around them—very few other characters to disrupt the symmetry. Or in other words: with few characters, symmetry seems to emerge by itself, even in the absence of an aesthetics of symmetry.

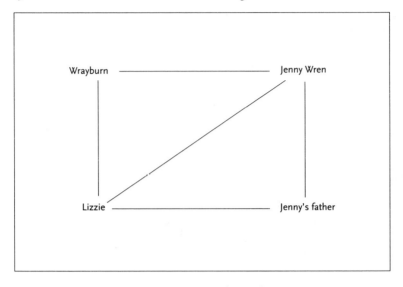

Figure 17: Our Mutual Friend, ii.2

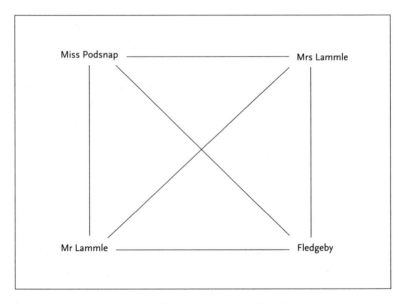

Figure 18: Our Mutual Friend, ii.4

An aesthetics of symmetry is on the other hand very present in Chinese literary culture, where readers of novels expect, in Andrew Plaks's words, that 'the overall sequence of chapters' will add up to a 'round and symmetrical number, typically 100 or 120'. The pronounced sense of symmetry 'provides the ground for a variety of exercises in structural patterning. Most noticeable among these is the practice of contriving to divide an overall narrative sequence precisely at its arithmetic midpoint, yielding two great hemispheric structural movements.'[10]

Hemispheric movements . . . Think of the rhymed couplets that serve as chapter epigraphs in classical Chinese novels: 'Zhou Rui's wife delivers palace flowers and finds Jia Lian pursuing night sports by day / Jia Bao-yu visits the Ning-guo mansion and has an agreeable colloquy with Qin-shi's brother'. A does this and meets B; C does that and meets D. As if the two halves of the chapter mirrored each other perfectly: 'A very earnest young woman offers counsel by night / And a very endearing one is found to be a source of fragrance by day'. 'Parallel prose', as Chinese aesthetics calls it. So you take *The Story of the Stone*, use bold edges for the first half of the chapter, dotted edges for the second half, and . . . Figures 19–22.

Chinese novels should have *more* symmetry than European ones. But no. And the number of characters is probably again the reason: if with few characters symmetry emerges almost by itself, with *many* characters it becomes implausible. It is one of those cases where size is not just size: it is *form*. But what does this form mean? Dickens's symmetry is clear: it indicates that, below the surface of social interactions, there is always a melodramatic substratum of love or hatred ready to erupt. A-symmetry?

---

10   Andrew Plaks, 'The Novel in Premodern China', in Moretti, ed., *The Novel*, Princeton 2006, vol. I, p. 189. See also Plaks, 'Leaving the Garden', *New Left Review* II/47 (September–October 2007).

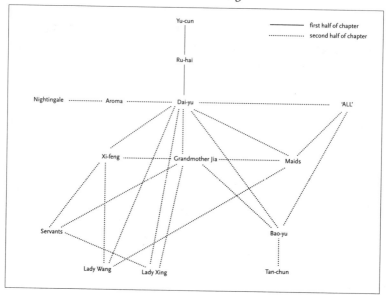

Figure 19: The Story of the Stone, Chapter 3

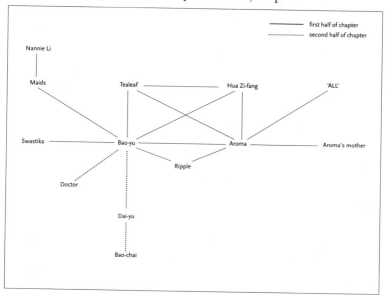

Figure 20: The Story of the Stone, Chapter 19

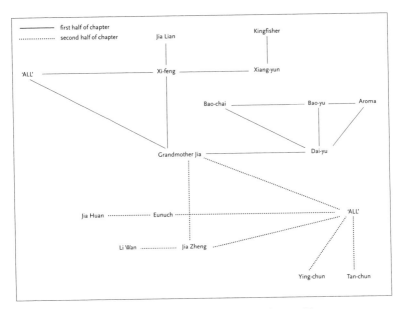

Figure 21: The Story of the Stone, Chapter 22

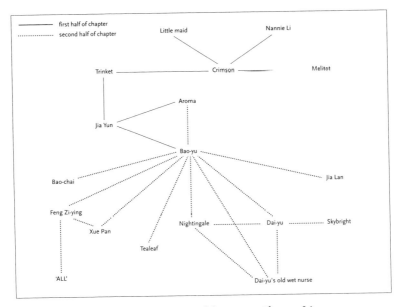

Figure 22: The Story of the Stone, Chapter 26

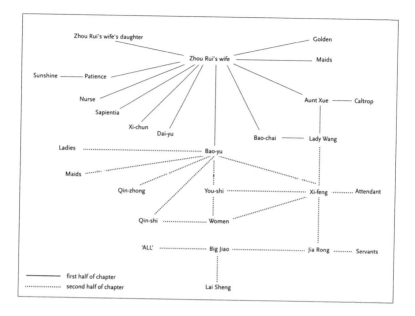

Figure 23: The Story of the Stone, Chapter 7

GUANXI

First half of the seventh chapter of *The Story of the Stone* (Figure 23). Zhou Rui's wife, who is a member of the staff of the Rong mansion, must report to Lady Wang on the visit of a distant relative; she does not find her in her apartment, asks about her, is sent to other parts of the compound, is given some errands, inquires about some new faces and about people she hasn't seen in a while, is asked to intercede for her son-in-law . . . and so she ends up meeting a dozen characters—or more exactly, *speaking* to a dozen characters, she meets about twice as many, while another twenty or so are mentioned in the various conversations.

Nothing major happens here: people talk, walk around, play *go*, gossip . . . No interaction is crucial in itself. But taken together, they perform an essential reconnaissance function: they make sure that the nodes in this region are still communicating: because, with hundreds of characters, the disaggregation of the network is always a possibility. We are close to one of the most distinctive keywords of Chinese culture: *guanxi*: something like 'connections', translate Gold, Guthrie and Wank; part of 'a specifically Chinese idiom of social networks . . . linked to other building blocks of sociality such as *ganqing* (sentiment), *renqing* (human feelings), *mianzi* (face) and *bao* (reciprocity)': a world which is 'neither individual- nor society-based, but *relation*-based'.[11] And these relations are not a given, they are an artefact; 'manufacturing obligation', 'chain of transactions', 'indebtedness', 'consciously producing' connections—this is the lexicon of *guanxi*.[12]

A chain of transactions that generate indebtedness: in Chapter 24 of the novel (Figure 24), Jia Yun, who is a poor relative of the Rong-guo house, is looking for work; he asks Jia Lian but receives only vague promises, so he turns to his uncle Bu Shi-ren, who owns a store, hoping to get some perfumes on credit to use as presents. Bu Shi-ren says no, Jia Yun walks away and bumps into a drunk, who turns out to be his neighbour Ni Er, a racketeer; Ni Er finally lends him the money, and Jia Yun buys a present for Xi-feng, who is in charge of the finances of the clan. This is how *guanxi* works—and this is what creates the asymmetry: a character rallies all its resources in order to 'manufacture obligation', unbalancing a whole cluster of interactions in the same direction. Ideally, in the long run *guanxi*

---

11   Thomas Gold, Doug Guthrie and David Wank, 'An Introduction to the Study of *Guanxi*', in Gold, Guthrie and Wank, eds, *Social Connections in China: Institutions, Culture, and the Changing Nature of Guanxi*, Cambridge 2002, pp. 3, 4, 10.

12   See Gold et al., 'Introduction', p. 6; Mayfair Mei-hui Yang, *Gifts, Favours and Banquets: The Art of Social Relationships in China*, Ithaca, NY 1994, pp. 6, 44, 125; and Andrew Kipnis, 'Practices of *Guanxi* Production and Practices of *Ganqing* Avoidance', in Gold et al., *Social Connections in China*.

will produce reciprocity, and hence symmetry: but at the scale *of the chapter*, asymmetry is exactly what we should expect. And, needless to say, a story which is unbalanced at the local scale, and balanced at a higher one—this is interesting. Even more so, if in Dickens we were to find the opposite configuration: symmetry in the chapters—and asymmetry in the plot as a whole. We'll see.

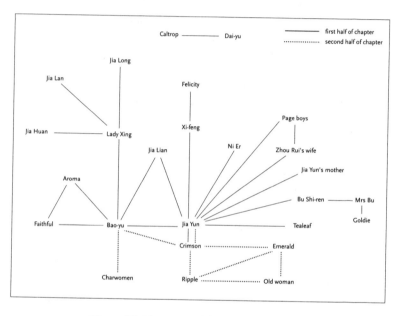

Figure 24: The Story of the Stone, chapter 24

FRUITFUL DOING

In the last two figures, I have focused on how individual behaviour contributes to the shape of the network; now I'll turn the matter around, to see how the overall network of *The Story of the Stone* shapes individual characters in a specific way. Bao-yu, in Chapter 8, is a good instance of this (Figure 25): as the chapter unfolds, he takes part in three distinct episodes: he has an important encounter with his predestined bride Bao-chai, which is catalysed by her maid Oriole; then he gets drunk amidst the banter of the characters around him, despite Nannie Li's vigilance; finally, he throws a tantrum with his maids, until Aroma threatens a general desertion. Three episodes; all mediated by different characters; each of them bringing out a distinct side of Bao-yu (naive lover, sensuous youth, petty domestic tyrant) due to his interaction with a different cluster of characters. And the same happens in every chapter of the novel: its huge pack of characters is re-shuffled, the new 'hand' forms new character-clusters, which generate new features in the figures we already knew. Novelty, as the result of recombination: in the first twenty chapters of the novel, Bao-yu speaks to fifty-four characters, and not once does the same group re-form around him.

Now, Bao-yu is arguably the protagonist of *The Story of the Stone*: the male child born under very special auspices, and expected to do

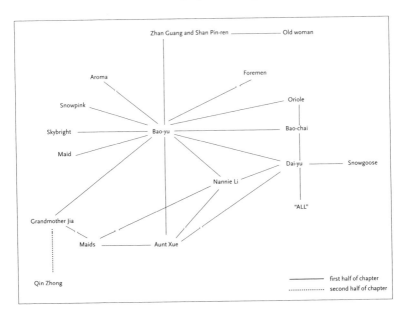

Figure 25: The Story of the Stone, Chapter 8

great things for his family. But what a strange life, for a protagonist: constantly summoned by this and that relative, kept under supervision, asked to perform all sorts of duties—even the many delightful opportunities he is offered come usually with constraints attached. The protagonist, yes, but not free. The protagonist, *and therefore* not free: because he has a duty *towards the structure*: towards the relation-based society he is part of. 'The One *for* the Many': Elizabeth Bennet, not off to Pemberley on her own, but kept at home, to shape the life of her sisters.

A different role for the protagonist, resulting from a different set of narrative relations: what networks make visible are the opposite foundations of novel-writing East and West. One day, after we add to these skeletons the layers of direction, weight and semantics, those richer images will perhaps make us see different genres— tragedies and comedies; picaresque, gothic, *Bildungsroman* . . . —as different shapes; ideally, they may even make visible the micro-patterns out of which these larger network shapes emerge. But for this to happen, an enormous amount of empirical data must be first put together. Will we, as a discipline, be capable of sharing raw materials, evidence—*facts*—with each other? It remains to be seen. For science, Stephen Jay Gould once wrote, fruitful doing matters more than clever thinking. For us, not yet.

LIBRARY, UNIVERSITY OF CHESTER

Index

Note: Page numbers followed by *f* and *n* refer to figures and footnotes respectively.